D1268977

1295

A CENTURY OF PROTESTANT CHRISTIANITY IN JAPAN

is published in cooperation with the

Japan Committee
Division of Foreign Missions
National Council of the Churches of Christ in the U.S.A.

M

Iglehart

A Century of

PROTESTANT CHRISTIANITY

in

JAPAN

Charles W. Iglehart

CHARLES E. TUTTLE COMPANY

Rutland, Vermont   Tokyo, Japan

Published by the
Charles E. Tuttle Company
of Rutland, Vermont & Tokyo, Japan
with editorial offices at
15 Edogawa-cho, Bunkyo-ku, Tokyo, Japan

Copyright in Japan, 1959
All rights reserved

Library of Congress catalog card
No. 59–11758

First edition, 1959

Book design & typography by
Roland A. Mulhauser

Printed in Japan by
The Dai Nippon Printing Company, Ltd., Tokyo

To

E. T. I.

Brother and Yoke-fellow

CONTENTS

5

CONTENTS

Chapter Three

A GROWING MODERN NATION-STATE
1882–1909

The Church in Modern Society

Chapter Four

EXPANSION TO EMPIRE
1909–1937

The Church Under Responsibility

Chapter Five

TOTAL WAR, DEFEAT, OCCUPATION
1937–1952

The Church Under the Cross

6

CONTENTS

Chapter Six

RENEWAL AND ADVANCE
1952–1959

Japanese Christianity Faces the Future

FOREWORD

A Century of Protestant Christianity in Japan has been written by Dr. Charles W. Iglehart in the first instance at the request of the Christian Literature Commission of the National Christian Council of Japan, as part of the Centenary Campaign of that body, culminating in 1959. A number of historical statements have been issued in the Japanese language, but it was felt appropriate that there be a factual and comprehensive account in English of the Protestant Christian movement in Japan on the occasion of the 100th anniversary of the beginning of such work. This is especially important since there has been no such account to our knowledge written since the excellent two-volume history by Rev. Otis Cary prepared at the end of the first fifty years of Protestant Christian work.

The Japan Committee of the Division of Foreign Missions of the National Council of the Churches of Christ in the U.S.A., whose membership embraces more than twenty North American mission boards and agencies with work in Japan, including all those boards which began their work in the early years of the hundred year period, heartily endorsed the proposal of the Literature Commission and asked Dr. Iglehart to undertake this work. The support of these boards has made it possible to proceed with the project.

The Japan Committee wishes to acknowledge with gratitude the hard work and devoted spirit with which Dr. Iglehart has carried out this assignment; one for which his personal commitment to the Christian cause, his deep love for Japan and its people, and his long years of eminent service in that country fitted him uniquely. Deep appreciation is also due Dr. Floyd Shacklock, Executive Sercretary of the Committee on World Literacy and Christian Literature of the Division of Foreign Missions, for his helpful contributions in making publication of this book possible.

We commend it to the reader with the conviction that this history will fill a long-felt need and will for many years provide an informative and discerning source of information concerning Protestant Christianity in Japan. Most of all, it is our prayer that this work may provide an additional resource in the great mission of winning Japan and her people to the cause of Jesus Christ.

WALLACE C. MERWIN
Secretary, Japan Committee

PREFACE

In 1959 Japan completes a hundred years of history as a modern nation, and with it the Protestant Christian movement reaches it centennial. The first missionaries entered the country with the enacting of the historic treaties in 1859.

The theme deserves exhaustive treatment in a well-documented history. In the short space of a single century Japan travelled the long road from the society of the Middle Ages to the highly articulated life of a modern nation-state. She entered the arena of world struggle, and won victories over China and Russia. Expanding into an empire she aspired to the role of the re-organizer of the Asian world. Pursuing the aim of national fulfilment through successful wars, she fell to defeat. She received the stamp of a foreign military occupation with its imposed revolution. Her return to national autonomy finds her facing renewal in a new Asia and a new world.

Even a cursory view of the scene drives home the impression that Japan's fateful course has been, not the eccentric flash of a meteor, but a well-defined orbit of progressive change into which the peoples of our modern world are being drawn. Driven by common impulses and forces they are moving from the static life of yesterday to the dynamic but dimly understood world of tomorrow. Somewhere along this crowded course all the nations are struggling forward toward fulfilment. Jostling, colliding, madly swerving away from catastrophe, they pursue their way. The story of Japan's modern century when adequately told will furnish a classic saga of twentieth century humanity.

In this ferment and fury of change the Protestant Church in Japan has come to birth, grown to maturity, and achieved some degree of acceptance in its society. It has thrilled to the successes of its people, and grieved in their sorrows. Suffering with them it has given its witness and ministered to human need. Its story, if fully recorded, would offer a transcript of the typical situations facing most of the "younger churches" of today. It is in just such conditions of change and tension that Christianity must find a way to live its life, and to give its testimony to the Gospel. No branch of Protestantism in any part of the world has as yet found a solution to these baffling problems, though many are bravely struggling toward one. The small minority Protestant churches of Japan have at least faced them, period by period in their changing aspects, and they have survived. Their history deserves a full recording for the world to ponder.

There are good prospects that adequate historic studies are in store. Both among the younger Japanese Christian scholars, and among foreign missionaries and other western students a new interest in the Japanese church in its society is clearly discernible. Before long a body of published reference material may be expected. On the basis of this deeper research and study a more adequate interpretation of Japan's modern century, both for the nation and for the

12

churches, may be gained.

In the meantime the present volume is offered for the non-professional reader as a brief survey of the scene. It follows the main highway of accepted facts and events, and is without the apparatus of documentation. The chapter divisions and subdivisions trace broadly the major changes in Japan's history, each covering approximately a quarter century. The story of the Protestant Christian movement is interwoven in this context, though not in every detail does it correspond in reaction to the national trends.

Especial thanks are due the editorial committee which under the direction of Dr. Floyd Shacklock kindly charted the course of the study and gave constant counsel. Dr. Franklin D. Coggswell rendered editorial assistance in the reading of the final draft. The author, however, must assume responsibility for the text.

February, 1959   CHARLES W. IGLEHART
New York City

CHAPTER ONE

THE OLD JAPAN

Soil and Climate for Protestant Christianity

LAND AND PEOPLE

The Japanese have for twenty centuries inhabited the rocky reef that skirts the Asian mainland. Such a people must have had a distinctive history and were bound to be carrying up to the modern period the deposit of a precious spiritual heritage and national experience. Some knowledge of this is essential to any understanding of Christianity in their modern period.

Like a pendant the long archipelago swings from Kamchatka and the Kuriles, curving down onto the Philippine chain and off into the South Pacific. Japan's four main islands stretch for fifteen hundred miles at about the center of this arc, in the temperate zone. The Japanese people are in many ways insular. They are homogeneous, compact, loyal, conscious of their own identity and used to long periods of isolation. But like all islanders they have had open gateways into and out of their alloted land space, through which many streams of new life have flowed during their history.

The islands of Japan are open to the south, and the most

rudimentary ties of the Japanese people seem to be with the folk of that vast island area. In the racial blend there is a clearly recognizable Malay or Southern element. The most common folkways share the oceanic pattern. The pavilion-like houses of light construction, the belted robes for clothing, the rice culture, the clustered village life, all speak of the south; and so do the sunny disposition, the swift mobility, the keen zest for life combined with a fine capacity for repose, and also the skills and resourcefulness in the use of simple materials. The Japanese people love the open air, enjoy an intimacy with the natural world, and are completely at home in or on the water. This is the elemental form of the modern Japan of world trade, of the Japanese fleets, and of the people in a relaxed mood.

From the south they get their earliest and still perhaps their deepest religious impulse. The idea of *"mana"* is familiar in the Oceanic world. In Japan this mysterious dynamism is called *"Kami"*; the element of power that inhabits and activates all unusual objects and persons. We may call this primitive animism; in Japan it has come to be called Shinto, "the Way of the Gods." It lives in the village shrine with the patron deity and the year-round festivals of the food cycle, and in the household shrine, recalling the presence of the ancestors. At its peak in veneration stand the Sun-goddess and the Chieftain of the tribe. This religion originally carried little or no content of philosophical ideas; it taught no ethical code, but was engaged in purely for practical results. By the proper manipulation of the *kami*, life might be persuaded to move on. With the passing of the centuries, Shinto has undergone changes, but it still maintains a place of dominant influence upon the nation.

Again, the islands are open to the north, either directly from Kamchatka by the land chain or through the Korean

peninsula and across the straits to Central Japan. The
Northern Asiatic strain appears in the other type of Japanese, the ruddy, sturdy stock. The disposition that goes
with it is more slow and even stubborn, and has a great
capacity for endurance. Yet beneath a surface stolidity
there slumber volcanic elements. These under pressure may
be unpredictable and violent.

From the north comes another spiritual heritage in
shamanistic religion. Life on the uplands and mountains
of the Asian heartland turned mild Buddhism into the
tantric system of Tibetan Lamaism; and of primitive animism it made a dark cult of demon-possession, with the
dancing medium, the transmitter of oracles, visions and revelation. These elements have tended to reappear in modern
Japanese sects.

The islands are too restricted in area to permit a moving
tribal life in the saddle with pitched tents for shelter, but
deep in the racial memory of the people there is a yearning
for the range of the prairies. A kind of nostalgia has turned
their minds toward the mainland during all the modern
period. It has given an emotional support to Japan's modern
wars, most of which have centered in this region. The north
is the Japan of fighting men, of feudal chivalry on horseback, and of the Japanese Kwantung Army. It is the Japan
of struggle for survival by food supply and raw resources,
of tension and combat, of explosive force and of conquest.

Cultivated and refined Japan looks to her west. There
broods China, the mother of far eastern civilizations, un-
approachably great, and fertile in the good things of the
spirit. Century after century the tides of culture have poured
in from China, providing nourishing elements for the less-
developed capacities of the gifted Japanese people in the
formative periods of their history. Each phase of special
creativity has been greeted with eager response, and usually

adopted. An infusion of Chinese language elements enriched the early Japanese speech, and the Chinese ideographs became the accepted medium for writing it. Chinese literature and calligraphy were appropriated. A bewildering array of artistic expression came with the introduction of Chinese culture. Even the social and political organization of China were copied, but most important for our study is the religious contribution received from Japan's great neighbor.

Every aspect of the religious life of Japan shows this debt. The basic folk-faith of China was a hierarchy of relations to deity. The villager and householder dealt with the nearby spirits of the earth and wind; the official higher up made his offerings to loftier gods; while the Emperor stood alone at the national altar and did obeisance to Heaven. This idea of handling the affairs of religion strictly at one's appointed level runs deep in Japanese religious behavior, as does the place of the Emperor as high priest. Also, a half serious dealing with good and bad luck, with the points of the compass, and with the calendar and zodiac have a considerable place in the everyday life of the ordinary person in Japan, as in China.

Confucius with his clear pattern for the right deportment of the gentleman encompassed the world of manners and to a degree took over the ethical life of Japan. His teachings gave strength to the family system, and placed ancestors in a firm position of reverence. On the other hand Lao-tze and the Taoist mood of *laissez faire*—has a place in Japan's heritage, as well. A passive reaction to life, a floating with the current, or a bamboo-like bending with the storm is not uncommon. Buddhism has deeply confirmed this disposition.

The first Buddhist priests brought from China during the sixth century, instruction and training in architecture, painting, carving, bronze-casting, tapestries, silk culture, and much more, in the wake of their faith. For the first time Japan was introduced to persons who joined religious observance with philosophy and learning in one total view of life. The scriptures became a fountainhead of scholarship for thirsty minds. Adherence to this highly developed world-faith made the Japanese kin with fellow-believers in Korea, in China, in India; and through Persian channels gave them contact with some of the splendor of ancient Greece.

Throughout its history Japan nevertheless has had the ability to close the gates at will, and it has done so over and over again. It has seemed to possess a built-in monitor which has given warning when the point of assimilability was about to be reached. Perhaps all nations possess this power, but in the case of the Japanese people it has been spectacular and recurrent. Their history could well be written from the standpoint of these repeated oscillations and their results. During the periods of assimilation the foreign elements formerly adopted have undergone change, and have been re-shaped to native use and form. This took place in all the arts and skills.

It is especially noteworthy in religion, where the Confucian center of emphasis was shifted from the parent-child to the ruler-subject relation. In Buddhism a pessimistic philosophical skepticism gave way to a simple religion of assured salvation in a paradise of bliss. Thus different observers see quite contradictory aspects in the life of Japan. Some note the fact of appropriation of outside elements; and they call the Japanese imitators. Closer students of Japan, however, see the genius for selection, appraisal, recreation and utilization for their own purposes. They would say that no people on earth have displayed more versatility in cultural achievement or greater genius in developing a unique civilization. In any event, Japan has constantly imported from abroad, yet the inner core of the changeless Japan is more precious to most Japanese than any importation ever can be.

What is this core, and how does it act as a lodestone to pull back to center every oscillation in history in relation to the outside world? Perhaps the clue can be found in the land itself. Island life is limited. It tends to throw people back on one another and to produce a tight social organization of mutuality. This intensity of group consciousness is increased by the meagerness of natural resources. Japan's island area is almost too small for survival, and it cannot expand with population growth. The islands themselves would not have survived if they had not been a rocky reef jutting everywhere into mountains. A few small plains, narrow glens running up the steep hillsides, and a scant surface of precarious soil is all that nature has given.

With these uncertain resources a sense of crisis and of danger is ever present. The forests must be kept full and healthy, generation after generation. The rainfall is abundant and must be channelled and controlled. Soil erosion is a constant danger, and the terracing of the slopes must be kept in repair. Fertilization must return to the soil every year what has been used. Rice, the most rewarding but the most demanding of crops, requires the incessant toil of hand gardening. Since there is little room for grazing, the meat supply has had to be wrested from the depths of the ocean; a task calling for reckless daring and dogged, patient toil. Terrific labor and ceaseless vigilance are the everyday lot of the ordinary Japanese.

Thrift, resourcefulness, and the austere discipline of hard living have had to be harnessed to group loyalty if the people were to survive. It is inevitable that after centuries of such experience the nation should deeply cherish its own way of life. The tried and tested paths must not be lightly abandoned. Yet always some of the people have been on the lookout for increased resources and for better ways to utilize the old.

A GLANCE ALONG THE CENTURIES

The earliest history of Japan was written on the plains, mostly in the far south and west. There the clans first had their grouping. Gradually the Yamato tribe extended its range, moved north onto the main island and built its capital in Nara in Central Japan (710). Modelled after the China pattern, court life began to take form about the person of the chieftain, who soon began to be termed Emperor. Dynastic histories were compiled, running back to the semi-historic founder Jimmu Tenno, into the period of legendary heroes, and then to the mythological deities on the Plain of Heaven. The imperial line has continued until this day; and the eighth century compilations of genealogies and traditions have never been more influential in Japanese life than during this modern century.

A new capital at Heian, or Kyoto (794) became the center of the life of political and cultural Japan. The palace remained there with the court until the Restoration in 1868. The arts developed, religion thrived and the lodestone of changeless Japan found there its permanent home, periodically brought into use to restore order when the ancient ways were endangered. The emperor himself seldom exercised the functions of government. A dual system developed, in which the ruler became a symbol of authority and even of worship, while someone else actually administered the affairs of government. Regents were frequent, sometimes they too had their deputies. Shadow government became a national tradition.

In the twelfth century a military genius set up a "camp government" not far from the present Tokyo. He was the first *Shogun,* the one who ruled in the name of the emperor. For two centuries (1188–1333) this simple proto-feudal regime lasted, and it left a legacy of faith in the honesty and efficiency of military men. It then gave way to two centuries of civil wars between the great families and their retainers (1333–1574). By this time a true feudalism was developing, and a pyramidal society was taking shape. Politically it was a time of treachery, of cruelty, and of callous neglect of the emperors. But it was during this period that the culture of Japan came to magnificent flower. Buddhism not only had its own prestige, but by a simple formula it had adopted as incarnations of the "Buddha principle" all the heroes of Japan's past, as well as the deities of the Shinto pantheon. It held the religious field in undisputed control, as it repeatedly has tried to do in the modern century.

The period of political anarchy was brought to an end by the emergence in succession of three of Japan's greatest heroes. Starting from his holdings in Central Japan, Nobunaga Oda widened his power by battle and treaty. His most stubborn opposition came from the massed strength of the Buddhist priests in Osaka, whom it took him ten years to bring under control.

Just at this time there came to the southern gateway in Kyushu a wave of European invasion. First, Portuguese traders "discovered" the country in 1542. Then in 1549 there appeared under Portuguese auspices a small dark-robed Spanish monk, Francis Xavier, accompanied by two foreign assistants and a Japanese. With dauntless courage he visited the miniature courts of one clan chieftain after another until several of them gave him patronage and permitted him to spread his teachings, and to baptize. Eventually a number of chieftains and their retainers came into the Christian faith.

This event and the period following are extremely important for our study, as in many ways they offer a background of what was to happen to Christianity three centuries later. The repercussions they left behind set in motion again the same chain reactions of suspicion and opposition. Nobunaga, seeking strength to combat the Buddhists and with an eye to possible foreign help, favored Xavier and his mission. Even the capital at Kyoto seemed open to Christian evangelism. Then Nobunaga was killed, and his ablest general Hideyoshi Toyotomi succeeded to power. For a time the new strategist appeared to show goodwill to the Christian mission, but as he extended his domains he came up against the far-off chieftains in western Japan who were Xavier's patrons. They, had mixed motives. Among them were men of genuine religious conviction, but they were also ambitious for political and military power. They were eager to develop trade with the Portuguese and they had begun to employ them for the making of firearms.

These latter concerns disturbed Hideyoshi, who decided that Christianity was subversive and inciting to division among the chieftains, all of whom he must control. His first repressive orders were issued rather casually, and were not seriously enforced. They were disregarded by the Christians until suddenly he ordered the execution of a number of Japanese Christians and foreign priests. He then found himself facing a new phenomenon in Japan's religious history— martyrdom for the faith readily accepted by even plain common people. He also learned of the supreme loyalty of the believers to an ecclesiastical head in far-distant Rome. Hideyoshi died before he could undertake a consistent policy of extermination of Christianity, but his successor set that in motion. The arrival of Spanish monks from the Philippines and their strife with their Portuguese confreres began to cause a scandal. But what was more serious, unfriendly Dutch traders were saying that behind the merchants were great nations with powerful and ruthless rulers determined to conquer the east. It was charged that their method was first to send mild men of religion, and then later to come with soldiers for military conquest.

After Hideyoshi's death at the fateful battle of Sekigahara in 1600, his successor, Ieyasu Tokugawa consolidated the feudal Japan which was to last till 1868. In that battle nearly thirty thousand from the Christian clans fought and were killed on the losing side. These reasons and the fact that by this time there was a community of perhaps three hundred thousand of these people of alien faith and unyielding conviction, led Ieyasu's grandson in 1638 to bring the matter to a conclusion. He sent a force against a protesting group who had gathered behind the walls of the old Shimabara castle in west Japan. They resisted until the last one of these thirty-seven thousand Christian defenders was killed. For decades there followed a relentless hounding of Christians, the only choice given them being that of apostasy or death. Christianity disappeared from the scene.

This episode of history might have been recounted from the viewpoint of the heroism and devotion of the Christians, an aspect that has elicited the admiration of many non-Christian Japanese in recent decades. But the prevailing impact left on the Japanese mind over the centuries has been that Christians are people of strange disobedience, of alliance with subversive elements in Japanese society, and of direct connections with conquering powers from the West. Since the Christians themselves believed in the miraculous potency of the cross and of their treasured relics, it came to be thought, also, that Christianity was black magic. That, it was supposed, must explain the believers' unaccountable inflexibility in the face of opposition and persecution. This fear and hatred of Christianity was a tragic legacy from Japan's first chapter of the foreign Christian mission and it came to life with redoubled force in the modern century.

In 1638 by fiat of the Shogun,—in the name of the Emperor,—every gateway of Japan was tightly closed; Naga-saki, alone was opened to an occasional Dutch or Chinese ship. There the few traders lived as virtual prisoners. They obtained this trading concession by strictly disavowing any relation to the Christian mission; but even so they met with contemptuous and humiliating treatment. The westerners and their religion were now excluded, and Japan moved into two centuries of determined seclusion.

CHAPTER TWO

COMING INTO MODERN LIFE

1853—1882

Protestant Beginnings

BEFORE THE TREATIES

1853–1859

Planning a Beginning

In July, 1853 Commodore Matthew C. Perry appeared at the head of an American naval force and anchored off Uraga in Yedo (now Tokyo) Bay. He insisted on presenting to responsible authorities a firm request for relationships between the two countries. He then withdrew to the Loo Choo Islands for the winter, returning for his answer in February, 1854. The blow struck Japan like a tidal wave, and soon the dikes of seclusion were down and the nation itself was launched on the unruly waters of modern life. It found the new course with such swiftness and precision as to excite the wonder of the world.

The feudal system left behind him by Ieyasu, founder of the Tokugawa Shogunate in 1610 was a highly efficient organization of the nation. From his massive castle in Yedo

26

he and an elaborately organized bureaucratic staff held the lines that ran out to the 250 separate fiefs. The lords were divided between the "hereditary" ones who were kinsmen or allies of Tokugawa, and the so-called "outer" ones who had offered resistance. The strongest of these outer clans were in far western Japan. All rendered service and paid taxes in terms of their rice crop; all were compelled to maintain residence in Yedo for regular periods. A heavy spy system kept rebellion down. The pattern was rigid, and seemed trouble-proof; but with the turn of the nineteenth century it had begun to show signs of weakening.

The very distance from Yedo of the outer chieftains in the west made them largely autonomous, and the continuous journeyings to and from the capital kept them informed of conditions over a great area. Gradually a money economy began to emerge, and the cities of Osaka and Yedo burgeoned into wealth and strength. Great merchant houses gathered capital, and soon came to control the national economy. Manufactures were carried along the national road system to the corners of the nation. The cultural life of the time gives evidence of the luxury and indolence of the warriors (*samurai*) who had become softened through two centuries of enforced peace. Wealth was shifting to the common people of the cities who spent it in new recreations, dramatic amusements, and night life. The immemorial ranking of the warriors and farmers above the merchants was being overturned. A pattern of life was taking shape that was no longer feudal, but of a modern type. The "outer lords" were chafing to match strength with the static Shogun government. Japan was ready for a new chapter in history.

During the months of Perry's absence a slogan, the first part of which was "Expel the Barbarians" was on everyone's lips. Fomented by the western lords, this agitation was

27

intended to embarrass the Shogunate. But also it answered to a general demand that the wave of expansion from Europe should not be allowed to wash onto the shores of Japan. The fate of Indo-China, India, and China had become well known.

A second half of the slogan was "Revere the Emperor". Two recent trends in the thought life of Japan had greatly enhanced the prestige of the Throne. One was from a succession of Shinto scholars who wrote commentaries on the early classics. These called for a restoration of the pure Shinto doctrines of the unique sacredness of the emperor, the land and the people. The other trend came from a massive history of Japan in process of compilation by Confucian scholars under the patronage of the Lord of Mito. This, study by a different path led to the same conclusion; that the dynamic center of national life could be only in the living emperor and his ancestors.

As yet, no political implications of these revolutionary thought currents had been carried into action. But the slogan had great force. Bowing both to the court and the great feudal lords, the Shogun during the intervening months took a poll of opinion, only to receive a verdict of rejection of Perry's proposals. This left the government without support at home for making the concessions to superior force which it was compelled to do. Perry returned with his larger fleet, the Shogun's government submitted, and a treaty was made. It provided for humane treatment of shipwrecked seamen, fueling privileges for foreign ships, and the opening of intercourse with the West. Simple though it was, this treaty called for a representative of the American government to take up residence in the country.

Townsend Harris came as consular agent, later to become American Minister. A dismantled temple at Shimoda, on the tip of a peninsula facing away from Tokyo, was found for him. By his integrity, his patient perseverance and his Yankee wisdom he accomplished what the trained negotiators from Russia and Holland had been denied. In 1858 he obtained the official signature to Japan's first treaty of navigation and commerce. This was the opening wedge, and soon all the nations of the West had won similar treaty rights.

In the meantime, a Christian concern for the sending of a mission was mounting in America, and various sporadic attempts had been made to get through the closed gates. Missionaries from China in 1837 had attempted a friendly expedition in the ship *Morrison* but had not been permitted to land. In 1845 the Loo Choo Naval mission had placed a missionary in residence in Naha, but his efforts had met with failure. Japan was not yet ready to open to Christianity.

Japanese visitors had an opportunity to see Protestant worship in action when, in 1854, the Sabbath was observed on the American ships and a Christian service was held on deck. The naval band led the singing of "All people who on earth do dwell" to the astonishment of the crowds on shore. Perry was very circumspect, knowing of the Japanese hatred of the Christian religion. By government permission a burial service was held for an American seaman. But the naval expedition came and went without any further reference to religion. On Perry's ship was a young marine, Jonathan Goble, a Baptist, who had enlisted in order to see for himself what openings there might be for Christian work. On his return he took ministerial training, and in 1860 went back to Japan as a missionary. In various relations and fields of work he rendered good service.

With the arrival of Townsend Harris the stage was set for a Protestant beginning. Personally he was a Christian gentleman of conviction. He maintained his own Episcopal service regularly, with his one interpreter, Mr. Heusken, as the congregation. Officially he was determined to see that no mediaeval restrictions on religion should get into the new treaties. He managed by great skill to obtain permission, not only for the residence of foreigners in assigned settlements, but also for the unrestricted practice of their own faith, and the erection of suitable buildings for it. Furthermore he gained the explicit permission for them to bring into the country and to sell anything they pleased, with the exception of firearms and opium. There was no embargo on books. These provisions opened a direct path for the first period of foreign missionary life in Japan.

Between 1856 and 1859 there was a good deal of coming and going of foreign naval vessels, most of them based on China. Although the Japanese government was opposed to any contacts with the Westerners, and though public clamor decried it, yet there were many eager spirits, mostly among the young *samurai* who welcomed it, and took great pains to get acquainted. They came aboard the ships, asked to be shown books, and received their first lessons in English, the commander of the ship himself sometimes doing the teaching. Some of these classes continued for weeks at a time. And the Bible was often used as a textbook. In Nagasaki the governor sent a group of young officials to request instruction in English.

The prelude to the sending of the first Protestant missionaries took place in Nagasaki in 1858. The treaties had been agreed to, ratification was quite certain, and the laws were to go into effect the next year. The ship *Powhatan* was entertaining Japanese officials. In the company were the ship's chaplain, Rev. Henry Wood, Rev. Mr. Syle, the chaplain of the United States Consulate, and S. Wells Williams a China missionary who had come on *The Morrison* twenty years before. He had never lost his interest in Japan and had learned enough of the language to serve as chief interpreter for Perry on his expedition. Now he was back in Nagasaki, keen as ever for the starting of Christian work. The officials were urgent in their requests for teachers, offering to employ Chaplain Wood at once.

When the dinner party was over the three Americans had a conference. Each had the same impression; the time was already ripe for recruiting Protestant missionaries for Japan. They agreed to send an urgent appeal to the missionary authorities respectively of the Episcopal, the Presbyterian and the Dutch Reformed churches of the United States. All three Boards responded and immediately began to take action. In a matter of months six men of peculiar fitness had been found and were in preparation for sailing.

Three years previously, the missionary society of the Protestant Episcopal Church had sent two promising missionaries to China. They were both transferred to Japan. John Liggins was a man of keen insight, as his letters home during his few months in Japan show. Unfortunately he was in poor health, and soon had to return to America, where to the end of his life he promoted the cause of Christianity in Japan.

The other Episcopalian was Channing M. Williams. Kindly, gentle, evangelistic, he gave to Japan a long lifetime of devoted service. He there became the first bishop of the Episcopal Church, established its first school, and helped lay the foundations of the Japanese church. He, too, revealed deep insights in his early correspondence. In the midst of hostility and rejection from high and low he prophesied that there was a middle class emerging, that they would be of open mind toward Christianity, and that they would come to be the backbone of the Christian movement. All of these things later came to pass.

The Dutch Reformed Church found three recruits, who came with their families. Dr. D. B. Simmons after a year of missionary service in Kanagawa went into general medical practice.

Samuel R. Brown, a former China missionary, was pastor of a church and headmaster of a school in Connecticut. An exceptionally able teacher, he had already reached the age of forty-nine; but he left his work and joined the Japan mission. His peculiar capacity to attract and inspire young men is still a legend in Japanese Christianity. He is viewed as the greatest of the early missionary schoolmen.

The most brilliant and conspicuous man selected for Japan by this church was Guido F. Verbeck. Born and educated in Holland, he was just finishing his work at Auburn Seminary; the only really young man among the six. His unusual gifts called him to places of responsibility in planning and counselling with national leaders; a status not ordinarily given to foreign missionaries in Japan. For years, with the consent of his Board, he was loaned to serve the Japanese government at its highest level as counsellor to the makers of national policy. He then quietly returned to service of churches and schools within the mission. He had the stature of a giant.

The Presbyterian Board also called a veteran, a former missionary in China, Dr. James C. Hepburn. At this time as a very successful physician in a city of Northern New York he was well-rooted at home. Though forty-five years of age, he closed out his practice and again faced the Far East from which he had already had to retire because of broken health. Hepburn gave thirty-three years of service to Japan. His versatility as physician, linguist, educator and church builder made him the most venerated of all the early missionaries. He was widely loved and trusted.

LAYING THE FOUNDATIONS
1859–1872

Missionary Activities; First Converts

With the operation of the treaty of 1859 the modern revolution swept in on Japan. The early stages were a time of maneuvering for position, and of coalescing of the scattered groups and individuals into the power centers for action. The chieftains of the "outer clans" of western Japan, anti-Shogunate and opposed to the opening of the country looked for ways to assert themselves. In 1860 a Satsuma (Kagoshima) procession returning from Tokyo came upon a small party of British persons on horseback. Furious at their failure to dismount, the Japanese retainers attacked them and killed a British subject. In the same year the Japanese statesman who had signed the treaty was assassinated by a similar band at the palace Gate in Tokyo. In 1863 the American interpreter Heusken was killed. Choshu (Shimonoseki) guns fired on foreign vessels.

Since the Yedo government was unable to maintain order the foreigners decided on direct reprisals. British ships bombarded Kagoshima and forced the payment of an indemnity. At the straits of Shimonoseki, Dutch, American and French vessels demolished the clan forts which had fired on Western vessels. This so chastened the outer clan leaders that they at once dropped the "expel the barbarians" from their slogan. Instead they substituted "crush the Shogunate", and thereafter concentrated all their efforts toward the defeat of the Tokugawa regime for the control of the nation. In fact, from this time on they heatedly espoused the cause of opening the gates to the Americans and Europeans.

In the meantime the six missionary units—two single men

and four married couples—had come and settled in the places appointed for foreign residence. Liggins, Williams and Verbeck went to Nagasaki; and Hepburn, Simmons and Brown settled near Yokohama. At first they all were housed in Buddhist temples. Sometimes an unused temple was assigned them; in other cases the missionary occupied part of the building while the remainder continued in religious use. The purpose was two fold. No better arrangement could have been found than to sequester the obnoxious foreigners in the large enclosure of a non-residential building so that they could have no everyday contact with ordinary Japanese people. Also, the Buddhists all through the centuries of seclusion had been commissioned to keep the records of vital statistics for all classes, including the checking on their religious affiliations. It was they who annually brought the image of Christ on a metal plate for each householder to come out and trample on, in token of his hatred of the foreign faith. They were suitable espionage agents to keep watch on the missionaries.

During this period of three or four years of almost complete isolation the missionaries were not idle. In Nagasaki, although the official attitude toward Roman Catholic Christianity was rabidly hostile, the Protestants were treated quite tolerantly. Local authorities wanted to exploit the foreigners' knowledge of English, and sent young men to them for instruction. Verbeck for several years held regular classes for three Buddhist priests, though in their case the purpose no doubt was to get information to use against Christianity.

Near Yokohama, Hepburn at once opened a small clinic. He immediately engaged himself, as did most of the first missionaries with attempts at Bible translation. One can imagine how difficult this was, since almost a year went by before any language teacher could be obtained, and then he proved to be an informer. The home was always open for anyone who might brave the uncertainties of the Westerner's threshold; and occasionally one did. In several cases, Japanese who became Christians later told the missionary that they had come ostensibly to be instructed, but really with the intention of ridding their country of the evil foreign priest.

Conditions were not conducive to easy intercourse. Yet the primary concern for the welfare of the Japanese people and the evidently sincere kindness of the newcomers led, in numerous instances, to the beginnings of lasting friendships. A quaint observation was made by one who visited Hepburn's clinic: "There is a suspicion that he is a Christian, but he does not act like one at all; and he certainly is a wonderful foreigner." In the meantime the wives, often more quick in making friendships than the official relationships of their husbands permitted, no doubt were gently making their way into the hearts and lives of some persons who came and went to the homes.

Soon there were children in the missionary families, and they must have become incomparable ice-breakers in the chilly neighbourhoods.

The arrival in 1861 of Rev. James C. Ballagh of the Reformed church was a welcome reinforcement. He ranks among the "greats" of the first period. His preeminence was in the field of Christian character, piety, prayer life, and a most humble assiduity in service to anyone in need.

A change came in 1862, when provision was made for a settlement of foreigners in Yokohama. It was scarcely more than a fishing village, but it was better than a lonely temple, for Japanese people did live nearby. The Hepburns moved to Yokohama in 1862, as did the Ballaghs, and they were joined by the David Thompsons of the Presbyterian church. Hepburn erected a special building and set up a permanent dispensary and clinic which he conducted with remarkable results for sixteen years. His home classes blossomed into a school in which Ballagh and Thompson joined forces. This was the forerunner of the Meiji Gakuin University in Tokyo.

With more adequate clerical help and assistance in language study Hepburn in conjunction with Dr. Brown, turned seriously to Bible translation work. His monumental English-Japanese, Japanese-English Lexicon of forty thousand words began to move forward to its publication in 1867. In 1860 the first Protestant services had been held in the various legations. In 1862 regular services in English under Brown's direction were held in Hepburn's building while at Nagasaki in the same year a similar building was under Brown's direction were held in Hepburn's building, for the religious services of foreigners were clearly within the purview of Townsend Harris' treaty; and no complaint was made, not even, when, a little later, Japanese Christian groups began to use them for their worship.

During the next four or five years (1864–68) the struggle for control of Japan's advent into modern life shifted in an eddying whirlpool. Steadily the western or "outer" clans pressed their advantage against the Shogun's government, defeating his forces here and there in sporadic fighting, and campaigning with their war-cry "Honor the Emperor, Down with the Usurpers". These outer lords went to Kyoto and there directly arranged for the Emperor's signature to the treaties. Thus at one stroke they committed themselves to the revolution, and espoused the cause of the Emperor as its head and center.

The exigencies of events helped bring the Tokugawa regime to an end. There had been three long reigns of unusually able emperors. When in 1867 the last of them died it brought to the throne a young man of fifteen years,

Mutsuhito, who became the Emperor Meiji. This instantly precipitated the issue of his position in the changing Japan. During the previous year the Shogun had died.

The succession to the Shogunate fell to a young lord of Mito, whose famed ancestor had promoted the compilation of the *Great History of Japan* with its high estimate of the Imperial system. The implication of this clearly was the restoration of the emperor to power. Also the strength of the outer chieftains was too great longer to resist. In 1867 Keiki, the last of the Shoguns handed his resignation to the Throne.

During this period the Protestant mission effort was moving forward. It had as yet no involvement in the Japanese revolution except as the treaties gave the foreigners permission to reside in the country. The swirling currents of opposing factions and views threw the mission enterprise this way and that, now giving encouragement and now threatening failure. No Japanese voice could be heard with a good word for Christianity, the hated and forbidden faith. The utmost that any responsible leader would yield in accepting the inevitability of contact with the West was that it offered some techniques that might be useful. Few attributed any spiritual quality to this imported civilization.

A moral philosopher of that day wrote advising an active acceptance of the open door policy, saying that the wise man "employs the ethics of the East and the scientific technique of the West thus bringing benefit to the people and serving the nation". Yet even this view was so unpalatable to the public that this philosopher was assassinated in 1864.

At more humble levels, however, things were stirring. James Ballagh found a teacher, Yano who had been officially assigned to him as his language instructor. In his spare time Ballagh set him working on the Gospel of John, more for Yano's spiritual benefit, Ballagh later explained, than for any intention to publish the work. In time the seed fell upon good ground and took root. In 1864 Yano fell ill and from his sickbed sent for the missionary and requested baptism. Ballagh, taken aback, consulted Yano's wife and sons who to his astonishment agreed. He then asked the opinion of his seniors Hepburn and Brown, and they advised it. So, in fear and trembling at the possible consequences of this open defiance of the law, he administered the rite.

Yano died within a few weeks, strong and triumphant in his new-found faith. His family was not punished. Hepburn spoke exultingly of the fact that whereas in China, missionaries had had to wait ten long years before the firstfruits of harvest, here in scarcely five years God had already given the first increase. He went on to say that if the proscription sign-boards prohibiting Christianity were not posted throughout the land all Japan within a few years might well come to kneel at Jesus' feet. Hepburn was encouraged the same year to publish his Christian tract: *An Easy Introduction to Christian Doctrine*. This must have required courage for it was palpably an evangelistic effort and could bring conviction of crime upon anyone who possessed it, as well as on the author.

In the same year, 1864, a youth was deeply stirred by reading an English textbook which spoke of God as the creator of the universe. The young man, Shimeta Niishima determined to defy the law and escape to America. He went to the northern port of Hakodate. Three years previously the Russians had opened a consulate there and its young chaplain Nicolai at once evinced an interest in the Japanese and their conversion. He was another foreign missionary who ranks among the early giants. Speaking humanly, by his single efforts the Eastern Orthodox church was founded in Japan. It grew to be a community of over thirty thousand.

While Nicolai was still in Hakodate, young Niishima presented himself and offered to act as teacher. The city was a remote port, and the surveillance was not strict. Possibly Nicolai knew of the youth's plan and assisted it. At any rate Niishima got off on a merchant vessel and soon found himself in Boston. In the home of Mr. Alpheus Hardy, a Christian layman, he found direction for his spiritual pilgrimage and became a Christian. As "Joseph Hardy Neesima" his name was to become familiar to a generation of Christians on both sides of the Pacific.

The story of the Roman Catholic work lies outside our field, but mention must be made of one or two events that bore on the total Christian situation. A year before the treaties were in force, in 1858, a French missionary priest was already in Yokohama, and the next year another priest was stationed in Nagasaki. This was the scene of the great work of Xavier and his successors. It was here that the martyrdoms had taken place. The priest Fr. Petitjean repeatedly went into the villages looking in vain for relics and evidences of the early believers. When in 1865 he completed the building of the Church of the Twenty-Six Martyrs, in Uragami, Nagasaki, he was visited after the dedication, by a group of country-women. They had watched, fascinated as he celebrated the mass, and then they met him, with muffled questions and conversation. When he had confirmed the use of the crucifix, his celibacy and the adoration of the Virgin they whispered: "Our hearts are as yours."

Over two centuries had passed since the last vestiges of a living Christian had been seen. These people could not have had a trained ministry, nor instruction in religion. Yet here they were, still clinging to their faith. They reported that there were many villages made up of Christians like themselves. Eventually more than 10,000 of such Christians revealed themselves to the priests. This is considered one of the miracles of Christian history by the Catholic church. The government eventually learned of it and it took action four years later when, in 1869, three thousand of these hapless people were driven into exile, scattered among twenty-seven clans all over Japan.

To return to the Protestant story; in this same period a prominent *samurai* and his brother became Christians and were baptized without any tragic consequences. Wakasa, the next in rank to the lord of the Nagasaki region was responsible for watching and guarding the bay, when, in 1855, he happened to see floating in the water a book that had fallen from the deck of a foreign ship. It proved to be a New Testament in Dutch. With help he read some of it; and so great was his curiosity that he sent to China for a Chinese Bible, and for years made its study his chief preoccupation.

When Verbeck came to Nagasaki, Wakasa sent a messenger on the first of many visits to ask certain questions about the Christian truth. For several years this strange long-range Christian counselling went on until one day in 1866 Wakasa, with his brother and two sons, presented himself in person. His retinue was so large that his visits had to be made secretly at night. Finally in Verbeck's home on Whitsuntide he and his brother were baptized. He reported his conversion to his chieftain who accepted the situation without administering punishment. Wakasa lived for years and maintained an unblemished Christian record.

Chinese Bibles and Christian literature had a large place in this early period, for educated Japanese were able to read the Chinese text. Long before there was any Christian literature in Japanese and when it could not have been circulated, Christian books in Chinese, printed in Shanghai were brought into the country. Townsend Harris himself ordered and distributed many copies of Martin's *Evidences of Christianity* in Chinese.

The fact that in 1867 Mrs. Hepburn was permitted to

open a school for girls in her home indicates that a new day was about to break for Christian work.

In 1868 the Restoration quickly followed on the resignation of the Shogun. The youthful Emperor was installed in the great Yedo castle which became the Imperial Palace in re-named Tokyo, and the era of Meiji began. It was revolution, of course, yet much of the old government structure was sound. Its dismantling and reconstruction was a matter of careful selection and re-use. Policy, too, had to be delicately balanced to hold in control all the various elements in society. Indeed, for the next four or five years, from 1868 to 1872, the differences and tensions in policy were in sharper contrast than ever before.

On the one hand, progressive trends were strong. The official formula now changed to "Open the Country, Press Progress". The Emperor publicly took the "Charter Oath" in which he pledged that "absurd customs of the past" would be abandoned, knowledge sought in all lands, and the people consulted in matters of national policy.

At the same time, however, the government issued a caution that the old prohibition of the Christian faith still held and would be strictly enforced. In fact, the public noticeboards were freshly re-posted. The following year was the time the Catholics trudged into exile. Shonan Yokoi, an advocate of friendship with the west, was assassinated.

In the midst of this heightened struggle of ideas and policies the little Christian fellowship moved cautiously. Many things were allowed by the authorities to pass unnoticed, under a kind of permissive disapproval. It was so with the first baptized converts, of whom there were ten by the beginning of 1872.* The numbers were evenly divided between the Nagasaki and Yokohama regions. In Hakodate,

* For names and identification see Verbeck's report; *General Proceedings Osaka Conference*, 1883. pp. 51, 52.

Nicolai in 1868 had won to the Eastern Orthodox faith his first convert, Sawabe who first came to assassinate him but was captured by friendship and the Christian witness.

A memorable statement was drafted by the missionaries and other foreigners meeting for the Week of Prayer in Yokohama in 1866, and sent to the churches of the west. It cited in clear terms the situation at that time, listing the gains and the avenues open for advance. Yet it did not evade the fact that all active missionary work was still against the law and would bring trouble on the converts, if not on the missionaries. It asked for prayer for direction and for opening doors under God's hand. The Church Missionary Society in England was deeply moved by the appeal, and presented the matter for prayer throughout the church. As a result their mission was founded in 1869.

This year 1869 also saw other reinforcements. The American Board (Congregationalist) sent as its first missionary Daniel C. Greene, who though arriving ten years behind the other giants, soon was taking his place at their side. His long life of service was a link with that earliest period, and he led a procession of stalwarts who opened a new field of Protestant operations in central Japan.

The work of the Protestants was coming out of seclusion and making at least a semi-public appeal, yet no one could be sure of consequences. As late as 1872 a language teacher of Greene died in a Kobe prison, his crime being that he had in his possession a copy of Hepburn's translation of the gospel of Mark. His wife, however, was released and immediately received baptism without further trouble. In Nagasaki the language teacher of an Anglican Missionary was spirited away to prison and taken through the city with an iron collar around his neck. It took nearly two years of persistent effort by Japanese friends to obtain his release.

For the Christians the year 1872 was pivotal. Till then

there was no Christian movement as such. The Christian converts were but ten in number, they were scattered, and only one or two were destined to play any historic part in the Christian story. In Yokohama the missionaries and other foreigners were celebrating the Week of Prayer under the auspices of the World Evangelical Alliance. The meetings reached a high degree of intensity. Before they were over, a number of Japanese students who were under the instruction of the missionaries asked to be allowed to hold such services themselves. They received permission, and started. Ballagh led in daily Bible studies, centering on the second chapter of the book of Acts. Day by day the spirit rose among these young men, as yet uncommitted to Christ, until finally they were on fire with earnestness, contrition and desire to become Christians.

On March 10th, 1872 Ballagh baptized nine of them. These he at once organized into a church, adding two older Christian men, one as elder and the other as deacon, Ballagh himself acting temporarily as pastor. The name chosen was "The Church of Christ", (*Kirisuto Kōkwai*). A creed largely taken from the one of the World Evangelical Alliance was supplemented by other articles having to do with a code for living. These latter were plainly the work of the Japanese young men, and indicate a leaning toward a somewhat nationalistic emphasis. In a few words the church polity was defined. Authority was vested in the congregation under the leadership of the pastor and elders.

In September, 1872, a noteworthy meeting of missionaries took place in Yokohama. The senior members of the Presbyterian, Reformed, and Congregational missions formed the voting nucleus. The chief purpose was to standardize the scattered efforts at New Testament translation which had been going on from the earliest years and now were beginning to issue from the press, piecemeal. With great team-

43

spirit all present decided on a fresh start, and a committee was organized.

Another action taken was in commendation of the basis of the first Japanese church, and of its name and polity. The resolution spoke of the diversities of denominations as being accidents that obscure the oneness of all believers. It approved of the simple form of church structure and pledged the missionaries to work for identity of name and organization in all future church developments. It was in a very fraternal and cooperative spirit that the Protestant movement came to its first major mile-stone at the end of this period, in 1872.

Dr. Verbeck in later summarizing the record tabulates the main achievements of the Christian mission to that date. The missionaries had managed to turn the edge of hostility, and were now liked by many of the public. The people had a changed attitude toward Christianity, and some were beginning to be inquirers. Christian literature in Chinese was being widely distributed. The missionaries' degree of acquisition of the Japanese language had become adequate for their work. Japanese Christian literature was started. Bible translations were being published. Dispensary work was prospering. Christian schools for boys and for girls were doing well, in numerous centers. Services in English for the foreign communities were publicly being held. The statement and appeal to churches in the West had caused heightened interest and added support from abroad. The harvest in conversions was being gathered. The first church native to the soil of Japan had been founded.

This was indeed a brave and auspicious beginning for a religion that was still proscribed under pain of exile and even of death.

CONSTRUCTION UNDER WAY
1872–1882

Early Life and Work of the Protestant Churches

The shifting struggle for national power finally centered in a group of young men less than a hundred in number, former *samurai* belonging chiefly to four of the outer clans. In recent histories these leaders are called the Oligarchs, and such they were. Within their ranks they had intense rivalries, but they stood together like a phalanx both in shaping the course of the modern revolution and in carrying it out.

In fixing on Tokyo as the capital, and in placing the youthful emperor at the center, they had determined both the political and the spiritual foundation for the new structure. By 1870 they were ready to dismantle and rebuild. The Shogun was gone. It was time for the feudal lords to hand over their authority; and led by the four dominant fiefs they did so. Next, the *samurai* as a class were gradually levelled into the ranks of commoners. At first they were permitted to leave off their swords, later these were removed by law. Feudal ties were cut by money compensations to chieftains and retainers. These were then commuted into bonds and annual pensions. Thus all became capitalists with a common stake in the new order.

The ordinary people were elevated to a new level of dignity. For the first time they were allowed family names of their own. In 1871 a system of general public education was started. The most drastic of all the changes was the national conscription system under which all feudal ranks and prestige for the former fighting man were swept away. In every major encounter during the seventies between this new national army and the old-fashioned warriors the peasants and townspepole won. Their use of fire-arms, too, displaced the old weapons of chivalry and speeded the change.

National unity was aided by the building of better roads, the construction of the first railway, installation of some telegraph lines and a system of swift postal messenger service. Industry, too, was set forward at new speed and in the direction of both light and heavy manufactures. Early in this period a national pattern of industrial development was undertaken. It anticipated the cartels of revolutionary nations today. Anything needed for national prosperity and safety was ordered into production and paid for by public funds. The slogan "National Prosperity-Strong Arms" put it succinctly. Basic economic development had priority even over national defense, and both took precedence over purely political matters.

A new tax system based on land values instead of the old unreliable crop levies gave a more solid fiscal foundation. An immense reservoir of capital was already stored in the vaults of the several merchant and banking families of the Tokugawa period. They were encouraged to expand manufactures and trade by government subsidies and also by the purchase at bargain prices of the government-founded industries. Heavy industry always remained under national control.

But at this point the matter of the treaty relationships with the Western powers blocked the way of progress. All the treaties were alike in two regards: they exempted foreigners from Japanese law, and they imposed such limits on Japan's power to tax imports as to make impossible any real competition in trade. These restrictions were galling to Japanese national self-regard, as they implied inferiority and established intolerable economic handicaps.

The Oligarchs, therefore, sent abroad a score of their

number accompanied by a large retinue. The mission was under Iwakura the president of the Council of State. The Japanese were not successful in obtaining a revision of the treaties. But they were able to scrutinize the life of the West,—its social and political patterns, and most of all its industrial and economic workings. They learned to appreciate Western developments, and they formed sound judgments as to those Western patterns which might best be adopted in Japan's various areas of essential change.

The Iwakura Mission everywhere ran into trouble over the restrictive rules regarding religion; and they were soon writing back urging their colleagues to remove the pressures on Christians. They wanted to be able to say that Japan already qualified as a modern state by its freedom of faith and religious toleration. When Iwakura returned in 1873 the proscription boards against Christianity came down. The government's face-saving explanation was that the laws were already so well-known that they no longer needed emphasis. With this change the Christian movement ceased to be outlawed; and the decade here under review became notable for its pronounced progress.

In 1873 a new surge of interest in Japan spread through the churches of the West. Perhaps it arose from the Iwakura visits to the major cities. Also in America the War of the States was over, and at least in the Northern and Middle Western states recovery was taking place. This one year brought in as many missionaries,—twenty-nine,—as there then were altogether in Japan. Some of these enlarged the ranks of the American Episcopal, the Presbyterian and Reformed, and the Congregational missions, but new groups also started work. These included missionaries of the Methodist Episcopal Church, the American Baptists, and the Canadian Methodists. From Great Britain came missionaries under the Society for the Propagation of the Gospel. During

47

the decade the numbers were steadily increased as the Evangelical Association, German Reformed and Methodist Protestant missions were founded.

In the open port cities the older missionaries found new freedoms, and a better reception for their work. Greene in Kobe was holding meetings in a shop on a busy street, addressing crowds of more than a hundred. In Osaka, several men were carrying on evangelistic work without molestation. In the interior cities others in medical service were permitted to reside. Even within the restrictions of the passport regulations, the major cities were, nonetheless, being occupied as the centers for the Christian church structure of the future. There was a concentration in the metropolitan areas of the east and of Central Japan, though the geographical spread extended from Hakodate in Hokkaido to Nagasaki in Kyushu. Of the total of eighty-seven missionaries, Yokohama had thirty-three, Tokyo sixteen; Osaka sixteen; Nagasaki twelve, and northern Japan two.

Wherever the foreign missionaries lived, teaching was sure to start. Enterprising Japanese young people gathered about them for study. In the homes, classes were formed and individual students were instructed as well. From these beginnings came the Christian schools. The first was opened in Yokohama in 1870, later to develop into the Ferris Girls School. During 1874 there were started the small beginnings which grew into three Christian universities in Tokyo: St. Paul's, of the Episcopal Church, Meiji Gakuin, of the Presbyterian-Reformed Church, and Aoyama Gakuin, of the Methodist Church. In the following year Doshisha, of the Congregational Churches was founded in Kyoto. A few modest school buildings were erected at this time, and the first dormitories were built to accommodate resident students. The Christian influence of early schools was greatly enhanced by the intimacies of life on the campus of a small school.

As for the more intensive training of the ministry, a beginning had been made in 1875 in Yokohama. In 1877 this school was merged with the Presbyterian united theological school in Tokyo. The Baptist Woman's Training School, also in Tokyo, was founded in 1875. Training of the clergy started under Church Missionary Society auspices in Nagasaki in 1877. A number of the other schools later developed theological departments.

In the extension of Christian educational influence there must be counted the work of missionaries, sometimes laymen, who were employed or who went to teach in Japanese private or public schools. Verbeck was a conspicuous case, as he was made head of one of the two schools which together formed the first Imperial University, in Tokyo. There were a number of other Christian teachers in general educational institutions.

In the mid-seventies the Christian movement gave signs of having taken root. Hitherto it had been largely the work of foreigners, exercising what initiative they could within the network of restrictions and prejudice. Now some developments native to the soil and climate of Japan were about to take place. They would furnish the leadership and set the patterns for the Christian movement for at least the first half of the modern century.

Outstanding in this period of Protestant history were the "Christian Bands", of which there were four or five. The first in point of time gathered in Yokohama. From the various clans, mostly in the north, ambitious young men came to the port city to gain contact with the Westerners who lived there and if possible to study English in preparation for a future role in the making of the new Japan. Most of those who came to Yokohama and found their way to the homes and schools of missionaries belonged to the "hereditary", or pro-Tokugawa fiefs, which were now out of favor as the outer clan Oligarchs took over the power in the nation.

They came as individuals with differing backgrounds, but many of them were of excellent families, already trained in the disciplined thinking and living of Japanese Confucianism. All, alike, were seeking a great future for their nation, and were eager to find strength to take their part in its realization. The half score of students who went through the spiritual experiences of conversion under Ballagh, Hepburn and Brown, and who were gathered into the first church, became the nucleus of the "Yokohama Band". They were joined by several others, notably by Masahisa Uemura, son of a high feudal family in Tokyo, and destined to become one of Protestantism's leading figures. The group became tightly knit together in mutual fellowship and common Christian experiences. They and the other Bands were literally the elite corps of a militant Christianity in the hostile society of their day.

A second Christian Band gathered in west Japan. In 1871 the lord of Kumamoto decided to establish a school of occidental learning. He went to Verbeck who recommended as its head Captain L. L. Janes, a West Point graduate. When Janes came he quickly displayed a vigorous Christian faith. Already incensed at having any foreigner as their school head, at this added affront of Christian witness the faculty resigned *en masse*. That left the school entirely in the hands of Janes, who reorganized it into a little West Point. Discipline, thrift, moral strictness, appointed duties and hard work for long hours were the rule. Yet never in the first three years he was there did he offer the suggestion that any student should become a Christian. Nor did he formally teach Christianity.

Finally, the unspoken pressure of Janes' influence upon the hearts of his students came to a boiling point, and at dawn one morning in 1876 thirty-five of them climbed the hill of Hanaoka and there took an oath of Christian fealty. It was couched in terms of national liberty, and yet had in it the drive of a universal Christian faith. Christ was to be their Lord, for the emancipation of their nation. This group included a score of Protestantism's famous figures. Perhaps most prominent of all was Hiromichi Kozaki, who had been a teacher in a neighboring school until the furor among the parents and neighbors over this Christian scandal had reached its height, when he joined the Band. Its members had to undergo severe persecution, but most of them persisted on their Christian course.

As Janes' period of service ended and the school was abruptly closed he commended the students to Niishima, who had recently returned from his years in America, and was then in Kyoto starting the Doshisha School. His story is filled with romance and chivalry;—his flight to the West, his finding a home with Mr. Hardy; then his education in New England at Amherst College and Andover Seminary. While in seminary he was summoned by the Iwakura embassy to act as interpreter. This he did, with lifelong advantages in his friendship with the nation's young leaders. When their trip was over and they wanted him to return and take a government post, he replied in true *samurai* spirit that he was an exile, having forfeited loyalty to any but the Lord Jesus Christ. He was ordained, and accepted as a missionary by the American Board, of which Mr. Hardy was the Chairman. In the Board's annual meeting before his departure he made an impassioned appeal for the establishment of a Christian College in Japan; whereupon an offering was taken and a grant was made for the project.

Through influential friends Niishima had finally broken the seclusion of Kyoto and obtained land facing the palace grounds, where in rented quarters he was trying to get the scnool established. It was fighting for its first breath when this infusion of new life came from Kumamoto. Doshisha, too, then became a kind of Christian West Point with the students themselves setting the pace of discipline; but always with Niishima ahead. No one could say that this was a foreigner's school. It had all the tang of Japanese *samurai* life in it. These youth had been carefully selected, for admission to Janes' school in Kumamoto.They were of as prime quality as those in Yokohama and if anything they possessed a still more intense spirit of heroic devotion to Christ and country.

The third Christian Band was in the far north. In the same year, 1876, the national government, having set up a Hokkaido Colonization Office, decided to establish in Sapporo of that northern island a higher school for pioneers majoring in scientific agriculture. They called President W.S. Clark of the Massachusetts Agricultural College as its head. His position was uncompromisingly Christian, and the authorities reluctantly had to yield to him the right to teach Christian ethics, since he said he knew of no other way truly to interpret the life of the West. Soon all of the first class of fifteen students had given in their names as desiring Christian baptism. They were moved by such enthusiasm that even after Clark had left, when his school year's contract expired, they themselves led the next year's entering students into the Christian life.

The Sapporo Band was different from the others, and yet it was like them, too. The lads were all carefully chosen from excellent backgrounds, but they were not from any one clan. It was an individual honor to get into the school. In that distant frontier town there was little opposition to Christianity, nor could the parents complain, for they had deliberately exposed their sons to the Western influence. The tension and costliness of the faith of the Sapporo Band was less than in Kumamoto. They represented a more placid and urbane type, such as Dr. Inazo Nitobe, for many years Japan's leading literary light in English, and long one of the Secretaries General of the League of Nations. Some of them were aggressively individualistic, such as the noted Kanzo Uchimura, of whom more later. The group included Shosuke Sato the future Chancellor of the Sapporo University, and Hokkaido's first citizen, as well as several other teachers prominent in the field of science and literature.

There were other Bands, less well-known, yet influential in Japanese Christian history. One in Hirosaki developed in connection with the To-O Gijuku, a clan institution, with a history of seventy-five years as the training ground for the sons of the local knights. Yoichi Honda was sent to Yokohama to obtain the services of an English teacher for the school. While there he became a Christian, and joined the church. When he returned to Hirosaki he took with him John Ing, an American Methodist missionary en route to China. Ing and his family were persuaded to go with this unknown youth to a still less-known field of service in Japan's back country. The result was that together they gathered a group of about fifteen students who soon were ready for baptism, which Ing and Honda administered. As Ing was soon to return home, in 1878 Honda, who had been made an elder in the Yokohama Church, obtained its consent to the affiliation of the group with the Methodists in Japan

Bishop Williams of the Episcopal Church gathered about him another circle of young men in Tokyo. These became the nucleus of the future leadership in the Japanese Episcopal church.

The next natural development to be noted in the Protestantism of this period is the growth and expansion of the churches. The beginnings had been made by missionaries, most of whom were of high caliber. They came from sound, responsible churches in the West. It so happened that most of them were from the United States. Their tradition was that of classical Protestant Christianity. New England and the Puritan tradition were predominant, though other strains were not lacking. A clear sense of church-centeredness was the common heritage of all the missionary groups. The relation with the potential Japanese Christian leaders, at that time disciples of the missionaries, was close and loyal. All these factors were favorable to responsible church growth.

By 1875, three short years after the first church was founded, Yokohama had twenty-five places of weekly Christian worship that were on the way to full church status. Tokyo had ten, the Kobe-Osaka region ten, and other places five. In Kyoto, Doshisha had sprouted three churches. By 1874 unpromising Nagasaki had one church. All over the country the stakes were being driven in for the future.

From each of these cities evangelistic efforts radiated into smaller centers. Missionaries now were by the tacit permission of the authorities beginning to leave their homes in the ports and concessions areas and to travel into the interior. Sometimes they found the ground strangely prepared. In one mountain region a Japanese Bible colporteur had done all the essential training of a solidly true Christian group whose members a missionary later baptised.

The important new element in this growth was the leadership of the Japanese. Soon Doshisha had graduated its first class of fifteen, all of whom went into Christian work. In Niishima's clan home at Annaka a completely self-supporting church was formed. Students' summer evangelistic trips became the practice. The first country trip had been made in 1873 by two students starting from

54

Tokyo. In 1874 the Yokohama Church had sent out, on its own charges, five teams of student evagelists into the Tokyo Bay area. Presently they were planting churches, and serving them. These were not all small congregations. In some cases more people gathered for worship then than do now in the same churches.

It was a time of construction of church buildings. Some of the old ones still remain, and their large size is testimony to the wide range of interest Christianity exercised in the early days of Japan's modern century. In the one year of 1879 the entire Christian membership in the nation increased by sixty percent. This was not a mass movement into the churches, to be sure, but it was rapid individual growth.

During these years three major Japanese denominations began to take form, each deriving most of its leadership from one of the Bands. The Yokohama group chiefly manned the churches which became the "Church of Christ in Japan". In 1876 the missionaries of the American Presbyterian, Dutch Reformed, and Scottish United Presbyterian churches met and organized themselves into a "Council of the Three Missions" for the purpose of forming a single Presbyterian-Reformed denomination. Meeting again in 1877 with the eight elders of the local Japanese churches they set up the church on a national scale, with a total membership of 623. Two,—already trusted evangelists,—were ordained, and the first of Protestantism's indigenous branches took form on a nation-wide scale. It bore the name "United Church of Christ in Japan".

In the Kobe-Osaka-Kyoto region, the Congregationalist missionaries committed to the local churches the autonomy of their system, but these churches were bound by spiritual ties which led them some years later to adopt the national organization. Their two first leaders were Niishima and

Paul Sawayama. The latter, a saintly, sensitive man returned from study in America to establish in 1874 the first church in Osaka. He was an ardent advocate of totally self-supporting Japanese Christianity, and he so infused this spirit into his congregation that the Baika Girls School was launched with no outside assistance.

Niishima's primacy was in the Doshisha rather than in direct church life. His Christian character so impressed itself on his students that to this day the graduates refer with veneration to the founder and the Doshisha spirit which he exemplified. Although the Kumamoto Band was school-centered, yet it was to them and to later Doshisha men that the Congregational churches looked for their pastoral leadership.

The Hirosaki Band went on to fructify the Japan Methodist Church through all its history. Over two hunderd men and women passed from the Christian schools and the church in Hirosaki into full-time Christian service, all over Japan. Their revered leader was Honda.

The Sapporo Band, on the other hand, was destined to write another kind of chapter in Protestant life. Under the most individualistic of them all, the pioneer Uchimura, they formed themselves into a congregation after their own devising, having the Bible and early Christianity alone as the guide. With even President Clark the laymen gone, they had no visible ties with any church structure or tradition. After an unsuccessful attempt to fit into the connectional system of the Methodist denomination, they decided to walk alone, and declared themselves an independent body. The members took turns directly services, though in reality Uchimura was pastor. This project set the first pattern for Uchimura's more radical movement, which has continued until the present as "Churchless Christianity".

In 1874 the leaders of the two Yokohama and Tokyo

churches and those of the two in Kobe and Osaka made an attempt at organic union. The first church in Yokohama called itself by the generic term "Catholic" (Ecumenical) Church. The Missionary Conference in Yokohama confirmed this as their policy. This was done in highly commendable and irenic spirit, and if it could have been made effective a miracle would have been performed. But in fact the missionaries were the architects of the first churches and each had his own denominational background, and backing. These early ideals of supra-denominationalism were all but impossible of implementation, for each Japanese church was already related through its missionary affiliation to one particular denominational tradition. With all the goodwill in the world, that stubborn fact emerged as soon as any coalescing of the church organizations was attempted.

As to the constitution of the first church in Yokohama, the description of the church authority as being "in the hands of the pastor and elders with the concurrence of the brethren" certainly suggested a congregational pattern with the primacy in the local church, yet the place of the elder implied a Presbyterian tradition as well. On the basis of this over-simplified and ambiguous formula the churches of the Tokyo-Yokohama region and those of Kobe and Osaka went their two separate ways. The Yokohama Church established as its branch Tokyo's first church. On December 30th, 1873, the Presbyterian missionaries in pursuance of instructions from America organized a Presbytery, which the related Japanese churches joined.

In the meantime the missionaries in Osaka and Kobe had founded their two first churches, according to the Congregational pattern familiar to them, and which they thought to be identical with the Yokohama type. Thus within a matter of months the two traditions had carried the groups apart, and when they tried to get together, each side was astonished at the failure of the other to keep its agreement.

This did not break their cordial Christian fellowship. It was simply the first of many instances where the young church was swept by the traditional currents into positions most of its members might never have selected if they had been making church history from a fresh start.

Japanese ministers and laymen had their first experience of a national conference in the Fellowship Meetings, in Tokyo in 1878, and again in Osaka in 1880. This became an event recurring every year or two. Only a score or so of those attending were delegated from twelve cities, but many hundreds came to the meetings. Other meetings open to the public became the order of the day. There were sometimes evidences of local opposition to Christianity, but more and more the Christians were being permitted to give their testimony; the public evincing real interest, and numbers going on to conversion. The year 1880 saw the celebration, in a National Conference, of the completion of the translation of the New Testament. Another conference in 1878 had set up a permanent committee with the entire Old Testament as its next assignment.

The enrichment of Christian hymnody was under way, though not yet far advanced. The earliest attempts of foreigners to translate such hymns as "Jesus Loves Me" and "There's a Land that is Fairer than Day", are still the theme of amused recollection by Japanese Christians. These products must have been a strain on the feelings of the early Japanese Christians, but perhaps not much more so than the idea of singing in public worship at all. This cut across Japanese reserve and customs. All the denominations however, soon had persons working on their compilations of songs for worship; and the time was to come when some of these would be assembled into hymn collections as excellent as those found in any country. The first hymnal with notes was issued in 1878, there being at that time one or two books containing as many as fifty hymns.

Christian literature up to this period had not developed much beyond the stage of tracts and simple evangelistic presentations of Christian teaching. The heavy apologetics were to come later, when intellectual opposition took on more formidable proportions. The foundations for publishing were laid by the American Board mission with their own press. In this enterprise they offered encouragement to a Japanese layman, to take it over when he was able to do so. In 1875 they started the publication of the first Christian periodical, the *Weekly Miscellany*. The members of the Bands, it was said, would go without food to get hold of every issue. In wider circles the periodical exerted a strong influence.

In 1880, in Tokyo, under the leadership of Kozaki the first Young Man's Christian Association, was formed. With him as chief editor the group started its weekly, the *Cosmos Magazine*, which for many years was one of the most widely read periodicals in Japan. Though the number of publications was not yet large, the beginnings of a creative literature of high quality had thus been made.

Sunday Schools were beginning to be held informally in the homes of the missionaries, Dr. John C. Berry being credited with the first in 1874. By the 1880's they were everywhere appearing as a strong adjunct to evangelism and church life.

In social service outreach, the churches had scarcely made a beginning. Yet in this early decade there were more medical missionaries with dispensaries than at almost any subsequent time. Hepburn's clinic was the pioneer. J. C. Berry of the American Board immediately on arrival went to work in Central Japan, and soon his lines spread widely. In Kobe he gained the privilege of lecturing to government medical students in surgery, with dissection. He opened branches with official approval around the Inland Sea, and at other interior points. Everywhere Dr. Berry exerted a deep influence on Japanese physicians and on the authorities. Other physicians of the various missions were stationed in the major cities. Later developments saw a lessening of medical missionary service, but there is a new resurgence of interest in it today.

The forces in Japanese society that reacted favorably or unfavorably toward the nascent Protestant movement were of great import in this first quarter-century.

The government attitude was plainly equivocal. It certainly was not friendly, yet it had to watch for repercussions abroad, so it exercised caution. Under the surface some encouragement was probably given to Japanese groups hostile to Christianity while at the same time a position of official tolerance was taken. The Ministry of Education was prone to hold up passports for travel into the interior. Not infrequently local government officials would openly oppose Christian undertakings, though sometimes they were over-ruled by Tokyo. No doubt the foreign consulates were at times called on to exert pressure for fair dealing toward the Christians. One of the things still quoted with glowing appreciation by Japanese Christians is that Hepburn and Ballagh and Brown refused to request diplomatic protection or immunity of any kind for themselves or their student charges. It was thought to be the mark of a true *samurai* to face hostile circumstances, and the early missionaries were of the heroic stamp to follow that tradition.

Among the intellectuals, mostly professors in the emerging Imperial University, there were able antagonists who wrote against Christianity. On the other hand there were the "liberals" who sometimes took up the cudgels for Christianity. They centered in a group formed in 1873 under the name *Meirokusha,* (or "the 6th of Meiji-ers"), as this was the year the Western calendar was adopted, and it symbolized to them Japan's joining the currents of the world's culture. Their periodical *Meiroku Magazine,* featured innovations in thought and manners. Chief among these men was Yukichi Fukuzawa, founder of Keio University, and of the *Jiji Shimpo* daily newspaper, also the author of many books. He was utterly without interest in religion, except as it might be turned to possible use in statescraft. He swung back and forth like a weather-vane. Each book and every editorial had its effect on the still pliant Christian organism. In 1881 he was opposing the new faith. On the friendly side was Keiu Nakamura, head of the *Doninsha* another college in Tokyo. He actually had been baptized by Dr. Cochran of the Canadian mission in 1873, and more than once he came out in appreciative interpretation of Christianity as the mainspring of Western civilization and personal character.

The Buddhists always had to be reckoned with. They were in an unenviable position, representing the old and nearly moribund religious system of the uneducated common people. It was to Confucianism and revised Shinto that the intellectuals looked. Unable quickly to produce new, trained intellectual leadership, the Buddhists resorted to shock treatment for the Christians. There were some treatises written against the Christian faith. But for the most part the opposition was by direct action. When there would be a public Christian lecture meeting, rowdies sometimes would be brought in to cause trouble. Mobs in the city of Niigata destroyed the Christian dispensary, and by mistake killed an innocent citizen thinking him to be the Christian pastor.

Interment and funerals in the ancestral cemeteries connected with Buddhist temples were, and still are, a matter of embarrassed tensions. On Niishima's death in 1890 his body was not admitted to burial beside that of his own father in the family plot. At times Buddhism was officially utilized by the government. It then treated Christianity with scorn. When, in turn, it was disestablished and thrown on its own resources, it became bitter in competitive struggle. Yet later there were drawn from among its priests several of the most perceptive of the Japanese Christian ministers.

Within the ranks of the Oligarchs a factional struggle reacted upon the Christians. The Iwakura embassy did not include all the contenders for power. Those who were left behind soon tried to seize leadership in national policy-making. Learning of this the embassy returned and restored order. Of the disgruntled ones, several resigned from the Council of State and organized political resistance. Among these were Taisuke Itagaki and Shigenobu Okuma. They never were able to match in strength the two great leaders, Hirobumi Ito, and Aritomo Yamagata, who were to dominate Japan for the coming decades. But both Itagaki and Okuma long maintained a vigorous opposition as the men next in power and influence. They both deeply favored Christianity and repeatedly lent it their support.

At this time their strategy was to take up the cause of the common people in what was known as the People's Rights movements. They urged the early drafting of a Constitution, demanded more local political autonomy; and each organized his own political party to promote the cause of democratic action in opposition to the Oligarchs in power.

Whereas the official stressing of the unequal treaties, with its waves of anti-foreignism, militated against the churches, this movement for political rights, plainly an idea from the West, led many people to look with goodwill and interest on the missionaries and the Christian movement. So it was that winds favorable and unfavorable swept over the scene.

Yet the Christian church had been planted. That was the

great achievement of the first period. There had been enough opposition to challenge the young Protestant movement to meet it, while in the process sufficient new strength was given to send it springing forward in the next period of national development.

Japan had gone a quarter-century into its new life. In the classic pattern of all modern revolutions the new ways were introduced by a few leaders. The cities as the centers of the industrialized society were coming to embody a new culture. A modern state was in the early stages of construction, though not yet organized on a democratic basis.

There were many incongruities, as the new moved in upon the old. The rural people were slow in comprehension of what was happening; they were being dislocated by the changes, but were not greatly benefited by them. A new ideology, that of Japan's unique "National Structure," was being developed for national strength. In the Throne the new Japan was seeking to find its central lodestone of strength. It was still groping for a consistent, thoroughgoing revamping of life in a pattern that would preserve all the best of the old and also that of the new. Not even blue-prints had as yet been made. Only basic goals were clear.

In this world, Christianity had come, unsolicited and unwanted. Even the Western culture was scarcely desired, and its religion was, by many, feared and hated. Yet, it could not be kept out, and Japan was slowly beginning to come to terms with it. The missionaries proved to be not undesirable visitors; on the other hand they had much that progressive persons valued. The first Japanese converts, too, were persons of good standing, of high character, and many of them, had unusual gifts. The schools were acceptable, and medical service was still more so. Christian periodicals were in the lead among intellectuals.

Christianity was almost exclusively a part of the new

Japan. It had little place in the old world of the farmers, the small shopkeepers of the country towns, or in village life. Its roots could not be deeper than those of its members in the cities, and their roots were not deep. It did not grapple with the knotty entanglements that Shinto wove about the householder and neighborhood, nor with the Buddhism that held in its embrace the generations of ancestors gone by. It was moving into position in a network of local churches under trained ministers in the western pattern. Little if any real adjustment to soil or climate had as yet been made.

CHAPTER THREE

A GROWING MODERN NATION-STATE

1882—1909

The Church in Modern Society

PEACEFUL CONSOLIDATION

1882–1889

Rapid Growth

As Japan entered its next phase of modern life the lines straightened out into directions that were to be characteristic of most of the century. The pattern was one of normal, peaceful revolution from the old to the new. Among the Oligarchs, Yamagata, the military genius, was to take his dominant role in the next, more aggressive period, but for the present it was Hirobumi Ito the civilian who had the stage.

By strong financial measures the budget was balanced, inflation stopped, and the economic life made firm. The Bank of Japan stabilized the currency. Cotton and silk industries were encouraged. Foreign traders were to be supplanted by native merchants. Notice was given the small army of technicians and advisers from the West,—at times said to have been nearly five thousand in number,—that they were to be eliminated. Japan was getting ready to guide her own course. The government next turned to the formation of the new political structure for the nation.

The situation was urgent for the active campaign of the opposition was being supported by a rising tide of discontent, largely among the heavily taxed farmers and small-townspeople. The foreign unequal treaties, however, could not be revised until Japan adopted a more modern pattern of laws. It was therefore decided to prepare a Constitution, and public announcement of its promulgation in 1889 was made. Ito was to be its architect. In the meantime elected provincial assemblies were tentatively set up. At the national level a Cabinet of Ministers of State was formed, with Ito as Premier. This was the beginning of responsible government, but it still had slight relation to the public will, for, like all the other changes of this period, it came entirely from above.

At the same time, stern measures were taken to put a ratchet on the wheels of progress. The People's Rights Movement was held under control by a law censoring publications, and another one regulating all public meetings. Yet, notwithstanding its turbulent elements, Japan was really doing well. This period of mid-Meiji is spoken of as a kind of national springtime. The mood was enthusiastic, youthful, and self-confident. Nothing that modern nations possessed or had accomplished seemed impossible for Japan. There came into blossom a flowering of acceptance of the West and all its ways. It was one of the oscillations toward an openness to new things characteristic of the people in their past history. It proved to be of short duration, and it took curious forms, but while it lasted it was a dynamic force, directly bearing on Christianity.

The people at large had now for nearly thirty years been exposed to the West. With fear and repulsion they had expected the worst, but nothing had happened. No foreign power had threatened Japan's sovereignty. There was no general invasion by Westerners, though all supposed there would be when the treaties were revised. In fact even the new activities and teachings of the Christians were not too offensive; and in general public opinion many of the missionaries and Japanese Christians were regarded as admirable people. At any rate the Christians opened windows onto the Western world where, both in the past and the present, a fascinating scene was open to view. In a spirit of self-confidence many Japanese were ready to emulate the West.

It was in court circles that the adoption of foreign ways began. By 1885 the government was encouraging westernization. Prominent persons were affecting western dress, and a whole new vocabulary was coming into the Japanese language. A semi-government official center was established where all the activities were in western style. The ladies were encouraged to discard the kimono and learn the European hair-dress. The Premier held monthly parties at which diplomats and their ladies intermingled, thus showing that Japan could qualify as the equal of the "civilized" Western peoples. Uemura poked fun and poured scorn on the whole thing. It must have been quite a picture to have seen the stern *samurai* Ito or the ascetic Yamagata who would never be seen in public with their own wives embracing Western ladies, in their valiant efforts at a polka. This did not last long, and it serves as a kind of comic interlude of relief in Japan's modern drama.

Another cause for the turning toward the West was the place that the new public schools and their curriculum had in the life of the people. In the early years American Readers were in use, either in English or in literal translation. The teachers and the students were receiving lessons in political democracy and in personal morality from these imported text-books. In them were set forth the character and teachings of Washington and Jefferson. Most of all, Abraham Lincoln and the emancipation of the slaves kindled their admiration. Among the more advanced groups in Japan, the French Third Republic of 1875, was an exciting event, as were the changes in the new nations coming to life in Europe. A humanistic patriotism based on the writings of Rousseau and on the Enlightenment philosophers captured the minds of intellectuals.

Another cause and effect of this wave of westernization was the place of women in the new Japan. Asiatic feudalism reserved for women a most inconspicuous role, and Japan was still largely feudal at heart. But gradually the opening of doors to the young men and their fathers permitted the sisters and mothers to pass through. Girls were admitted to the grade schools. They read the same stories that their brothers were reading. They soon discovered the place women have in all civilizations tempered by Christian traditions. It was too soon for any political action, but spiritually the women's revolution had begun.

One more of the phases of societal life that affected the development of Protestantism in this period was the changing position of the old religions. Nn nation in revolution can avoid dealing with its traditional religious systems. In the struggle for power the vested hierarchy of an ancient religion sometimes offers the most stubborn obstacles to change, and has rough treatment. Sometimes it is the other way round, and it furnishes a ready instrument for use by the new regime. It will then be utilized. In Japan during the eighties various policies were tried.

Buddhism was the faith of the common people, and indeed the formal faith of all the people. Among its fifty sects everyone could find a congenial home; or at least one's ancestors had done so and that was enough for continued affiliation. During its thirteen centuries it had gained wealth, privileges and prestige. Could such a network of power be made responsive to the swift decisions and experimental actions of the early Oligarchs? They thought not, and so during the 60's they all but outlawed official Buddhism. Finding, however, that Buddhism was offering no opposition, they shifted their policy, and during the 70's tried the expedient of combining the three traditional faiths, Buddhism, Confucianism, and Shinto, in one single institution called the Great Religious Bureau, with branches throughout the country. But the essential universalism and passivism of Buddhism did not mingle well with the Japanized Confucian system nor with the ardent neo-Shinto cult with Emperor veneration as its center. It proved impossible to mingle these divergent blood types in a single religious transfusion.

In the 80's, therefore, a different policy was adopted. All religion was declared disestablished. This reduced Buddhism to the status of a voluntary faith. Confucianism was ruled to be a philosophy, which in Japan it is. As to Shinto, it was declared to be the immemorial way of life for Japan and the Japanese, not a religion at all but the divinely-appointed "Way of the Subject". All this was clarified in future decades, but it began to take form as national policy in the period now under review. This is the religious framework in which Protestant Christianity has had to find its place and exercise its ministry throughout the modern century.

In April of 1883 a noteworthy conference was held, the Second Missionary Conference in Osaka, the one in 1872 being counted the first. It is considered a landmark because of its thoroughly representative make-up, and its unhurried proceedings, well prepared for, and recorded in a volume of nearly 500 pages.

There were about a hundred members, women almost equaling men in numbers. They represented a score of missionary and Bible societies, with all the divergent national and denominational backgrounds then represented in Japan. A spirit of amity ran through the entire conference, This was a source of astonishment to non-Christians who had supposed that all these different evangelizing agencies were engaged in internecine warfare.

Hepburn, the dean of the missionary community, presided. Verbeck read a painstaking history of the missions up to that time, a document which is the nucleus of all the histories we now have in English. The agenda covered what a missionary conference would today; obstacles to evangelization, education, ministerial training for men and women, self-support in the churches, language study, missionary itinerating, medical missions, health of missionaries, a Christian literature and principles of translation. In 1883 it was not considered an anachronism that such subjects should be discussed, papers read and conclusions arrived at almost solely by missionaries, without the participation of Japanese.

This Conference registers a stage in the devolving of responsibility from missionaries onto the indigenous Christian movement through which missions in all countries must pass. It was still early to look for guidance to the young men and women of Japan whose introduction to this alien religious world dated only some six or seven years back.

The Osaka Conference registered no sign of tension between missionaries and the Japanese leaders, most of whom were still of the early group of proteges. It was however an instance of parallelling organization and activities, of policy-making and of planning which went on in the Christian movement in Japan for several decades.

The mood of the conference was optimistic, radiant with hope and warm in faith. It did not suggest any changes in denominational lines, nor any radical new departure in church relationships. There were no serious theological debates, and no deep rifts of outlook.

During these years, along with recruits for the older missions eleven new ones came in. These included missions of the Disciples, the Friends, and the Church of England in Canada. One noticeable addition was that of missionaries from three American churches in the south, the Methodists, Presbyterians and Baptists. Just recovering from the disastrous war and its tragic aftermath, they now came to join the Protestant forces.

Another addition to the missionary body was the first foreign mission sent by the recently formed Evangelical Missionary Society. It represented Liberal Protestantism in Switzerland and Germany, with an acceptance of the critical study of Scripture and a broad view of the non-Christian faiths.—something quite new to the earliest missionary force in Japan. Even if these newcomers had been cooperative in spirit, they probably would have been welcomed by the older missionaries with a guarded enthusiasm, but in their own countries they had achieved their position by battle, and they seem to have carried their armor with them to Japan. When in 1885 they were augmented by the Unitarians from America who disavowed any missionary activity at all and defined their aim as only fraternization with the non-Christian world, the lines came to be clearly drawn. Looking ahead it may be said that the early tensions between these "liberal" workers and the other missionaries in later years completely disappeared.

By the end of the 80's the missionary force had expanded from 145 in 1883 to 363 in number; their places of residence from 37 to 89; and the outstations related to the churches,—

the great majority of which still were centers projected and cultivated under missionaries' direction,—had leaped from 83 to 448. It was a busy time of seed-sowing and harvesting.

In May, 1883, in Tokyo, the third of the national Christian Conferences was held by the Japanese churches. Ministers and laymen attended. Delegates came from all over Japan. In addition, hundreds of non-delegated persons were in attendance. The sessions were largely given up to addresses and preaching.

The conference proper ended on the Sunday with Niishima preaching. A Communion service followed in which over three hundred persons participated. In a huge, rented theater for five nights there were public preaching services with a score of speakers. Each one was a tested exponent of the faith, competent to express it with convincing effect on persons who had never heard it before. Night by night the numbers increased. On the last evening, the doors had to be forcefully closed on over three thousand people with crowds milling about outside.

There was another particular feature of this period. During the meetings of the missionaries in Osaka, and again during the Japanese conference in Tokyo the spiritual tone had reached a high pitch. Ballagh had preached a sermon on Acts 1:8, recalling the events of 1872 when after the Week of Prayer in Yokohama the fires of spiritual "revival" had come to flame. He had also reported that a similar thing was happening again in Yokohama. Celebrating the World's Week of Prayer of the Evangelical Alliance some seamen in the port had come into a fresh experience of God's saving grace, and had kindled a spirit of longing, contrition and of spiritual regeneration in the group. The meetings had continued from January till March, the movement, in the meantime spreading to some of the girls' schools in Yokohama, then to Aoyama Gakuin in Tokyo, and to other centers. There were intense emotional upheavals, much confession and restitution, and moving testimonies to the joy of the new life in Christ.

The revivals jumped from the Tokyo-Yokohama region to Central Japan and in 1884 enveloped Doshisha College. Here once more, the January prayer meetings could not be stopped, but ran on until March, with the entire school swept by the spiritual excitement. The authorities sent three representative students to report to the churches, and tried to get the rest of the student body to resume academic work, but without success. A respite of one week was taken, after which, with the baptism of two hundred students, things moved back to normal schedule. In 1886 a similar movement struck Sendai, putting all the church life on a new level of strength. Nagoya which had always been uphill territory felt the lift, and Nagasaki, another hostile citadel opened to the spiritual forces in a new way. In Oita in Kyushu it led to the formation of the Oita Band centering in Dr. Samuel H. Wainright of the Southern Methodist Mission.

This demonstration was so different from the usual course of the Protestant movement that it raises the question as to how it came about. Perhaps Ballagh was particularly used of God at this juncture. Certain it is that he felt divinely guided in his part in all the associated movements of those early days; and his special stress was upon the witness of the Holy Spirit in the inner life. But the broader question remains. Would the Japanese people respond more readily to an emotional appeal rather than to the customary rational presentation of the Gospel? Up to this time the missionaries, although of varying temperaments, had tended to explain and expound, their appeal being made to reason and to common sense.

The popular religious cults throughout the Tokugawa and early Meiji eras exhibited a great deal of emotion. Ecstatic experiences with dancing marked their rites. In recent years this feature has been prominent in many of the new cults. But as a rule Christianity has been conventional in deportment and just a little on the starched side. This seems to be the way most of the pastors wish it; they want the waters to run deep, but prefer not to encourage too much overflow of emotion. This revival period in the life of Japanese Protestantism was viewed from the German Evangelical position as having been the result of the peculiar temperament of American and Anglo-Saxon Christians, and as being a very dangerous phenomenon. The rank and file of Japanese Christians, however, generally look back on it as belonging to the springtime of Japan and of the church; a blessed time of refreshment and replenishment for persons who were in constant spiritual suffering for their faith and who could expect only more difficult encounters ahead.

The changed national attitude of openness had an effect on the evangelistic strategy of Christianity in this period. For one thing, the method of witnessing through large public meetings came into general use. Already, in 1880 there had been a successful two days meeting in Uyeno Park, Tokyo, where there were said to be four thousand people gathered in the open air to listen. It was the first experience of a Christian mass meeting, and the public reception was uncertain. But it had been immensely successful. At the time it was regarded as a mile-stone on the way to public recognition of Christianity.

Christian lecture meetings in rented theaters became an expeditious way of reaching multitudes of people. The buildings were always large, provided with stalls where families or parties would come, as to the Japanese dramatic performances, for stays of long hours. They were accustomed in going to the theater to bring their refreshments, solid and liquid, and to disport themselves without too much reference to the stage unless it caught and held their attention. One can imagine what nerve it took to announce a serious religious meeting, especially a Christian one, in such surroundings. Anything might happen. People were curious, they wanted to know more about the West and its ways, and they came in crowds. Some had deeper spiritual reasons, and still others had already been touched by Christian influence, and intended to go farther. Sometimes it was the local church that made the arrangements.

All this presented a great challenge, and the missionaries and their Japanese associates undertook the work in earnest. One result was that the early missionaries learned to think and talk in Japanese on their feet. And the inexperienced Japanese began to do the same. They learned how to catch the crowds and how not to lose them. They showed great skill in telling Bible stories and became adept in handling hecklers. In this hard school they strengthened their own faith in action. Not all were equal to this kind of tussling with the public, but many early missionaries recalled some of these "native helpers" or evangelists as among the finest and bravest witnesses the Japanese church ever produced. In the early years most of the acknowledged leaders of the church, both ministers and laymen, were masters of the public platform.

A number of cities were in the habit of holding expositions for purposes of encouraging industries. Christians would rent a pavilion, and serve there in shifts, keeping up a barrage of short addresses, hymn singing, and student testimonies all day long and into the night. Such meetings are still held in many provincial towns at times of festivals and other celebrations.

Another marked feature of this period was the rapid expansion of the church membership. People did more than merely listen; they went on to baptism and church admission at a new rate. In seven years the adult membership rose from a little over four thousand to thirty thousand. The number of churches multiplied threefold, as did that of ordained ministers. The body of evangelists increased still more rapidly, from 100 to 409. In evaluating trends it is of great importance to take account of the unordained ministers, or those partially ordained as evangelists. The settled pastors, as a rule are inside the fort, holding it, and their work is indispensable. It is the evangelists who are on the skirmish line. They often suffer disparagement and loss of morale by not being given full status in the church constitution, but a young Christian movement that does not have them in large numbers usually is not registering much growth.

Most of the evangelists were associated with a particular missionary who had a plan of Christian outreach for his region. Some of these teams covered wide areas and set the lines for what later became a network of churches. In illustration one case comes to mind, though it belongs to a later time. H. H. Cook based on the city of Yamagata in North-Eastern Japan, would load his motorcycle with bundles of Christian periodicals and his violin, and with a Japanese colleague, set out systematically visiting the towns and villages of that area. Wherever there was a reader of his magazine he visited him and where two or three would gather he held a meeting. Back he came, again and again, stirring up interest, encouraging lonely converts, organizing study groups, enlisting subscribers to the periodical, training young leaders for Christian responsibilities, until in many of the fifty centers he had on his heart and schedule new churches came into being.

Many of the church members in the 80's were young people. Some were students from the Christian schools. A great many girls and women were now opening their minds to new impressions and were attending public meetings. The wives of missionaries and of pastors were active in all sorts of ways to cultivate and serve the needs of Japanese housewives and mothers. In addition to Bible study, classes for cooking and dress-making were being held, and Christian societies were organized.

In this work a new kind of minister came upon the scene. Women missionaries found their opposite numbers among the young Japanese women who volunteered for Christian work. Prepared in one of the several Women's Training Schools they became worthy colleagues for work in evangelism, personal counselling, or the conduct of Bible and other classes in Christian nurture. During the seven years from 1883 on the number of such "Bible women" or women evangelists advanced from thirty-seven to a hundred and twenty-five. Not all of them were on the frontier. Many served well-developed local churches as visitor, leader of religious education, director of work for women and city evangelist. The period when the woman evangelist was made to be the trusted associate pastor of the growing local church came later; in the earlier years her place was usually by the side of a much beloved and loving foreign woman missionary.

Not all such growth was due to missionaries' efforts; it was to a large extent traceable to the leadership of the pastors and their congregations.

At the end of the seven years in 1889, there were many more churches than at the beginning, and also the average membership of each local group had risen from 42 to 106. Self support, had surprisingly gained ground. In 1882 there were but 15 unaided churches to 80 receiving aid. In 1889, 153 stood on their own feet, to 123 that received assistance, or considerably over one half. And this was at a time of many newly-born churches.

Japanese Christianity unlike the beginnings of the church in some other countries never had a "people's movement". Its first leaders and many of its members were *samurai* who, though they scorned wealth were the privileged intellectuals of their time. In the new modern Japan, some of them had gone into professions and business, and had prospered. Now they were the responsible laymen in the churches. One such church, Bancho Church in residential Tokyo, included numerous national figures in business and political life. Members of the Court, the cabinet and the diplomatic service were in the congregation, some of their wives being Christians. It gave a certain prestige to associate with people of the international circles represented by the pastor, H. Kozaki, and his members, particularly at this time of pro-Western sentiment.

In the development of civil government some pastors and church members took a conspicuous part. Yoichi Honda was the first president of the Aomori provincial assembly. He and others were in the People's Rights Movement, being known as "People's Warriors". The Oligarch Itagaki who led this movement openly commended Christianity, helped found the local church in his home city of Kochi and advised several of his political followers to be baptized,—though he himself never was.

Among the cultural liberals, too, this was a time of approval, somewhat patronizing to be sure, but apparently genuine. One educator advised the adoption of Christianity as the national religion; what he called "protective coloring" for Japan in dealing with the Western nations. A professor of the Tokyo University advised Christians bravely to make a bid through their schools for the allegiance of the best minds in the nation, inasmuch as Christianity was bound to become one of the major faiths of the people.

It was among these liberals that the new German Evangelical mission had its most enthusiastic welcome. They attended the lectures by the founder, W. Spinner and assisted him in opening a school for the training of young men in the doctrines of his church. A number of young Japanese later to be famous in literary and social work were for a while members of this church.

When A.M. Knapp from America came introducing Unitarian Christianity, President Fukuzawa took him to his heart, brought him and other missionaries of that group onto the faculty of his Keio University, and gave them full moral support. A number of persons who had already been baptized, but who were restless within the framework of the traditional theology and church regulations became members of the Unitarian church in Tokyo. Among them, Isoo Abe and others were famous in the social movements of the next decades. They took over the *Cosmos Magazine* and made it their Unitarian organ of opinion.

To be sure there were adverse currents affecting the churches. The government noticed the Christians' affinities with the progressive movements and checked closely on some of the leaders. Honda was forced to resign from the principalship of a Christian school. The layman Kenkichi Kataoka who technically violated the Peace Preservation Law by insisting on entering Tokyo to present a memorial to the government, was arrested and sentenced to a year in prison. The police refused permits for Christian open-air meetings as possibly being subversive of law and order.

The Buddhists also increased their opposition. They renewed the rowdyism of the 70's in a nw movment slurringly called "Exterminate Yaso", using the vulgar pronunciation for Jesus' name. This was carried on by itinerating priests, and consisted of open attacks on churches, systematic braking up of meetings, and general intimidation. At this point the authorities usually stepped in and gave protection. Sometimes good sportsmanship on the part of the public gained a hearing for the detested faith.

Conventional Buddhism had its back to the wall, fighting to retain a foothold in the new Japan, and also to combat the alien Christian religion. At the same time a renovated Buddhism was beginning to show itself. Priests who went abroad were amazed to find in English and German universities scholars who knew more about original Buddhism, its texts and languages than they did, who were limited in knowledge to its Chinese background. That gave them a new sense of the dignity of their own religious tradition. Some who tried to put into effect basic reforms in Japanese Buddhist sects were repudiated, but many agreed in utilizing the new currents of life in the old faith to block off Christian progress. Their periodicals carried on a constant flow of hostile articles, and numerous books were put into circulation aiming at the defamation of Christianity. There is no evidence that they had much effect. At the close of the decade the Buddhist leaders were launching a new movement "Reverence for the Emperor; Veneration for the Buddha; Indivisible". From this time, however, there are signs of adoption by the Buddhists of Christian techniques, a trend which later became much more pronounced.

In all this situation the Christians were not without public champions of their cause. Through their already popular periodicals, Kozaki, Uemura and others broke lances with their opponents. With vigorous writing, sarcasm and humor they often carried the day. Kozaki's *A New View of Politics* and *The True Line* by Uemura had a wide circulation.

The major Protestant denominations were building bone structure as well as muscle and nerve energy. Each by now had its framework of organization extending all over Japan. They became known as the "Big Five"; a term, of course, relative to the small size of the entire Christian movement.

The Congregationalists had the head-start, because of their early organization in 1877, and the building up of an active Home Missionary Society to extend their borders. Strong in Central Japan, with the prestige of Doshisha and Kyoto, they had wide frontiers. A galaxy of able missionaries loyally supported their independence and branched out into various fields of auxiliary service.

Abreast with the Congregationalists in numbers and due to grow still more rapidly was the Presbyterian-Reformed Church with five strong missions in support. An all-encompassing geographical area had been staked out, cultivated, and by now was covered with a network of churches on their way to complete autonomy. It was a most admirable framework for a national church, which with an unusual leadership of ministers and laymen was on the way to a splendid history in Japanese Protestantism.

Next in size, and rapidly growing was the Methodist work. It was not yet organized into one body, but the three supporting missions observed a division of areas of cultivation fraternally agreed upon so as not to overlap, and all had similar outlook and polity. It could therefore already be viewed as one Japanese denomination, which it became in 1907.

The fourth was the Holy Catholic Church (Anglican-Episcopal) aided by four missionary Societies. Bishop Williams had laid down his episcopal responsibilities, and they passed to Bishop John McKim who for over half of Japan's modern century superintended one or more of the ten dioceses of the denomination. Bishop Bickersteth came from Great Britain in 1885, and by 1887 had brought together the related groups in the formation of the Japanese church. In this church, too, as with the others, a Home Missionary Society under the Japanese churches was immediately organized.

The fifth group was the Baptists. Their geographical spread was very wide and the line was sometimes thin, as was the case with the Methodists. They were more consistent in maintaining the autonomy of the local church than were the Congregationalists, so that the Japanese churches never became one cohesive body as did the Congregational Churches. This may have been a source of ecclesiastical weakness, though the Baptist witness has always been faithfully given.

In 1886 a renewed effort was made to unite the Congregational and the Presbyterian-Reformed churches. Separate commissions were raised, then joined. A plan was passed back and forth with changes and modifications. Finally it was adopted by the Presbyterians but at the Congregational assembly of 1888 it was tabled for further study. The matter was then dropped. By common report, it was Dr. Niishima who caused the failure. It is said that he personally was favorable to the union, but that as a *samurai*, largely responsible to the American Board of Missions, he felt it disloyal to abandon the Congregational polity, as the new plan would have done. How far regional clannishness as between Kyoto and Tokyo, and the differing loyalties of the Yokohama and the Kumamoto Bands may have exerted an unconscious influence, must be left to conjecture. The fact remains that never during Japan's Protestant century did two major denominational families voluntarily unite.

In 1884 the Fourth National Christian Conference voted itself into the World's Evangelical Alliance as the Japan organization, and with this structure served all the denominations until 1906, when it dissolved. In 1911 it was succeeded by the Christian Church Federation until its transformation in 1922 into the National Christian Council. Thus for three quarters of its century Protestantism in Japan has had something of a united voice and action.

From the start missionaries and churchmen had been concerned to possess the text of the Scriptures in suitable Japanese. In 1888, at the commemoratory service in Tokyo, Dr. Hepburn, the Nestor of the movement for nearly thirty years, stood in the pulpit holding in one hand the New Testament, in use for eight years, and in the other hand the newly finished Old Testament. It had been a great undertaking, and it was well-done.

In the task foreigners and Japanese formed an indivisible team,—the missionaries dealing with the Biblical languages, and the Japanese with literary usage and style. Before the New Testament was finished and throughout the Old Testament sessions the Episcopalians were enthusiastically in the work.

The development of Church music was also progressing during these years. Missionaries in Nagasaki published a really modern book with over two hundred hymns and tunes, liturgy and worship services. Also a joint committee of the Congregational and Presbyterian-Reformed churches published the *New Selected Hymnal* probably the best collection both of music and of hymns produced in Japan up to that time. Uemura's translations were of the highest literary quality. How these same few church leaders found time and strength for all such tasks is a mystery, but their versatility seemed almost without limit.

During this period in the 80's more schools came into being, notably North-Japan College in Sendai, the leading Christian school in North-East Japan. Aoyama Gakuin moved onto a 25 acre campus in Tokyo, and Kwansei Gakuin was started in Kobe, later to share with Doshisha the leadership in Christian education in Central Japan. Numerous Christian schools for women were established, including Kwassui Jo Gakko, Methodist, in Nagasaki; Hiroshima Girls School, Southern Methodist, in Hiroshima; Toyo Eiwa,

Canadian, in Tokyo; and Wilmina Girls School, Presbyterian, in Kyoto.

Protestant social outreach resulted in a variety of new institutions. Medical work continued. Dr. Berry's recommendations to the government for prison reform had not only been largely put into practice, but in the process he had inspired Taneaki Hara to commit his life to a ministry to ex-convicts. As a prominent layman, Hara was a leavening influence upon all the denominations in their outlook on under-privileged people. Another product of this same movement was Kosuke Tomeoka, the founder of a home for delinquent boys. Work for the relief of lepers was begun, and the first training of the blind was begun. At Okayama, another work of social rescue developed in the Orphanage founded and carried on till his death by Juji Ishii. This, too, came to be a kind of lighthouse pointing the way for all denominations in future social work.

In 1886 Miss Mary Leavitt of the Woman's Christian Temperance Union visited Japan, where she laid the case for purity, peace and temperance upon the women of the Christian churches. Mrs. Kaji Yajima, the head of a girls' school in Tokyo, was challenged to organize a chapter of the organization in Japan. She not only did this, but gave herself heart and mind to the cause for the remainder of her long life. She has been followed by a noble line of successors who have never for an instant given up the fight for purity.

Thus Japanese Protestantism passed through its first summer harvest. It proved to be a brief Indian summer followed by early frosts, but it stands as a period to which Christians may look back with nostalgia and pride. Perhaps never again in Japan's modern century was the church so close to the intellectual, the political and the social leadership of the nation, nor did it ever again attract quite such wide attention and interest. Never again was it so near to a mass movement in growth. It probably did not again register so high a level of spiritual experience on the part of the ordinary members of the churches. An imposing roster of names among both ministers and laymen was posted. Its accomplishments in proportion to its size were impressive. It offers an example of a normally developing Christian movement in a nation passing swifty to modern statehood. Viewed across the tumultuous events that followed in the next decades, this period presents an idyllic scene, scarcely again to be repeated.

REACTION AND TENSION
1889–1899

Retarded Growth in Church

Toward the end of the 80's the pendulum swung back, as it was bound to do. The Japanese people threw off the eccentric aping of the west, and with momentous tasks ahead they turned to a more serious concentration on them. A resurgence of Confucian studies caught the public mood with the slogan "Preservation of our National Values".

The new Constitution was promulgated by the government in 1889. Prince Ito its designer had gone to Germany in 1882 as the country most likely to offer what Japan would wish, and there for several months he had studied and observed every detail of the Prussian pattern. This intensive indoctrination had equipped him later not only to utilize every feature of the national law to advantage, but also to become the author of a voluminous set of commentaries on it.

At the center of the new state structure was the Emperor, the source of the national dynamic, who alone could give this constitution to his subjects. The instrument was brought into being by first creating a Privy Council through the emperor's command and selection, and then by submitting the document to them. This small group continued to be a most potent element in Japanese national life. Ito was always chairman, and the Oligarchs all belonged. In its secret meetings policies were fixed, and the shifting ministerial assignments were agreed upon. By this time the Oligarchs were middle-aged men, ripened in experience, and skilled in administration. They were autocrats, men of iron and utterly committed to what they believed to be the national welfare. Whatever faults they had, they were above petty corruption, and no scandal was associated with them. They surrounded the Emperor, set the nation's course, and through a large corps of civil servants supervised all administration.

In the meantime the Emperor had another still smaller, informal group for consultation, and these may originally have been chosen by him. They were the Elder Statesmen, who on a personal basis could be called on for advice at the highest level of urgency, or when a deadlock had to be broken. A further concentration of power lay in the armed services. Early in the period an Imperial Rescript for the Army and Navy was issued in which they were characterized as the Emperor's left and right arms, with the safety of the nation committed to them. That, of course, gave them the right of direct access to his person for confirmation of all their policies, and made it possible totally to by-pass any other procedure.

With this complete inner system of authority, there was really little need for a Constitution, nor for a Representative Assembly, but since the clamor for it was general it was provided. A Diet of two houses was set up. The Lower House of three hundred members was elected by certain land-owning voters, who at that time comprised about one per-

cent of the population. Its powers were strictly limited.
Even in case of its failure to pass a budget, the government
could proceed with that of the preceding year.

The Upper House was composed of the five ranks of the
nobility and other persons chosen by the Throne. Their
powers included an effective veto on the Lower House. No
reference was made to a Cabinet, but there was to be one,
operating under its own rules, and really not accountable to
the Diet at all. The ruler was to name the premier and his
chosen colleagues, the ministers of state. Courtesy called for
their attendance at Diet sessions and the answering of
questions, though in times of tension they often declined to
do either.

From the beginning the opposition was represented by
political parties, and indeed the history of much of the Diet
has been one of its warfare against the Oligarchs. When its
pressure became too obnoxious the simple procedure of
dissolution proved effective. Few politicians could long
endure frequent general elections with their strain and
expense. In the first decade these came every year or two.
Prince Yamagata soon took over as premier and resorted
to harsh policy measures, even to the employment of professional bullies, to control the elections. Bloodshed and rioting
were common. From the first, too, the practice of arbi-
trarily using the seal of the Emperor came to be employed
with conclusive effect. Most features of the system carried
on up to the end of the Second World War. Notwithstanding
the limited functions of the Diet, it did constitute an organ
of popular opinion, and at times it exerted some real influence in the public life of the nation.

The leaders were concerned to infuse the new body politic
with a spirit of loyalty. This spirit was to be in no sense
new, but a distillation of the ancient heritage of Confucius
and Shinto, addressed to the national situation. It took the

form of another Imperial Rescript, this one on Education, issued in 1890. The injunctions to moral conduct are sound, beginning with duties to parents, then to neighbors, friends and to the public welfare and common interests. It continues "always respect the Constitution and observe the laws: should emergency arise, offer yourselves courageously to the State, and thus guard and maintain the prosperity of our Imperial Throne, coeval with heaven and earth."

Copies of this Rescript were issued to every public school. It was ceremonially read on all national holidays. Special instructors interpreted and applied it in classes, with approved textbooks. Gradually it came to be the sacred testament of modern Japan, stamping its imprint upon every child and youth during all the school years. The reading of this Rescript scroll was augmented by the issuing at this time of official portraits of the Emperor and Empress. Their use developed into a ritual event tantamount to worship. On special occasions they were unveiled while the students stood with heads bowed low. In later revolutionary situations of other nations the emotional power of the use of portraits has been demonstrated. Seventy years ago in Japan it was an innovation, and terribly effective.

Social and economic progress was that of a fast-growing modern State. Silk and cotton mills were springing up, literally in the fields. Perhaps half the labor force consisted of farmers' daughters needing a dowry before marriage, or bravely attempting to pull the household out of debt. They lived in dormitories, worked interminably long hours at low wages, and often with tragic effect on health and morals. There were as yet no labor laws nor organizations to protect them, and the paternalism of the owners was only occasionally benevolent. The big industrialists were steadily growing more powerful, with government aid supplementing increasing profits. They were building up a strong merchant marine, and were pushing mining, and the making of steel. Heavy industry was beginning to produce a new type of laborer and with him emerged problems of housing, health, and labor relations entirely novel to the nation.

The country needed the reservoir of technical skills and capital now accumulating, for population was rising. From the twenty five million of 1850 it climbed to over forty million at the end of the 90's. For the first time in history the rice crop had to be supplemented by purchased food. Japan had crossed the line from an importing to an exporting nation with its balance of trade. This changed the national outlook, and eyes scanned overseas horizons for natural resources, and for markets for finished products.

The region most obviously in view was Korea, the next-door neighbor. It not only offered resources of its own and was the gateway to greater ones inland, but the control of it seemed essential to a curbing of the expansive aggression of the European powers.

China, in her historic role of arbiter of the Far Eastern world, stood in the way of the nation's policies. Disregarding this, Japan had obtained a treaty with Korea, to which China never agreed. Finally, in 1894, on the occasion of some civil disturbances in Korea China sent in troops to restore order. Japan rushed an expedition across the Straits, and the two armies were face to face. Fighting followed, and the issue was quickly settled. Japan's energy, skill and equipment were more than a match for the antiquated forces of the ancient empire. A peace humiliating to China was made by the Treaty of Shimonoseki in 1895.

Japan had won her first modern war. It cost her little and brought great and immediate gains. The reparations she received more than paid for the financial outlay while she obtained control of Korea and the strategic Liaotung Peninsula. Of all wars, that sort is the most deceptive. It shifted Japan from low gear into high as a modern nation, called for more speed, for stronger controls, for heavier military power, and for more ambitious expeditions toward farther national goals.

There were, however, other contenders in the field. It was not in the plans of Russia for Japan to hold Liaotung, the gateway to the rich lands of South Manchuria. In concert with Germany and France she intervened and forced Japan's relinquishment of this territory. In compensation Japan was given Formosa, and Southern Sakhalin, as well as the Kuriles in the North. There was a deep sense of anger and bitterness at the cynicism of the western Powers in the pursuit of their national self-interest in the naked power struggle for Asia. The experience convinced Japan's leaders that the only way to national fulfillment in the modern world was through successful wars carried on with ruthless strength. They renewed the old slogan with intensified meaning "Prosperous Country; Strong Arms", and set out to be ready for the next round, with Russia over Korea.

Such was the situation in which Protestantism found itself during the 90's. Consisting, as it did, of Japanese people living in their own world it reflects all the events and trends we have noted. The coming of missionary recruits and the opening of new missions went on without much reference to the Japanese political and economic scene, but their work soon reflected its trends.

A number of new missions came, including, from America, the Scandinavian Alliance, the Christian and Missionary Alliance, and from England the Evangelistic Band under the direction of Barclay Buxton, who was for years a stimulus to the higher devotional life of all the churches in Japan. The United Lutheran Church from the United States opened work, chiefly in West Japan; the Seventh Day

Adventists established themselves in Tokyo, where they have continued to serve the medical needs of Japanese and foreigners while carrying on their own Christian work. The United Brethren and the Universalists rounded out the Protestant Church emphasis. The work of the Salvation Army was introduced, from Great Britain. Then, as later, they ran into trouble with the authorities over their military terminology, ranks, uniforms, and close integration with the West. Especially did their periodical the *War Cry* puzzle the Japanese with its apparent belligerency. Their works of mercy, however, and their efforts especially for the rescue of victims of the brothels swept away all misunderstandings with the ordinary people. A mission to railway workers was started, and an entirely new venture was the launching of the *Gospel Ship* under the capable skipper-missionary Captain Luke Bickel upon the waters of the Inland Sea. He pushed it among the islands where no Christian had ever been seen, and by his indomitable labors built up for the Baptist church a scattered but vigorous Christian community.

Evangelistic work was pressed more widely than ever. The lines were extended to reach the remnants of the prehistoric Ainu people in Hokkaido, by the Anglican missionary John Bachelor. The Bonin Islands also were visited by Anglican workers. The Baptist, Methodist and Anglican missions all began regular Christian work in Okinawa. This new activity was made possible by the leniency of the Japanese government in issuing passports freely from 1894, when the agreement to revise the treaties was made, without waiting for the stipulated five year period to elapse before their coming into effect.

But notwithstanding the fact that the missionary force had now grown to 723, the Christian advance dragged. The rate of adult baptisms per year which in 1888 had been about seven thousand, toward the end of the 90's fell to less than three thousand. Church membership up to this time had been doubling every three years; now it took twelve years to accomplish the same result. As later years showed, even this was not insignificant growth, but it was in marked contrast to the period just preceding. Persons still became inquirers and a good many received baptism, but the number who fell away or had to be dismissed was disappointingly large. In some of the years it was said to be sixty per cent or more. One missionary in a report in 1893 referred to the situation as not so much hostility as complete stagnation. In his district, of the 117 accessions to the church it had been necessary to drop 73 persons.

The causes for this recession may be attributed in varying degrees to the trends already indicated. There was a recoil from over-westernization, and Christianity was still a Western faith. The fervent patriotism of the time had its effect. The conservatism of the old family system had not disappeared, nor had the hold of the Shinto shrine or Buddhist temple in the home village. The Buddhists at this time were thoroughly aroused and fighting Christianity with all their force.

Preoccupation with the oncoming political changes, the new Constitution and the recurring elections, supplanted in public interest the large meetings conducted by Christian evangelists. When such meetings were held they often were broken up by deliberate opposition, but more often by the disrespectful and vulgar heckling of the kind then current in political meetings. Some government officials were well disposed, but most of them were not friendly. Pressure came from the police in the matter of refusing permits for meetings. Some school authorities discriminated against Christian teachers or students. The army was very hard on soldiers who showed any interest in the new faith.

Within the churches, too, were forces at work that retarded growth. The new liberal theology was unsettling the minds of some of the ministers, and the current scientific and rationalistic outlook, deriving mostly from Europe, was deterring the intellectuals from easily accepting the traditional presentation of Christianity. Many avowed Christians had never made a really deep commitment, and in the various categories of the Parable of the Sower, they disappeared. Defections due to moral conduct were not unusual, for standards of the young churches regarding smoking and drinking, sex relations, and amusements were extremely rigorous.

The Japanese churches and their leaders exhibited sensitive reactions to all the trends that were sweeping the nation. They followed the general mood in a new attitude of criticism toward the missionaries whose training and competency, they thought, were scarcely adequate to the new demands. Perhaps there was a basis of truth in this. There had been very rapid expansion of missions. In the United States in the 80's and 90's missionary societies had no systematic recruiting methods or tests; there was little missionary training, and even theological education was not always demanded of the ministry.

In Japan there were then no adequate facilities for language study. One of the most prominent and sympathetic of the Japanese church leaders said in 1896 that few of the members of the mission could converse easily in Japanese or were able to understand the real conditions and needs of the Japanese people. They were preaching sermons ground out with an "assistant" or "native helper", but they had never been given the training required to orient them deeply in Japanese life. This, of course, does not apply to all. It is recorded with full recognition of the devotion and consecration of the missionaries of every period, and of the linguistic facility of many.

93

To catch the drive of the Japanese discontent regarding Westerners one must go deeper than languages, for often a missionary who cannot speak the language at all has endeared himself to the people beyond all thought of criticism. The foreign mission as conducted seventy years ago, carried with it an implied sense of the superiority of the Western culture as well as of the Christian religion, and by inference, of the missionary himself. This extended not only to "the heathen", to whom frequent references were made in the Osaka Missionary Conference of 1883, but to the Japanese colleagues as well. In the Bible Translation reports, the members are referred to as "assistants", whereas in Japanese thinking they are among the immortals.

Most of the Japanese leaders had by this time been in America and were shocked by the deeply divided Negro-White civilization. They came back with a sharp eye for the slightest indication of disparagement of Japanese in the thinking of any foreign missionary. If the nation would not tolerate unequal treatment from the Western powers, neither would the high spirited church leaders who were already making a greater sacrifice in becoming Christians than their foreign colleagues realized. Some missionaries did fully sense this climate, and cordially accepted it. In the discussions of the early conferences, still preserved, both points of view are represented.

This emotional recoil was in part a reflection of the general turning of interest from America toward Germany. It was the period of Germany's great contribution to Japanese national reconstruction. A German professor of law in the Imperial University had made one of the four drafts from which the final text of the national Constitution was formed. From the Christian movement in Germany had recently come the new type of approach, that of the German Evangelical Society. They came, they said, not to convert but to confer. There was to be no overlordship of anyone's faith, but rather, an exchange of religious beliefs. The other religions were to be studied and respected, not demolished. Toward the Japanese Christian associates they consistently maintained a fraternal attitude.

This was a most attractive innovation, and especially so to those who had already been drawn in their reading of European works toward the modern scientific views, and were impatient with the general lack of knowledge or interest in this field on the part of their Western missionary colleagues. It was even before this time that Uchimura was devouring the works of Kierkegaard, and Kozaki was lecturing on the social philosophy of Karl Marx.

Tension was appearing in the area of church relationships with the missions. Each of the major Japanese denominations was affiliated with at least one foreign mission, and in some instances with four or five of them. These missions were really churches in so far as they were doing evangelistic work. They also operated schools and other institutions. Year by year their size was increasing; they had large budgets administered by themselves, they made their own plans for expansion of church life by selecting the communities to be evangelized. Inasmuch as their work was on the frontiers of outreach while the Japanese pastors usually had all they could do to maintain their local church, it was the missionaries who determined the lines of the boundaries, and eventually of the make-up of the church-to-be. In a word they were the engineers of the church itself, not in its thought life nor spiritual trends but in its actual physical existence as a collocation of local Christian communities.

This activity was precisely what had brought the Japanese denominations into existence in the first place, and it was one for which all were grateful. But times had changed. Now it was felt that the churches, already under the stigma of supposed dependence on the West, must become responsible for planning their own growth.

In 1894 the Presbyterian-Reformed Church declined aid for its Home Missionary Society and reconstituted itself as an all-Japanese body. This did not affect the other work done by the mission directly. The year 1895 saw a similar action by the Congregational Churches. They were of the hope that all work by missionaries in relation to the church might be subsumed within this organization. The mission felt that they must maintain the right of supervision "to ensure", as one wrote, "that the money intrusted to its care be used for propagating the fundamental truths of the Gospel." Probably the mission never realized the emotional effect on the church leaders of the clear implication that the missionaries had a more dependable fiduciary sense and that they were better judges of "the fundamental truths of the Gospel" than the church leaders. At any rate, the Home Missionary Society established its own independence.

A more dramatic episode illustrating this same field of tension with all its complications is that of the Doshisha University. It was founded officially by Niishima, and it would seem that he personally furnished the occasion in Boston which led the American Board to make it possible. Yet, associated with him from before its opening was Jerome D. Davis, who in Kyoto maintained one of the early missionary home-schools of the time. This was the physical parent of Niishima's Doshisha, and from the start the two men were a team. Who then really had founded the school?

It was a faltering experiment until the Kumamoto Band came and put it on its feet. So these men, later alumni, felt that it was their school. And they were the most self-confident and patriotic of any one group in Protestantism. Dr. Niishima had treasured the dream of university status, and had gone back to America to get support for it. He then

returned and scoured all Japan for subscriptions, finally enlisting even the Oligarchs, several of whom subscribed to
its financing. They were his friends of the years, but he had
undoubtedly made a case for the contribution which this
broadly cultural university might make to the nation at
large. In the effort he spent his strength, and in 1890 he
died.

About 1895 tension began to rise among the teachers, between the missionaries and the Japanese of an extreme
wing, liberal in religion and conservative in nationalism.
There is no need to trace the details, but in the process of
controversy the missionaries by vote of the mission withdrew, and all contact was severed. On the Japanese side
the trustees virtually abrogated the Christian basis of the
school's constitution substituting instead the Imperial Rescript on Education as the foundation for moral teaching.
The visit of a deputation from Boston failed to break the
stalemate. Finally in 1898 the missionary society made a
threat of legal action to determine who should control the
school. A former American Consul in Japan was sent out
as attorney. As the matter was now a *cause célèbre* Premier
Okuma brought it to a conclusion by obtaining the resignation of the board, a change in the administration and a
return to the former mission relationships.

Here in brief was the complex of irritating emotional
factors which in the late '90's harassed both missions and
churches as Japan moved away from its Western moorings
into the open sea, as a mature nation-state. There were
many other factors affecting the churches, of which perhaps
the chief was the new national Constitution, and its conservative interpretation. Christians had no question as to
the place of the Emperor. They loyally accepted his role as
that of the center and inspiration of life for the national
structure. Later this became a critical problem as he came

to be an object of worship. Probably at the time under review that interpretation was not yet generally put upon his
person. "The Imperial Will", however, was absolute in
authority, and that fact alone should have presented a problem for Christians, though they maintained that it was
not. They held that there was full place for loyalty to the
Emperor and to Jesus Christ as Lord. This was a time of
robust apologetic writing by Kozaki, Uemura, Ebina and
others of the prominent Christian pastors, as well as of
several laymen,—notably Soho Tokutomi,—who were editors of large daily newspapers. These writers were immensely influential; a bulwark of strength for the Christians in facing hostile attacks.

The point of central attention for the Christians, however, was Article XXVIII of the Constitution which read:

"Japanese subjects, within the limits not prejudicial to
peace and order, and not antagonistic to their duties as
subjects, shall enjoy freedom of religious belief."

Viewed critically and from the standpoint of the degree
of religious liberty accorded in many nations today, these
qualifications leave the way open for much repression, but
at that time the law was viewed as giving recognition to the
legitimacy of being a Christian in Japan, since obviously
neither Buddhist nor Shinto believers needed any such re-
assurance. The churches and schools felt as though they
were coming out of the catacombs. They engaged in a
tremendous celebration of thanksgiving. A little later Honda wrote of the joy of being able to cease swimming against
the stream of opposing sentiment in his native land.

In the Diet, from the first session on, the Protestants had
a contribution to make. Versed in debate, and many of them
politically trained Christian laymen, they were in their element. Thirteen were elected, as members. One, Nobuyuki
Nakajima was chosen Speaker, and another, Saburo Shima-

da was the Chairman of the Committee of the Whole. A third, Sōroku Ebara, kept his seat for years until elevated for life to the Upper House for meritorious service. In succeeding sessions Kenkichi Kataoka, the most prominent of them all, was Speaker. Honda would probably have been there, but the new law made it impossible for one to be both a clergyman and a representative, so he made his life decision and gave up politics.

Christians furnished what most members may have considered a joke, when invariably on the roll-call a temperance leader, Sho Nemoto, took the platform to recommend special action in outlawing juvenile drinking. After many years, such a law did finally pass. Madame Yajima of the WCTU managed to get before the first session her appeal for a law making plural marriage a crime;—the "One Man-One Woman" law. Christians in Japan have enjoyed a creditable record wherever there have been elections and legislative assemblies. The chief drawback has been that the Diet, and civil bodies in general except for a few periods have never exercised the highest powers in the nation.

Japanese Christians ran afoul of the new Imperial Rescript on Education when it was first issued. It was almost by accident, and it occurred not in a Christian school, but in the First Higher College, feeder to the Imperial University in Tokyo. The Rescript scroll rested on a pedestal and the hundreds of students were standing at attention as one by one the instructors on the platform stepped out and made a low bow in obeisance. Among them was Kanzo Uchimura, no longer pastor in Sapporo, nor in government service as he had been, but now teaching English. Uchimura had only a matter of seconds to see what was happening and to decide, as a Christian, what to do. Temperamentally a nonconformist he acted on first impulse, stepped forward, stood straight as a ramrod, and returned to his seat. The con-

99

sternation almost disrupted the rest of the ceremony. A Buddhist paper got the story and spread it over the country. Professor Tetsujiro Inoue of the Imperial University published a syndicated attack in six periodicals to prove that he had been correct all along in insisting that no Christian could be a good Japanese subject. Uchimura did not object to the Rescript at all. It was merely that he wanted to know what he was bowing about, and had not had time to make up his mind, so he had balked. Later he agreed to comply, but it was too late. He resigned from his teaching post, and the impression remained that Christians were disloyal.

The content of the Rescript, sentence by sentence, is impeccable ethics. Japanese Christians have never felt any spiritual antagonism to it, but rather have made it their own as loyal citizens. But it is the slant of the teaching behind it, rising in tempo and fervor with every crisis, like a barometer, and the ritualistic handling of the actual object that have raised a barrier to real freedom in school life for a conscientious Christian believer. It was intended so to do; for the basic purpose of the Rescript was to sink deep into the immovable past of ancient Shinto Japan the present foundations of the modern state.

The war with China pressed on the Christian movement from many angles. The Christians in service proved to be quite as dependable and brave as any, and they earned a new place of respect from officers and comrades. In fact after the war it was estimated that three percent of the army officers were Christians. At least two Admirals of the Navy became ardent members of the church. Others less high but later well-known were Tetsuzo Okada, who for several decades exerted a profound influence upon students of universities in Tokyo, and Major General Nobusuke Hibiki, who took an active part in the swift changes within the Christian movement in 1940 and 1941.

Uchimura had turned to journalism and he commended the war as a just one. It should be noted, however, that with his keen moral insight he later changed his views and castigated his country for making the conflict a source of wealth, and an occasion for the oppression of the Koreans. Such things were not openly said a few years later.

Christian civilians quickly went into action with a War-time Service Association and a central committee of which Honda was chairman. Arrangements were made for five chaplains to go to Manchuria, under army auspices, to serve the troops.

The women of the churches made and sent thousands of comfort bags, with articles indispensable at home but not included in the Spartan equipment of the army. Henry Loomis, of the American Bible Society was permitted to distribute vast numbers of free copies of Scriptures in all the camps. This service was greatly appreciated; even the Buddhists praised it.

Foreigners were welcome visitors in military hospitals at home, especially in Hiroshima which then, as in all later wars, was the arterial center for mobilization and debarkation. The Red Cross in Japan had just been established, and with that emblem as a text the Christians did some quiet evangelization. They also visited among Chinese prisoners of war. Thus Christians moved with their nation along the perilous current into and past the small war that brought everyone some advantage.

The organization of the Protestant movement was steadily taking permanent form. The Congregational group became the "Associated Churches" (*kumi-ai*) in a national organization. They adopted their own statement of faith, a well-phrased expression of Christian belief, liberal in mood and Scriptural in its basis. Leaders of the Presbyterian-Reformed Church, too, prepared a statement of faith, resting it upon the historic creeds that lay behind the special traditions of each of the affiliated Western churches. This was framed, as they explained, so as to be simple, confessional and irenic. The Episcopal church under the tireless Bishop Bickersteth assembled its forces, and in six dioceses directed by himself and five newly consecrated bishops moved out to become a church of national dimensions. The Methodists were showing evidences of wishing to unite in a single church. Japanese and missionaries were in favor of it, but more ponderous forces overseas counselled delay.

In the world of the Christian schools the tumult at Doshisha seems to have drowned the sounds of events taking place elsewhere. It was a period when the girls schools were enjoying growth. The five or six larger boys' schools related to the major denominations were beginning to develop college departments. The matter of administrative control was being dealt with in several of these schools by drawing up constitutions that provided for boards in Japan, with Japanese members as well as foreigners. Boards of directors in some cases fixed the local policies of administration while the actual ownership and final control was still with the sending society abroad. It was a step forward for Japanese to be participating in policy-making even to this degree. In some other cases, under the new laws, boards of trustees with full responsibility were being established. Gradually ownership of the property was transferred to these bodies in Japan, and thus the schools became legally indigenous. For some time the common pattern in the most advanced institutions was that one half the members of the board were missionaries and one half Japanese Christians. Within this framework it was possible later to shift weight to a Japanese majority membership without loss of momentum or of Christian responsibility.

As to the Imperial Rescript within the life of the Christian schools, it took its assigned place, and was regularly read and interpreted. Probably there was more of "national ethics" taught in expounding it than the missionaries knew, for neither they nor the Japanese Christian teachers were assigned the teaching of the Japanese classics under which this instruction came. The ceremonies at which the Rescript was read were opened with Christian prayer and hymn singing, and as a rule the atmosphere of the occasion was dignified but relaxed. Most of the Christian schools, however, made no move toward requesting the imperial portraits.

Beyond the mission schools significant things were happening among students. In several of the government colleges, such as the First Higher College and the Imperial University in Tokyo, as well as in the Sendai University, small Christian groups had developed and had maintained a continuous life across the changes of student generations. In 1897 John R. Mott made the first of his numerous visits to Japan. Lectures were arranged in nearly fifty public educational institutions, and everywhere he was well received. His commanding personality, measured speech, and style of expression were calculated to win student admiration. The national body of the YMCA was strengthened and given a wider horizon by affiliation with the world organization. Over the years it maintained a high level in foreign personnel, and enlisted many able Japanese as secretaries.

In 1889, Luther D. Wishard, International College Secretary of the YMCA, came to Japan and instituted the first summer conference after the pattern of Northfield. It was reported as a time of unforgettable impressions. Students from all over Japan were there introduced to the Japanese leaders, who had become nationally famous by their writings and speaking. Kozaki, always in front, elaborated a theory of inspiration of the Scriptures replete with knowledge of all the churning movements of current thought in

the West, but staying within the Christian lines in his conclusions. The second meeting in 1890 was even more kindl-
ing, with a massive battery of speakers dealing with every
aspect of Christianity and culture from ancient Greece to
modern Japan.

New currents of thought were flowing all across Japan,
and their influence was clearly felt within the Christian
movement. Like the Athenians the Japanese intellectuals are
quick in action, and in the 80's and 90's they were abreast
of every movement of thought abroad. They had followed
the new knowledge as it influenced the natural and social
sciences. Each new book by a leading thinker of the West
was eagerly awaited and read. The modern school of Biblical criticism, and the works of contemporaneous European
theologians had their vogue. In Tokyo a new prestige was
added when the Liberal German mission established themselves in Unity Hall adjoining the campus of Tokyo Imperial
University.

In these surging currents some of the Japanese ministers
were swept away from all anchorage, and left the church.
The first and most prominent was Tsurin Kanamori, who
wrote in 1891, his *Present and Future of Christianity in
Japan* in protest against the traditional positions, and withdrew from the church. As this was the first break in the
ranks, it came as a shock to the entire Christian community.
Later he returned to the same faith he had previously held,
and to another generation he gave the rest of his life as an
evangelist. In 1894 the prominent Christian, Tokio Yokoi
wrote an even more devastating repudiation of orthodoxy
in his *The Problem of Christianity in Our Country*, and
left the church, never to return.

From the early years individual Christians had undertaken works of charity and of social welfare, but in the 90's
a group began to be concerned about social change. They

belonged to the Unity Hall circle, and though some were
at first pastors of churches, they ultimately became university teachers and took their places as laymen. They subscribed to the Unitarian faith, and counted themselves as
within the body of the church. Their motive was compassion, and their goal was a gradual, peaceful amelioration
of the condition of workers through negotiation with owners and employers. They were optimistic and hopeful of a
better society by the power of "communal love". Throughout a long life Professor Isoo Abe stood as an organizing
center for all social forms of Christian action.

The movement had first organized as a center for social
studies, later it became the Association for the Study of
Socialism. At an earlier date these men had constituted a
Society for Forming Labor Unions, they did this with no
intention of radical action, but for purposes of negotiation.
Their motto was "Labor is Holy—In Unity is Strength". The
meetings were opened with prayer, and on Sundays sermons
were preached largely in this social context. Abe and others
went to America and there drank deep from the fresh
springs of the "Social Christianity", of Walter Rauschen-
busch. They came back to give guidance to the movement
as it reached a more active stage.

At the early period of almost every social movement in
Japan Christians played a prominent role. They were doing
this, however, as individuals. For the most part the Christian movement went its way not too much concerned with
social change. But Christians in general were not indiffer-
ent to human need. There were several great natural dis-
asters—the Central Japan earthquake, the North Japan
tidal wave, and a Tokyo earthquake. In all of these Christians rallied to give help.

Their concern for the sufferers, the expeditiousness and
efficiency of their work, and the kindly spirit in which they

dispensed their assistance made a national impression. Christian institutions of relief increased.

The Yokohama Blind School was started. Miss Riddell in Kumamoto began to systematize Christian efforts to aid lepers. The WCTU established a home for unfortunate girls, in Tokyo. A number of new orphanages began to spring up. Christians furnished some of the judges for the Juvenile Courts just established.

Moral reform movements were gaining speed. In the Hawaiian Islands, a Methodist evangelist to the Japanese, had led Taro Ando the Consul General into the Christian faith. As Ando's chief enemy was *sake*, his religious experience took the form of a temperance crusade for life. In 1898 he retired from government service, and with several others formed the National Temperance League of Japan. Soon branches were spreading all over the country. This was more than just a temperance movement. It was linked with Christian evangelization, and in many places resulted in the founding of a church or the strengthening of a Christian community.

The anti-brothel movement took root in one prefecture, Gumma, where Christian families had great prestige. The prefectural assembly voted the red-light districts out of existence. This was something new, and while it galvanized the brothel-keepers into political organization it also quickened the moral sense of the nation, and put Christians on the alert. The movement was not successful at a national level, but the local option plan of awakening public opinion by one campaign after another in different prefectures was later successfully followed.

The rescue of brothel inmates continued. In Nagoya, U. G. Murphy a missionary, decided to test a law declaring all contracts invalid if made with a person under twenty years of age. He was supported by a group organized among Japanese Christians, the law was sustained, and thereafter almost any girl might claim her freedom, for nearly all were minors in age. Unfortunately few of those rescued had sufficient intelligence or will power to persevere in obtaining and keeping their freedom. It was at this point that the Salvation Army workers assisted. They entered the precincts, made friends of the girls, encouraged them to stand firm, sometimes snatched them and walked them out. They then cared for them in the newly established hostels. This was dangerous, of course, and many Christian workers took hard blows. An indomitable national leader in this field was Gumpei Yamamuro, of the Salvation Army, and later its head. In a time of unfavorable reaction away from Western things, it was an inestimable boon for Christianity to be associated in the mind of the public with works of mercy and efforts at the moral reform of the nation. This more than any other one factor prepared the way for the gradual but steadily increasing acceptance of Christians in the years of the next period.

NATIONAL SELF-ASSERTION
1899–1909

Forward Under Pressures

As Japan crossed the dateline into the twentieth century it was accelerating its pace in every area of national life. The war with China of 1895 had immensely stimulated industry, manufactures, trade and economic life in general. There had been a great increase in wealth, and for many the scale of living had risen. But this did not reach everyone, and when the inevitable recession followed, there was much hardship, poverty and unrest.

In the political arena a change had come. The powerful

General Yamagata, his prestige enhanced by the successful war, largely disregarded the public will in his policy and program. But the other leaders realized that they must meet the opposition in the Diet by constructive party action. There followed a period in which new parties were organized. Christians were involved in almost all of them.

Overseas, Japan was trying to maintain a balance until she might be prepared for the supreme struggle ahead. In 1898, Japan and Russia, the two contenders for power, signed a mutual treaty of self-restraint. It, however, was far from a treaty of peace. In South Manchuria, Russia now held the very Liaotung peninsula which Japan had won. To match this, Germany seized great areas in North China, and Great Britain took another port. She already dominated the Yangtse River, with holdings in the China ports south to Hong Kong. France meanwhile was obtaining concessions in South China.

While these Western powers were carving up a helpless nation in Asia Japan was being left without any of the major spoils. She expanded her fisheries in the north, and began to develop essential industries in Formosa that were later to become a source of food and wealth. But this scarcely compensated for the sense of encirclement and apprehension that pressed upon government and people, for now another rival for power had been added.

The United States was just annexing the Hawaiian Islands and was soon to supplant Spain in control of the Philippines, with Guam and Wake as outposts of empire. This was far from being the same country that Japan had dealt with in 1853; modern statehood and empire were knocking at its door as well as at that of Japan. The old cry of "Manifest Destiny" was once again resounding across the nation. As yet without international experience or settled policy, except for its Monroe Doctrine of regional autonomy, the United

108

States now entered the China situation with a new slogan—the "Open Door" policy. Although it changed its interpretation of the meaning of the phrase several times, the unchangeable fact was that the United States was in Asia and intended to stay. Japan instead of facing a single front on the mainland now had to watch the entire horizon of the Pacific as well. There was but little time to enjoy the rewards of the past war, for events were pressing toward a more momentous struggle. An air of gravity and crisis pervaded the country as it faced the next decade.

Every department of government was straining to do its share for national unity and strength. Not least concerned was the Ministry of Education, always among the most important of the government agencies in modern Japan. Behind the establishment of the system of national education lay a fairly simple conviction that education was essential to a modern nation. The more progressive nations had such systems, and Japan heartily approved. Soon it became apparent that the public schools were the nation's most potent instruments for training in citizenship. As crisis followed crisis and the one supreme consideration was to instil loyalty on the part of every individual, the school system underwent changes necessary to perfect it for that task.

At the heart of the curriculum as its nerve-center was placed the sensitive subject of "National Ethics" or the teaching regarding the "National Structure". This ethical system was construed as being not religious. It must not, however, be thought that this was merely a device for by-passing the constitutional guarantee of religious freedom of belief. Much less was "National Ethics" viewed as being beneath religion or of minor importance. On the contrary, the official view of the makers of Japan's policy was that anyone might hold such religious views as he pleased provided they never touched the summit of Japan's life at the Imperial center. This was so far above the vagaries of a private religious faith that they could not be classed together.

Now that the educational system was fully in operation, molding citizens of the approved spirit and accepted duties, it was essential that no schools with any other goals should be encouraged. The Ministry would have been pleased if there had been no private schools. They had been useful twenty years before, but now they were regarded as a problem. Not only were they founded and administered on the basis of Christianity, a foreign religion, but that religion also presumed to determine all the individual's relationships, including his duties as a citizen. In Japan, that was intolerable for a subject of the Emperor.

With the growing sense of crisis the Diet tried to pass a bill prohibiting the founding of any more Christian schools, a measure which Soroku Ebara deftly managed to bring to defeat. Then another bill was presented. It provided that in private schools enjoying the privileges of public schools,—such as deferment of conscription, and admission to higher government schools,—no religious worship or teaching should be permitted. Although this also was defeated, the Minister of Education without further authorization issued a directive, Instruction Twelve, to all private schools announcing the provisions of the bill as a policy now in force. It is not difficult to understand the tensions that lay behind Instruction Twelve and the exceedingly apprehensive state of mind of the authorities of Christian schools at this time. Most of them decided to forego the privileges of the public system, to withdraw from it and to maintain the schools, hoping still to attract students. Actually, though, they made few changes in the curriculum, and kept their academic standards as high as ever. After two or three years in a more quiet time the Ministry began first to ignore the gradual re-introduction of Christian activities and then it openly permitted them. In a few years more a changed policy, of utilizing all religious faiths for national ends, led to positive encouragement of Christian work in the public schools. Of the problems facing every modern nation-state that of the relationships of public education, ethics and religion is one of the thorniest, and Japanese Christianity had to face it very early in its life.

At 1900 the Churches were staggering after the half-decade of reaction which followed the over expansion of the earlier years. There was some growth, but it was meager, nor were the strains all from the outside. Within the ranks of the leaders the theological rifts were threatening. Plainly the time had come for wrestling with the Christian message at a new dimension of depth. All the molders of opinion in the Christian movement were dealing with it in their periodicals, but chiefly the lines came to be drawn between two of the ablest men in the church. Ebina and Uemura were neighboring pastors in the uptown and student section of Tokyo. Each had his own personal periodical. Ebina's was *The New Man* and Uemura's *The Evangelist*.

The controversy centered about the person and work of Christ, and it raged for upwards of two years. Carried on at a high level of seriousness and courtesy it nevertheless opened up most of the issues that have had to be dealt with in historic Christianity from the time of Arius and Athanasius until today. It is noteworthy that neither man in presenting his case gave a merely scholastic repetition of the arguments of past thinkers, but rather each spoke and wrote out of his own innermost convictions.

Ebina, was a liberal Congregationalist, patriotic, keenly alive to new thought currents, and skilled in reaching the student mind by a rational approach. He presented Christianity as faith in God the Father-Savior, revealed through his greatest Son, and by the direct influence of the inner Presence through personal experience. His position was not that of humanistic Unitarianism, but of a Christ-centered liberalism. Uemura, in many ways the opposite of the graceful, bearded, eloquent Ebina, was pastor of the influential Fujimicho Presbyterian Church. Blunt, square-jawed, proud of his lack of ornamentation in speech, he nevertheless was one of the most formidable thinkers produced by Japanese Protestantism. His position was that of classical orthodox Christianity; and he drove it home in one powerful theological exposition after another. Of course there was no adjudication between the two, but when the wheels slowed down and quiet returned the young church realized that it had been through a long journey of stimulating and guided thinking as to just what should be one's personal faith within the context of the church life.

At this time, the Japanese churches, though struggling to maintain their own existence on a receding wave of public interest, assumed responsibility for at least some of the local churches and outstations started by the missions. And the churches were able to undertake the work of building and extension on their own initiative. It was inevitable that the general atmosphere of national self-consciousness should be reflected within Christian circles, and that there should be this increasing desire to be totally autonomous. It reflected a sense of growing responsibility on the part of Japanese Christians to their own society.

In 1900 a Missionary Conference was held in Tokyo celebrating the opening of the new century. Its delegates numbered 435, and there were 42 missions and agencies represented. The sessions lasted for eight days, and are recorded in a volume of over a thousand pages. The holding of such a meeting at all at this stage of Japan's Christian history is an arresting phenomenon. It was a Christian celebration not of foreign missionary work but of human history; yet almost no provision was made for any participation by Japanese. The conference throws a spotlight on the missionaries, missions and churches in their attitudes and relationships at the opening of the century. The missionary movement at 1900 was stronger and larger than ever before. More missions, more missionaries, more money, more work and more institutions marked the movement, which was on a spiral of growth greatly outstripping the capacity of the Japanese church to match.

There was a new spiritual dynamic as well. An upsurge of interest in the world mission had stemmed from the Moody revivals and had carried into the student Christian movements of America and Great Britain. Under the acceleration of the Mott-Speer-Eddy drive in the Student Volunteer Movement it reached its zenith. The most spiritually sensitive students in the west were being challenged to throw themselves into the evangelization of the world in their own generation, and with whole-hearted devotion they were enlisting for service. There were sixty such volunteers in the Tokyo Conference.

In this powerful foreign group, destined to do much to shape Protestantism in Japan there was a curious lack of questions at fundamental levels. Almost no discussion of the message as such took place, nor of its adaptation to non-Christian hearers. There was little reference to Buddhist thought or Confucian ethics or Shinto national philosophy. The reader misses any serious grappling with the problem of communication with non-believers.

On the program we find no reference to a study of the churches and their basic relations to the missions although these matters were engaging the acute attention of the Japanese Christians. Self-support was taken up, but only in the range of inducing the mission-aided churches to undertake

113

more of their own support. Where programs of work were studied it was almost solely in the context of unilateral responsibility of the missions. Remembering that the Japanese leaders had by this time had thirty years of experience and the church three decades of life, this strange moving of two forces within Protestantism on parallel but separate tracks seems an unaccountable fact. To be sure, in the every day work of many of the missionaries there was a genuine comradeship with their Japanese associates. The younger foreign workers were already showing a dependence on the ripened experience of their Japanese elder Christians. Yet a real dychotomy of authority as between missions and churches prevailed.

At the conference of 1900 a national organization of the missions was proposed, and a constitution presented. Two years later this body came into being, first as the Standing Committee of the Cooperating Missions, and later as the Conference of Federated Missions. It continued, holding annual meetings, initiating Christian enterprises, and speaking for the missionary body, until in 1936 it dissolved in favor of the National Christian Council of Japan. This organization did many useful things and built up missionary morale. In the long view, however, one cannot but raise the question: Did it not on the whole retard the process of complete absorption of all foreign elements within the Japanese Protestant Movement?

On the wider stage of history Japan was engaged at the end of the century in an international event that was to have great consequences. One of the last pitiful attempts of a wounded China to throw off foreign aggression was the lashing out of the "Boxers" against Westerners and particularly against the missionaries. The attack came to a head in 1899 when the imperilled foreigners gathered in Peking in a state of siege. An allied military force went to their rescue, and Japan joined the expedition. Her troops, which numbered about one half of all, carried themselves with courage but restraint, and when the siege was lifted they were promptly withdrawn. This disarmed all fears and gained the commendation of the other allies.

By 1902 the Siberian railway was linked to China. Japan felt that there was no time to be lost if Russia was to be kept from taking over the entire area so long in dispute. But Britain was as concerned as Japan regarding Russia's expansion, and in 1902 effected an alliance with this Asian neophyte in the world's councils of power. This alliance placed Japan in an almost impregnable position. In February of 1904 Japan struck in Manchuria. The fall of Mukden and of Port Arthur were the decisive victories by land, while in the Korean Strait the Russian fleet in May, 1905 was completely destroyed by Japanese naval strength.

President Theodore Roosevelt sponsored a peace conference to end the war. He mediated the treaty, and negotiated the final terms so that neither Japan nor Russia would come off sufficiently powerful to be an international danger for some time to come. Japan received no reparations. This led to riots in Tokyo, and the burning of a number of churches. The wave of disappointment, however, soon passed, and the nation with a new sense of its own greatness and of its world mission struck off for higher levels in the ascent of national expansion.

The first defeat of a Western power by an Asian nation was truly a watershed in history, and it was so recognized at the time. A thrill went through the life of every people from China to Suez as this first barrier to the irresistible onrush of Western colonialism was thrown up and the flood was held in check. The old nations of Asia tingled with the awakenings of new life and hope. They forgot all else except that Japan was now to become the champion of an emancipated East. From China streams of young men now came, as many as fifteen thousand at the peak in 1907, filling the student dormitories of Tokyo, eager to learn from their brothers who had stolen the lightning of the arrogant Western giants. What they had forgotten was that it was with the Western powers, not as an Asian blood brother that the Japanese had marched in the siege of Peking. So far as international relations were concerned it was not the lesson of freedom, but of conquest that the Japanese had learned from the West,—as tragic a paradox as modern history can show.

The Western powers all alike now realized that Japan was a formidable rival. With her foreign trade in cheaply manufactured articles, backed by strong government subsidies, and with her expansion in case of need supported by her highly efficient army and navy, Japan had become a contender of the first magnitude in the world arena. From this time American attitudes of patronizing friendship began to give way to suspicion, then dislike, and finally on to the ultimate clash of arms four decades later.

In Japan a new sense of self-assurance and national pride was noted. It could not have been otherwise. Judged by any current standards of achievement, Japan as a nation had in fifty years accomplished the impossible. Henceforth there would be nothing beyond her powers. She had never doubted the precious uniqueness of her past which she had brought with her into modern life. In addition she had now mastered the secrets of the West. This synthesis should make her the envy of mankind. Such was the mood in Japan during the first decade of the new century.

The reaction of Christians to the struggle on the mainland varied. There was the lonely prophet. Uchimura, who in disillusionment over any wars refused his consent to this one as it approached. He was on the editorial staff of a great daily, and was so conscientious that he handed in his resignation, on the grounds that no newspaper could refuse to support the national policy, but that he could not stultify himself by remaining silent as to his connections. From that time he renounced his prophetic role as a commentator on current events, turning to Bible studies instead.

Most of the Christians in the social action group, too, were in opposition to the war, Naoe Kinoshita, one of the most trenchant of their writers published a series of articles against it. But by this time they were on the periphery of organized Christianity, and some were under suspicion of disloyalty, so their influence on the rank and file of church members was not great.

In general Christians felt that whatever may have been the case with the Sino-Japanese war, this one with Russia had full justification as an attempt by the nation to recover its fairly-won position on the Asian mainland. Such was the official position taken by the church leaders and the denominations, and it probably reflected the general sentiment of the members.

The Japanese government feared Russian propaganda to the effect that this was a war between a Christian and a non-Christian nation, and took steps to refute it. Premier Katsura called Dr. William Imbrie, the veteran Presbyterian missionary, to an interview and urged him on his forthcoming furlough in America to assure the people of his country that this was in no sense a religious war, and was not waged against Christians as such. Also, a meeting of the several traditional Japanese religious bodies was held in Tokyo, and this conference issued a statement so similar to the government line that one may suppose the project to have been officially inspired. It asserted that this was not a religious war, but one engaged in solely for the defence of the empire and the peace of Asia. Dr. Kozaki, in his memoirs, recalls that his address went further and analyzed the struggle as between two civilizations, that of Russia belonging to the sixteenth century, while modern Japan fully represented that of the twentieth century.

The inter-faith group undertook the raising of funds for the rehabilitation of the Christian churches burned in the post-war riots. From this time on it became the custom in times of national emergency and war for such united meetings of representatives of the various religions to be held. The common element that fused all religious differences was the national interest.

Both the Congregational and the Presbyterian-Reformed churches organized wartime services and made declarations in support of the war. Through the Evangelical Alliance the Protestant churches set up a national Commission with Honda as chairman. The YMCA was given freedom to carry on a service of "comfort", not centrally religious but one of general welfare, to the men in Manchuria and North China. Informal religious work proved to be welcomed, however, and was performed. Three men, Secretary Hibbard, with two Japanese associates comprised the first team. Altogether there were 18 such teams. They asked few favors, provided their own quarters and had little equipment, but from the first they were received with gratitude by the lonely lads in uniform.

One special service was that of cutting hair. Hibbard said that day after day of long hours spent clipping the scalps of the boys he would turn in with both arms almost paralyzed. These selfless services of the "Y" men, Japanese and foreign, stirred the whole nation in a remarkable way. One of the first instances of recognition of Christian work ever made by the Emperor was a gift of ten thousand Yen in support of this wartime service. Since then the Household Department has repeatedly made gifts to Christian philanthropic enterprises in approbation and encouragement of their work.

At home Christian workers visited in the military hospitals, made bandages, sent comfort bags, helped care for the families of men at the front, and made offerings in support of the war. Benefiting from the experiences in the previous war the organization was improved, and the work was more efficiently done. The general impression that Christians after all were loyal subjects began to gain ground; They thus began to find a new confidence and rapport with their non-Christian neighbors.

The Forward Evangelistic Campaign of 1901–1904 was the most ambitious joint evangelistic effort the church had hitherto made. The motto for the campaign was "Our Country for Christ", thus the movement had its patriotic overtones. The campaign included series of mass rallies in the larger cities, visiting teams for single meetings in the smaller places, evangelistic appeals, the signing of cards, after-meetings for personal work, and the final follow-up assumed by local pastors. The results rewarded the careful planning and whole-hearted work of the speakers. Over three hundred churches participated, with three hundred thousand people in attendance, and fifteen thousand signed inquirers' cards. Over a thousand persons were baptized as a direct result of the meetings.

About this time a full-time evangelist of the Billy Sunday type came into action. Seimatsu Kimura returned from training in the Chicago Moody Bible Institute and introduced a people's approach into the more staid pattern of evangelism in the Japanese scene. He was emotional, vigorous in speech and action, colloquial, and with a sure aim at the target of the ordinary man. During a two-weeks series of meetings in a tent in Tokyo nearly one hundred decisions were made each night.

The separate denominations later followed with their own

forward drives. In the Congregational churches "Concentration Evangelism" meetings, were conducted, where in a selected church or group of local churches the pastors and laymen would be coached and prepared by prayer meetings for the arrival of a team of speakers. After the meetings the local church people led inquirers into church membership. It proved to be a very effective method, and it is the nearest the churches came to the "visitation evangelism" now gaining marked results in Japan. The Methodist church also launched a forward movement in which laymen took a conspicuous lead. With its thorough organization the movement reached almost every church in the denomination. "Extension Evangelism" was the name given the campaign in the Presbyterian church. The Christians of Osaka made an all-city project of the evangelistic center in the Osaka Exposition of 1903, with wide results and many decisions.

The title "Forward Evangelism" under which the inter-church campaign of 1900 went suggested a military campaign, and is an indication of the new courage with which Japanese Christians were claiming an accepted place in society. They were beginning to feel a responsibility for the evangelizing of their entire nation. It is true that they seem to have underestimated the deep resistance that even friendly hearers at a public meeting eventually offer at the point of accepting the Christian faith and entering the church. The decision-card scores were listed with much joy and confidence and as always they ran into huge numbers. But only the most minute fraction of such totals ever registered in the statistics of church membership.

This phenomenon is true of mass evangelism in the West; but much more is it to be expected in a country such as Japan where the old faiths still hold strong roots deep under the life of the family, the neighborhood and the village. The ancient systems may seem to be existing at a dying rate, but they never die. It is at just such a time as a vigorous Christian campaign that they pull themselves together to hold the lines. Life is a web of relationships through most of which the old religions are tightly woven, so that it is a terribly disruptive thing for an individual to tear loose and establish a new spiritual center in the Christian community. In the feudal days it would have been virtually impossible except as an entire community or clan moved together. In modern Japan individuals were coming to a point where they could make decisions, and they did make many serious ones. But of all relationships religious affiliation was the least private and the most strongly communal. Thus multitudes of people, mostly young persons and students in a genuine spiritual response signed cards of decision but only rarely could one muster enough courage to go on to a final commitment.

In 1904 the Young Women's Christian Association was established, and soon had a national organization. It was conspicuous in both its Japanese and foreign leadership. Caroline Macdonald of Canada and Michi Kawai of Japan could have led any world organization with distinction. They gave their early years of energy and devotion to the work for young women, both students and city workers, and set a standard of integrity that has made the movement ever since a ministering agency for human needs as well as a fearless exponent of social change. Later Miss Macdonald turned to the rehabilitation of ex-prisoners, and in that work won national recognition. Miss Kawai founded the Keisen school and college, combining academic studies and handwork for training self-reliant young women for the new Japan. The three larger branches of Methodist work combined in the establishment of the Japan Methodist Church in 1907, when Yoichi Honda was chosen as bishop.

Within the major denominations the movement toward

121

full autonomy and responsibility for church extension went on. Under a three-year plan of gradual transfer the Congregational churches in 1906 took over the support and development of the churches hitherto aided by the American Board Mission, leaving the less developed preaching places in the care of the mission. This program was carried to success by the Forward Movement in the churches, and it was made possible by a most commendable spirit of cooperation on the part of the mission.

In the Presbyterian-Reformed church a similar process was going on, but with much more tension. It was a struggle between a church led by men of stern independence and strength and a group of strong missions under like missionary leadership. Moreover, the denominational traditions of these two bodies throughout the world held the Mission organization apart from the churches as autonomous in policy and work. In 1897 the church synod had proposed a plan defined as "cooperation" in which all local church work aided by a mission should be administered by a joint committee of Japanese and foreign missionaries in equal numbers. This was rejected by the missions. In 1905 the missions made to the synod of the church a counter-proposal that missions should develop local churches until they reached one-half support, at which time they would be transferred to the care of the presbytery. To this the synod demurred.

At this time the Japanese leaders raised the question of the propriety of there being within the territory of the indigenous church an organization of affiliated foreign missionaries which really exercised the ecclesiastical functions of a presbytery or synod in founding, developing, aiding and directing local churches. It is probable that at this time no such question had been raised anywhere else in the foreign missionary world. It was basic to the whole progress of

122

mission and church relationships in Japan and for years it engaged the serious attention of both.

Eventually the 1897 proposal for administration of new church work by joint committees became the standard of cooperation fixed by the church. Of the six related missions three adopted it and three did not. The two missions of the Presbyterian Church in the U.S.A. (Northern) and the one of the Reformed Church, in the U.S. (German) placed all of their evangelistic and church work under a joint committee in which they had one half representation; while the two missions of the Reformed Church in America (Dutch) and the one of the Presbyterian Church in the U.S. (Southern) continued to do their work as before.

On the whole, both plans seem to have worked. In the areas where joint administration prevailed there may have been some tensions, but it was in a partnership of work that carried common satisfactions and loyalties. In the "non-cooperating" areas although there was no sharing of responsibilities there appear to have been deep personal ties of friendship between missionaries and pastors. Not all the church leaders, however, were pleased with either plan. The intensity of the general spirit of independence can be judged by the fact that in one area, the North-Eastern, there were so many pastors who opposed the principle of aid to churches at all, to say nothing of administration by a foreign group, that it became necessary within the same geographical boundaries to establish a second presbytery for those of that outlook.

Unquestionably the leadership in this movement of independence for the Japanese church centered in Masahisa Uemura. Almost without a peer as pastor, preacher, theologian, author, editor and dominating personality, he was viewed by his generation and by later ones as God's particular gift to the church during its formative years of crisis. He was relentless in his own standards of high quality, and impatient with anything less in others.

Uemura saw no reason for any policy of gradualness in the relinquishment of authority by the foreign missionaries or missions. He believed that the evangelizing of Japan could not be effected or ultimately hastened by assistance brought from abroad by foreigners, and offered largely on their own terms. He was deeply disturbed at a time of mounting national spirit by the indications that the missions were digging in for permanent occupation, and extending their power rather than diminishing it.

When, in 1904 as a professor of theology in Meiji Gakuin, Uemura learned that objection was being made to his use of certain textbooks in his classes, he withdrew, and with several associates he founded the first independent theological seminary in the Protestant movement, the Tokyo Shingakusha. The instructors, including himself, were volunteer workers, and the classes met in a corner of his church. From the start the work commanded respect for its thoroughness. No financial aid was asked or accepted, nor did more than one or two foreigners ever have a share in the instruction, and they only as lecturers. The graduates of this school over the years have been highly regarded as well-trained thinkers, with a firm theological rootage, a strong sense of the tensions and gravity of life, and a high idea of the national church and its responsibilities. Their convictions regarding church independence certainly have affected the entire Christian movement.

This pivotal subject of the place of mission and of church in evangelization cannot be left without presenting another aspect, which undoubtedly was always in the thinking of the missionaries. What would have happened if missionaries had not come in 1859 and later? Would there have been a church without them in 1872? Who carried the lines of the net out to the far reaches of the nation in the 80's, or stood firm when the tides receded? As the twentieth century opened what about the many hundreds of preaching places, and the churches that had not yet reached self-support?

It was reported that at 1900 four-fifths of all churches still were receiving some financial assistance; and obviously much of this came directly or indirectly from foreign sources. That had not been the case in 1886, but it was so in the lean years following. Should those churches have been permitted to disappear, or was it for the ultimate welfare of Protestantism that they be saved? But then again, did continued mission aid really save them or rather make them weaker? Thus the argument continued, the scales tipping now one way and now another in missionary sentiment, as well as in the judgment of many of the Japanese leaders.

In the life of the Christian schools, there may be seen the same emergence from the slump of the 90's into an onrush of new energy. By this time the pattern for the next half-century was well under formation. More and more, public education met all requirements at the elementary levels, and the urgent need for Christian primary schools ceased. Several hundred small day schools still were carried on, but almost all of them were under the care of two denominations, Episcopal and Methodist. They were in cities, and for poor children; scarcely more than day nurseries. Even these gradually disappeared from the records.

Kindergartens, however, were increasing. Miss Annie L. Howe of Kobe founded the first training school for Kindergarten teachers. This example was followed by several of the other missions, notably the Canadians in Tokyo, the Episcopalians, the Evangelical Association and later the Lutherans, who made it a special emphasis in their work. These local kindergartens, equally classifiable as church work or school work, became most effective seed-plots for

Christian nurture, and ran their rootlets into neighborhood families as no other Christian institutions could quite do.

The main strength of Christian schools was at the middle school level, with students ranging from twelve to eighteen years of age. According to the system of that time the boys middle schools and the so-called higher schools for girls, at the same age level, were separate. Of Christian boys schools there were fifteen or so, not large by today's standards, but with one or two hundred students each, and well suited for both high student morale and warm personal intimacies. It was among students at this responsive age when character was in the making, that Christian work proved most rewarding. Dormitory life, especially, was Christian in atmosphere.

Of the girls' schools there were forty or more, of about the same size, and with a still more permeating Christian climate and influence than the boys' schools. In some of them nearly all the girls were Christian by the time of graduation. Academic standards were not lowered to achieve that end. The leaders were for the most part Western women missionary educators who kept a fine balance between meticulous personal and class standards of discipline and a parental attitude toward the students. The Japanese faculty associates to a great degree also achieved this ideal relationship with the students. It was this unusual combination that won the admiration of non-Christian educators in the early days, and it still constitutes the chief attraction of the Christian girls' schools.

Time was found in the crowded curriculum set by the government to add courses in Western cultures as well as in the Bible. Some schools specialized in Western music, as for example the Miyagi Jo Gakko in Sendai, and all offered English studies. They were not disturbed by the government's Instruction Twelve, for military conscription was no problem. As women were not at that time admitted to the government colleges and universities they felt no disability. This fact of not being so tightly hemmed in by national policies as the boys operated then, and has done so ever since, to give to private girls' schools a place of comparative freedom for experimentation and religious influence. Their value in the making of modern Japan has been generally recognized.

Each of the four or five chief denominational groups had developed one or more major educational institutions. They were headed by Christian educators most of whom were men of national reputation. In Japan, the advanced state of the church had drawn some of the ablest men such as Uemura into the pastorate as their lifework. An alternative avenue of significant Christian service was found in the schools. These were not above and separate from a humble and struggling church community as in the case of some non-Christian countries. In Japan they belonged in the same world. The appeal of the schools was to the same intelligent, educated families of moderate means who were attracted to the churches.

By maintaining the government standards for general education the Christian schools offered the public educational facilities at a time when gaining entrance to a school above the primary grade was a difficult task. The public school system intentionally drew a line at the basic eight-year level, offering only limited facilities above that for middle school, still fewer for college, and only a very few seats for future civil servants in the three or four imperial universities. This sharp screening of applicants for higher education was suited to the civic and national purposes of a bureaucratic system; but it closed opportunities for many young men.

Thus the Christian schools met a real need of the community, and were welcomed. They also offered Christian facilities for the developing of character and for the training of professional leaders in the churches and schools of the future. At this time the schools were small, and the Christian activities were more forthright and official than they later tended to be when roots struck more deeply into neighborhood life and the support increasingly had to rest on Japanese friends and graduates irrespective of their religious faith. These institutions were finding their rightful place in the Christian movement in Japan where schools for general education can reach more widely and be welcomed with a clearer sense of gratitude from non-Christians than are the churches. Though never intended to do the work of churches they have been invaluable feeders and auxiliaries.

College departments though still small in size were beginning to gather strength. They usually served three purposes, and most of the schools maintained three divisions of study: theology, for the purpose of training the ministry of the church, English, which usually was a normal course to train teachers of English in middle schools, and business or economics, aimed at the development of businessmen of character. These were somewhat limited areas, selected because they fell within the range of the schools' modest resources to provide, and also because they were distinctly related to the needs of the Christian movement. A number of the smaller denominations had started ministerial training schools for men and women. The desire for a Christian university was expressed time and time again, but as yet no serious effort had been made to bring it to accomplishment.

The famine of 1905–6 in northeastern Japan was the occasion for swift and efficient relief from the churches. They went into action even before the government did; though public relief once started was so well administered that it gained the unanimous admiration of the Christians. A kind of teamwork followed that was characteristic of what later developed in many such situations. It was often the Christians who first would see some area of human need. Then the public agencies would take up the work. Especially in the cities, the social service departments soon came to be excellent in technique and spirit. Many of the early social workers in government agencies were Christians. A high state of collaboration has usually been the pattern between Christian social projects and the government.

In that first enterprise among famine sufferers, over two thousand children of impoverished parents in the affected areas were assigned to Christian nurture, and for a while resources were over-taxed. Twelve-hundred were taken into the Okayama orphanage and were tided over the crisis until they could return home. An equal number were kept at Sendai where, under the leadership of Miss Phelps of the Methodist mission in 1906, the Sendai Christian Orphanage was founded. All the local churches were behind it, and much of the support came from a fund raised by the *Christian Herald* in America. During this period the work for lepers, for the blind and for delinquent youths was expanded.

A great impetus to social work was given with the visit in 1907 of General William Booth of the Salvation Army. By this time the Army was pressing forward with its varied activities for human relief in Japan. General Booth caught the public imagination and he drew most enthusiastic welcomes in the many cities he visited. His tour was described as almost a royal procession; and those missionaries who were informed that they were to be his hosts in the various places recall that the General rather took for granted a treatment suited to royalty. But his works spoke for him, and the total effect of his visit was to set forward private philanthropic work in the nation, including all Christian social work projects.

Another visitor from abroad was Frank L. Brown the secretary of the World Sunday School Association. He encouraged the formation of the National Sunday School Association of Japan which was completed in 1907. Within each of the denominations a great deal of Sunday School work had been going on, and already the Methodists, Baptists, Congregationalists and Presbyterians were jointly publishing lesson helps based on the International lessons. In most of the denominations there were strong leaders versed in Sunday School work who were able to give direction and support to the new organization. Under a full time secretary, an expanded program of work was undertaken.

Another national movement just gaining headway was that for world peace. It came naturally as a reaction from the war, and as a reflection of the general mood of the time. Christian laymen, foreign missionaries and Japan's liberals in public life joined forces in organizing the Japan Peace Society in 1906. Count Okuma gave it his blessing and served as chairman, and Count Itagaki drew up a statement appealing to the West to unite in a study of the causes of wars and in efforts to forestall them. He listed national aggression as one and national exclusion policies as another, thus neatly balancing the sins of his nation and of America in a single formula. From the start Gilbert Bowles of the Friends mission gave unstinted time and strength to the movement.

The first time Japan became host to an international convention was in 1907 when the World Student Christian Federation held its conference in Tokyo. The delegates from many nations, the enthusiastic public meetings, with addresses by speakers from many countries, and the follow-up of evangelistic services among students made a deep and wide impression upon the public. Here was visible evidence of the high quality of character and of international ideals among the Christian youth of the world, something Japan had hitherto had no opportunity of seeing.

The Christian outreach through publications was being extended year by year. In a country where twenty thousand titles were being published in a single year it was certain that the Christian witness in print would be made. The Scriptures always came first in volume and in systematic distribution. In the early years few Japanese could be found who would stoop to the low status of a travelling trader by selling Scriptures. From the beginning the distribution policy of the Bible societies had been one of sale and not of free gifts, hence the circulation had been small. Men such as Jonathan Goble of the American Bible Society, and formerly of the Perry Expedition actually did the selling themselves. Goble led a horse and wagon through the streets and lanes of towns and villages, accepting the odium of a peddler, but getting the Scriptures into circulation.

By 1900, however, things had greatly changed. The three Bible societies,—American, British and Foreign, and Scottish,—made a joint plan of national coverage and seriously undertook supervised distribution by trained colporteurs. The Bible distribution then came to challenge men of quality to go into the work as a vocation and remain in it, combining Bible sales with continuous Christian witnessing to individuals. In 1905 and 1906 circulation of the Scriptures doubled and again doubled towards a million copies a year.

In 1903 the Union Hymnal was published, and became a rich possession of the worshipping Christians of Japan. Its preparation had been recommended by the missionary conference of 1900, an editorial committee representing the major denominations was formed, and two years later the completed book was published. Some of the earliest writers of hymns, Matsuyama for one, were on the committee, as was also Umenosuke Bessho a poet of rare gifts. Among the missionaries, George Allchin who had proposed and pressed the plan and Thomas MacNair of Meiji Gakuin gave it major service. A hundred hymns common to this book and *Hymns Ancient and Modern* of the Episcopal Church formed a useful link suited for united services of worship. In the publishing of the book the work was shared by the Methodist Publishing House and the Keiseisha, which at this time was probably the most vigorous Christian publishing house in Japan. Under the layman K. Fukunaga, and often in association with the Gospel Press of Yokohama under S. Muraoka, the Keiseisha put out numbers of Christian books, entirely on a commercial, self-supporting basis.

The time of spate for books, however, was to come a little later. The main emphasis in this period was on periodical Christian literature. The five or six weekly and monthly papers edited by the best known men in the Christian movement furnished the moving blood-stream for the growth of Protestant Christianity. They would have been a credit to the Christian community of any country. Over a hundred other useful periodicals of lesser influence also were in circulation.

As modern Japan reached her half-century mark she was arriving at maturity as a modern nation-state. The techniques, skills and organization of industry had brought her abreast of the world's most advanced nations. Politically she had erected at least the framework for a democratic political life. General public education had set a world record for total national permeation. A reasonably harmonious balance was being found between the culture of the past and the demands of modern society. In this the various religious strands were being woven without too great friction. Japan bade fair to become the model for ancient people in orderly evolution moving toward modern national life. The way had been blocked once and again by conflicts, but these had been successfully won. On the whole, the nation held the approbation of the world.

In this society the Christian movement was coming into its own. It was still small, still thought of as alien, and still subject to much hostile pressure. Insofar as the older elements of Japanese life retained their hold on the people, Christianity was under a severe handicap. It belonged to the new Japan. But Christian strength was concentrated in the cities exactly where the national life currents were running more and more strongly. Here was the creative heart of the modern nation. In that setting, the Christians, though few in number, were exercising a wide influence. Their leadership in the areas of public morality, and in many fields of social amelioration was conspicuous. Their schools were serving the nation. The clouds seemed to be rolling away, and a new, bright day of recognition seemed about to break.

Yet a price was being paid. The very hostilities of the earlier decades had bred a type of heroic Christians whom even non-Christians were compelled to regard with admiration. In the general movement toward recognition and acceptance a milder, more conformist pattern of Christianity was in the making. The crusading spirit of the early Protestants was yielding ground to a more pastoral sense of mission. Identification with fellow-Japanese, harshly denied in the earlier years, was now becoming a deeply treasured experience of the Christians. Protestant Christianity in Japan was on the way to being naturalized. Separatism was to be avoided. The message would be given, and service would be rendered, but from within the national family circle. In this mood the course was set for the events of the next decisive periods of national crisis.

CHAPTER FOUR

EXPANSION TO EMPIRE

1909—1937

The Church Under Responsibility

WORLDWIDE INVOLVEMENT

1909–1919

Protestant Christianity Takes Deeper Root

Modern Japan hurtled into its second half-century at breakneck speed. The spoils of victory over Russia lay temptingly near. Fifteen million people in Korea offered an unrestricted field for expansion, with the wide horizons of Manchuria beyond. Prince Yamagata and his triumphant armies had swept the field abroad and at home. Ito had been relegated to the post in Seoul as Governor-General of Korea. There he met with a new force in the determined resistance of the Koreans to Japan's pressures. As the greatest statesman of the Meiji era, he recognized the dawning of Asian nationalism in the peninsula, and counselled moderate action. But the military rulers in Tokyo, impatient of delay, drove him from office, failed to prevent his assassination in Dairen in 1909, and the following year proceeded to the out-

134

right annexation of Korea. General Terauchi was sent over to crush resistance, and set up the new regime. The dragon's teeth sown then came to tragic harvest later; but for the time being all seemed to be clear gain.

The economic strain of the war with Russia had almost broken the back of Japan. Now a recouping of expenditures was sought by advantageous trading with Korea and the appropriation of its resources. With the increased population at home and the poverty of domestic materials, the development and exploitation of the Manchurian resources was the essential next step. In 1911 the decks were cleared for this by Great Britain's renewal of the alliance with Japan, and by extension of the Treaty of Commerce and Navigation with the United States. The heavy industries of wartime were not dismantled but expanded; huge budgets for military and naval defense were passed, and a heavily-burdened citizenry was reminded of the old war maxim "In the hour of victory tighten your helmet-cords!"

The recorder of history is tempted to make the year 1912 the close of an age, for in that year Meiji the Great died. With his going an era did truly come to an end. Not only did the calendar change, but with the advent of the new period of Taisho the first classic pattern of the new Japan began to fade into the past. Only a very few of the former leaders were still alive, and they moved behind the golden screens, hidden from public view.

The die of destiny had been cast years before the Emperor Meiji left the scene. So gradual was the shifting of power in national decisions that no one can tell how influential he was in his later years. To be sure, his name was sacred, but it was being used by those who could possess his seal to enforce their own policies. His person was near-divine and to the last he made frequent appearances among his people. His influence never waned, and he may have exerted his will upon public policies for he had no counsellor whose face he feared. But there is no evidence that he was the propelling force toward empire. His demise must be recorded as having immense emotional and psychological effect on the people, but not as causing any sharp change in national direction.

Accompanying him to the other world went the national hero General Nogi and his brave, demure wife. As the gongs sounded the exit of the Emperor's funeral cortege from the palace gates, the two, in white robes, kneeling on the matted floor of their home with their short daggers, administered the rite of self-immolation, and went to join their Emperor. Amidst the struggling for power at Court, and in public life, in the Diet, in political parties, in business, and in much of private life this selfless act crashed home with an impact which that generation could never forget. The event deeply sobered the Christians, for seen from one standpoint it was suicide. But from the angle of Old Japan it could not be so viewed. For years to come the matter was held before the moral judgment of Christians in debate and discussion, ending usually in a suspended decision, but with profound spiritual appreciation.

The Nogi spirits were housed in a nearby shrine where to this day incense never ceases to rise, nor does the line of pilgrims end. The total influence of their act must have served to heighten patriotism, and increase the prestige of the army;—effects that were scarcely wholesome for Japan at that time.

The round of domestic politics went on, with the new political parties in the Diet fighting the government, and forcing repeated shifts of cabinets. Finally, in 1914 Okuma was called in to handle an unpleasant situation, as had happened in previous crises. Fate seemed to have put the helm of state into the hands of Japan's only liberal Oligarch just at the time when the pre-determined course of political action was driving the nation toward a reckless plunge into imperial expansion.

As soon as the European war broke out, in 1914, Great Britain requested Japan to enter it. No second invitation was needed, and within a matter of days all of Germany's former holdings in northern China as well as in the South Seas had been occupied by Japanese forces. Thereafter the industries of the country were kept at high speed supplying the sinews of war for the Allies, while the navy and merchant fleet patrolled the seas. This was the time of times to deal with a helpless China; and in 1915 the notorious Twenty-One Demands were delivered. In their sum total they would have meant economic, political, and spiritual vassalage. But China's own revolution of 1911 was already well on its way, supported by a groundswell of aroused national spirit. Japan had to yield ground on some of the demands, but enough were acceded to under duress to poison Sino-Japanese relations for the ensuing decades. Tokyo's makers of strategy in their frustration at the non-compliance of Korea and China could not see the irony of the fact that it was Japan itself that had helped break open the old world of Asia and release its pent-up nationalisms.

By 1915 the long period of mourning for Meiji was over, and the new Emperor Taisho was enthroned. The nation gave itself to rejoicing, living over its past in the historic rituals of state. Soon it was sadly realized that the new ruler was a semi-invalid in body and mind, unable to assume even ceremonial functions of office. In any event it would have been difficult enough for him to have succeeded such a figure as was his father, or to have faced the aged Oligarchs with authority. The nation in sympathetic loyalty built around him a wall of privacy and protection within which he might live his own life. At the same time official sanction was given to all decisions made in his name by Japan's real rulers.

This defensive situation entailed a still higher elaboration of the cult of emperor veneration, stereotyping it and removing it from any direct personal basis. The lectures that for years had been carried on at the Imperial University by Professor Yasoku Hozumi had laid the foundations for a mystical, religious view of the emperor's person. This was taken up by Professor Katsuhiko Kakehi who advanced it to the status of a theology, articulated by a Hegelian philosophy of national life. Thus all the materials for a later codification of the new emperor-cult were at hand when the era of Meiji came to an end. For Christians this presaged a new intensification of the problem of church and state.

In 1916 Japan obtained secret agreements with Russia and the other allies in support of her claim to holdings in Asia and the Pacific. The Ishii-Lansing understanding with the United States was also gained. The way to empire seemed safe and sure. But one more revolution was to come. Russia's upheaval in 1917 completely changed the outlook in both Europe and Asia. Seventy thousand Japanese troops were deployed into the Siberian region spreading as far west as Lake Baikal, guarding the railways, controlling all transportation, dominating the Allied Expeditionary force of Western nations, and in general replacing Russia as the overlord of north-eastern Asia.

With General Terauchi as premier the nation was driven so hard that riots broke out in the cities of Japan over inflationary costs of living, while in Korea the discontent became unmanageable. In 1918 the government fell, and for the first time a political party leader, Kei Hara, assumed the post of premier. The next year Baron M. Saito, a naval officer of high character, was made Governor-General of Korea. There, by a sympathetic administration, he did much to repair the damage wrought by the previous regime.

Victory came in 1918, and in January of 1919 the Paris

Peace Conference opened. Over the world a new age was struggling to be born. Although the nations were still counted as "Powers", and force had brought about the peace, yet international ideals hitherto unvoiced in world gatherings were clamoring for attention. The spiritual tensions were great. Japan shared these strains. The unwillingness of the other nations to include even a formal avowal of racial non-discrimination in the treaty was a grievous wound to Japan's self respect. The reluctance of these same nations to stand by the secret understandings regarding her place in Asia shook her confidence in diplomatic integrity, and China's skill in escaping from the grip of the Twenty-One Demands was an added cause of frustration. Yet it was in the new role of one of the "Big Five" that Japan found herself accepted at the round table, and eventually, too, most of her territorial claims were given consideration. The third of the nation's modern wars in close succession was turning into gold as the others had done. Japan was now fully recognized as an empire.

With the change in Japan's national estate Christianity moved gradually but surely into a new position within the life of the country. It was no longer under the ban, as it had been in the first quarter-century. Nor was it treated as an unwanted stepchild, as in the second quarter. It was now coming to be regarded as one of the dependable spiritual and moral forces in society. This had been given dramatic emphasis as early as 1911, when Christians were invited along with representatives of Shinto and Buddhism, to a conference sponsored by the government and known as "The Three Religions Conference." This was a tacit declaration by the authorities that Confucianism was no longer to be counted as one of the three hereditary faiths of Japan, and that Christianity was to take its place in that circle.

This recognition was all the more astonishing since one of

the occasions for the calling of the meeting was the shock caused by the announcement that there had been a plot against the life of the Emperor Meiji. In 1911 thirteen men accused of complicity in the case were executed; the leader being Shusui Kotoku. He was a theoretical anarchist who in earlier years had been in the group of social radicals, most of whom were Christians. Although he had never become a Christian it would have been quite easy for enemies of the church to have imputed guilt by association. Instead the official reaction was quite the opposite. Serious-minded persons realized afresh the need for strengthening the spiritual foundations of the nation, and some of them turned to religious leaders for that assistance.

The immediate occasion for the meeting of religionists was the visit of T. Tokonami, Vice-minister of Home Affairs, to America where he was much impressed by the spiritual force of Christianity. On his return he brought about the official calling of the conference. Sitting with thirteen Shinto and fifty Buddhist representatives were seven Christians,— a Protestant bishop, two pastors, two college presidents, and one each representing the Roman Catholic and Eastern Orthodox churches. The top men in government were there, and they made an outright appeal for the religious bodies to take their share in the moral guidance of the nation. The religionists on their side passed resolutions of appreciation of the government and of hope that the cordial relations would continue.

Opinion within the churches was divided as to whether the event was worth the cost. In proportion as the government interested itself in the role of Christianity in the national situation, freedom of initiative was likely to be curtailed. Uemura would have nothing to do with the movement, nor did Uchimura. But the general reaction among the church members was one of relief at the lessened pressures of misunderstandings, and of readiness to accept the full responsibilities of citizenship.

Meanwhile the Ministry of Education shifted position and began to urge a more active promotion of religious influence within the schools. Christian teachers were even invited to give moral lectures in some of the public schools. But this trend, also had its two sides. In May of 1911 the government issued the first of numerous advices instructing all schools to attend the ceremonies at the shrines. The churches found themselves facing an issue that was to plague them for all the rest of the modern period. The instruction construed the celebrations as "ancestor veneration", and thus avoided collision with the Constitutional provisions for freedom of worship. But Christians were not ready to participate in Shinto ceremonies of ritual, offering and prayer performed by the usual priests at the traditional shrines, no matter what they might be termed. There was immediate remonstrance from schools and churches. Dr. S. Motoda of the Episcopal church took a mediating position, distinguishing between "veneration" and worship; but he was almost alone. From this time on, many meetings were held to grapple with this baffling problem of Japanese national life, and earnest efforts were made to find a rationale of shrine attendance on the part of Christians without violation of conscience.

Protestant Christianity at this period had three distinct centers of organization. They were: the all-Japanese Federation of Churches, the all-missionary Conference of Federated Missions, and the joint Continuation Committee. Although they were interrelated, yet the activities of each were somewhat distinct from the others in scope. They, therefore furnish a convenient basis of classification for the events of the decade in the Protestant movement.

THE FEDERATION OF CHURCHES was formed in 1911 after the disolution of the former Evangelical Alliance in 1906. The Federation carried on the annual Week of Prayer in January. It concerned itself with public affairs, such as the Three Religions Conference, the matter of Shrine attendance, and wartime activities. It established liaison with public men when broad issues were at stake, and it served to mobilize sentiment in the churches for the national welfare. The anti-brothel campaigns, as well as temperance activities, centered there.

The nagging problem of denial of Christian burial in the Buddhist cemeteries continued unsettled. To appeals for moral support government officials merely replied; "Be diplomatic in your approach, and if necessary set up your own cemeteries",—somewhat poor comfort for Christians who were being stopped from joining their ancestors of past centuries in the family burying-grounds. Another problem was that of marriage to non-Christians. Most of the churches did not take a firm position on this matter, and increasingly they were losing their members by marriages outside the faith, with the attendant failure to establish genuine Christian homes. As the service of counselling and advice regarding the selection of mates is one of the very serious responsibilities of pastors in Japan, the Federation took action urging more positive practices of Christian choice.

With the enlarging borders of the Japanese empire the church felt the call to move out to the frontiers. No doubt the government, too, was glad to have this happen. Under the auspices of the Federation, Christian leaders undertook extensive travel assignments, visiting Japanese colonies overseas and encouraging missionary activity in them. Bishop Honda and Dr. Kajinosuke Ibuka of Meiji Gakuin, Tokyo made a number of goodwill journeys, combining attendance at world conferences with lecture tours abroad. The one who found this work most congenial and did it well was

Dr. Hiromichi Kozaki. He had close friends in government, in army and navy, and among influential men of affairs, all of whom were ready to support a wider outreach of Japan under Christian leadership.

Kozaki's visit to the Hawaiian Islands with religious meetings among the Japanese there resulted in the formation of the Hawaiian Missionary Association, 1903, and the establishment of a school at his Reinanzaka Church in Tokyo for the training of evangelists for this work. When in 1919 Japan was given a mandate by the League of Nations over the former German holdings in Micronesia the government asked Dr. Kozaki to make provision for the continued administration of Protestant missions there. This work had a history of American Congregational beginnings, but Dr. Kozaki rather quaintly notes that it was not convenient to consult the Japanese Congregational Church authorities and so he proceeded to make the arrangements himself. He formed a strong committee of Japanese ministers and laymen, sent one on a tour of inspection, presented to the government a budget calling for a suitable annual grant in 1920, launched the South Seas Evangelistic Band and again, in his own church, he established a school for the training of its Japanese missionaries.

Christian history in Micronesia offers an interesting example of missions following the flag, and of the uncritical attitude toward this taken both by governments and by Christians. When United States trade entered the Pacific world the American Board established and maintained missions in the Marshall and Caroline Islands, particularly in Truk and Ponape. After the Spanish War the United States government acquiesced in Germany's moving into the region, and the Christian work was taken over by the Liebenzeller Mission. When Germany was ousted it was taken for granted by the Japanese authorities that the Christian mission was to continue, and that it was to be tax-supported. This was done, and apparently with excellent practical results. The annual reports over the years,—until flags and mission administration again changed in 1945—show steady growth.

Other projects of Christian outreach engaged the interest of the Federation of Churches, although these were not always directly under its care. With the annexation of Korea, Torajiro Watase of the Congregational Church conceived a plan for mission work there. Obtaining the financial backing of Japan's four or five leading industrialists, he gathered teams of young ministers,—mostly Doshisha graduates,—and in 1911 established a chain of churches in the Peninsula. Within six years they numbered over one hundred, with fifty Korean pastors and over twenty thousand members. In the turblent period in Korea during and after World War II this Christian community seems to have disintegrated.

The Presbyterian-Reformed Church sent workers to Formosa, chiefly for Christian efforts among the growing Japanese communities. With the increased interest in the Asian mainland, the Japanese Churches moved into action. The secretary of the Federation, Kikutaro Matsuno, visited the main centers of Manchuria, and Coastal China to encourage the small communities of Japanese Christians in each city, and to help plan for the organization of churches. By 1919 there were a million of such Japanese settlers divided about evenly between Manchuria and China. This sizable field for missionary work was gradually entered by the Japanese Christian movement.

The stream of emigration to South America had started and by 1918 twenty thousand Japanese laborers were concentrated in the plantations of Brazil; but the churches could as yet send only occasional visitors. The YWCA did, however, set up a "highway of friendship" in 1919, for the "picture brides" going to America, with briefings, send-offs, and receptions on arrival. These services were intensely appreciated.

Troubled because "until now Christians of Japan and China have ignored one another", the Federation of churches sent a deputation to Shanghai in 1916 to carry the greetings of Japanese Protestants; but with no visible reciprocation. The next year a joint delegation including three well-known missionaries and two Japanese leaders attended a national meeting of Chinese Christians. They extended an invitation for a fraternal delegation to visit Japan in return. None came.

The revolution of 1911 in China syphoned off most of the thousands of Chinese students who were in Japan. They hurriedly left for home. It was said that these Japan-trained students comprised seventy per cent of the members of the first National Assembly, and sixty per cent of the first officials in government. YMCA Christian work continued among those students who remained. It should not be forgotten that during this period and the next decade Sun Yat-sen repeatedly took refuge in a hide-out in Yokohama, and that Chiang Kai-shek obtained his higher training in a military college in Japan.

The CONFERENCE OF FEDERATED MISSIONS,— formerly the Standing Committee on Cooperating Christian Missions,—was in a sense the opposite number of the Japan Federation of Churches. From its first session in 1902 it had become the accepted clearing-house for the missions and their common work. Virtually every mission in Japan was represented, with thirty-one sending regular delegates. By a careful avoidance of even the appearance of being a super-mission, or of imposing any credal tests for membership it provided an efficient instrument for counselling, fellowship, and for voluntary cooperation where desired. Just once, in

145

1915, there was a flicker of theological disputation, and one delegate withdrew, but for the rest of its history it was completely harmonious. It took its work seriously, and it had numerous distinctively missionary functions, although in many ways it did parallel the proper work of the Japanese Federation.

A glance at its committees and agendas of discussion indicate the chief fields of concern. There was the publishing of the annual year book, issued first at the incredible price of ten sen (five cents). The editors almost kept up with the expansionist policies of the Japanese government, for in the 1911 volume the title was changed to "The Christian Movement in the Japanese Empire", and reports of the Korea Christian Movement were included. The task of keeping the "home church" informed was further aided by the publication of the *Japan Evangelist,* and later of the *Japan Christian Quarterly.* These also served the foreign missionaries in Japan.

Japanese language study was systematized by the Conference and courses were fixed, with examining standards. Then followed the establishment of a school in Tokyo for language study. It came to be viewed as an agency for international cultural understanding. In later years, under the directorship of Darley Downs, Congregational missionary, and with the support of some of Japan's best-known men of affairs,—notably Baron Sakatani, mayor of Tokyo,—this Institute of Japanese Language and Culture rendered outstanding service. Its worthy successor with new facilities, in Tokyo, was still ably continuing its role in 1959. Branch schools over the years have been set up in other cities. There have also been some language schools under other mission auspices.

The work of community or union churches came within the purview of the Conference. These churches were organized in port cities and other centers where English-speaking Westerners lived. At times there have been as many as thirty in Japan. Only a few have maintained full-time pastors. As a rule missionaries have carried the brunt of the work. Pastoral care and Sunday School instruction for Westerners, and worship services in English have given these foreign institutions a valuable place as auxiliary to the main work of the Christian movement.

The Committee on Speakers from Abroad sponsored the visits of numerous church world leaders, working in co-operation with the Federal Council of Churches in America. Visits such as that of Drs. Shailer Matthews and Sidney Gulick in 1914, were an attempt to contribute to the improvement of Japan-American relations.

Beginning with a Committee on Christian literature, the Christian Literature Society came into being in 1910 with Samuel R. Wainright as the moving spirit. It was not destined to play quite the creative role which similar national Christian literature organizations have done in China or in India, In Japan by this time there were nearly a score of general publishers issuing Christian books and periodicals, as well as Japanese Christian publishers and other missionary and church publishing agencies. But the new society focused attention on the need for common effort by all the missions, and it did provide some unique services in Christian literature production. Particularly noteworthy was the work of E. L. Walne of the Southern Baptist Mission in pushing distribution to a scale hitherto unreached.

The magazine *Morning Star* was issued in huge editions and distributed to over fourteen hundred of the sixteen hundred public high schools of Japan. A generous mission gift made this possible, but it was the statesmanship of Christian teachers that saw the new opportunity for religious influence in the government schools and seized it.

The missions reflected currents of missionary emphasis and activity in the West. It was a time of great missionary enthusiasm, and also of hearty cooperation among the denominational boards. In preparation for the Edinburgh Conference of 1910 and in its follow-up a number of worldwide goals for Christian evangelization were set. The task was then seen largely as one of geographical extension, as a field to be "occupied". The "forces" were viewed chiefly as missionary forces, and the field was one to be occupied by them.

From 1911 on, the Conference and its committees were busy with the problem of "Survey and Occupation", of "Comity", and of a "Distribution of Forces". The country was divided into twelve major areas, each with a regional sub-committee for study. Conferences were held and the work of survey was allotted. Then report meetings followed with charts and graphs, statistical tables and maps, population figures, and computation of missionary percentages. It was almost a purely quantitative appraisal, with its counting of heads and measuring of square miles. The impression made on a young missionary at this time was that the task of Christianizing Japan awaited only the willingness of the churches of the West to send more missionaries, so that more places could be "occupied" and the legends on the maps re-colored.

Japanese Christian workers were not ignored in the studies, but notes in the surveys such as "No missionary and only 7 or 8 workers" were indicative of the comparative rating of personnel. For the first year or two there was no participation in the committees or conferences on the part of Japanese churchmen.

Over a period of several years considerable numbers of missionaries spent many hours in this sincere attempt to re-plan strategy so as to cooperate with less over-lapping, to plan future expansion with mutual comity, and to set forward the Kingdom in Japan with a more realistic sense of responsibility. We cannot say, therefore, that it was time ill-spent. But it was not an outgrowth of a felt need among the Japanese Christians, and ultimately it had little chance of life in it.

When the Japanese church leaders joined in the studies they did so on invitation of the foreigners, responding with courtesy and a degree of interest. But as members of the living organism of Japanese society they knew that their mandate to witness to their people could never come from the West, nor could it ever be as simple as it was then being construed to be. In the Japanese records of this period one finds only the slightest reference to the project.

The CONTINUATION COMMITTEE was a third center of Christian cooperation at this time. It was a conjunction of the streams represented by the Federation of Churches and the Conference of Federated Missions. Following the World Missionary Conference of 1910, a central Continuation Committee had been set up for the purpose of carrying out the plans projected by the conference. There was at that time no world-wide organization of the Protestant churches or missions. John R. Mott as chairman, within the several years following the conference visited the major countries of the world, encouraging in each the organization of a similar Continuation Committee.

In 1913 Dr. Mott came to Japan, where in fourteen days five successive conferences were held; one with missionaries, one with mixed groups of educators, one with Japanese church workers, a joint conference of all these, and one on Christian Literature. Japan had been represented at the Edinburgh Conference by Bishop Honda of the Methodist Church. Dr. Ibuka of Meiji Gakuin, Dr. Tasuke Harada of Doshisha, and Dr. Yugoro Chiba a Baptist leader. The effect of that world meeting was reinforced by Dr. Mott's reports and interpretations; and steps were proposed by him for implementing its findings in Japan. The Japan Continuation Committee referred to above was the result. It was made up of missionaries and Japanese in equal numbers, with co-opted members at large.

The report of the meetings published in 1914 covers the entire spread of missionary interests including mission support, increase of staff, extension of student hostels, and scholarships, union in theological training, a Christian university, Christian literature, improved Japanese language study, the development of city institutional churches, provision for a national secretary for education, and steps toward cooperation in all evangelistic work. These causes, excellent as they are, so closely match the concerns of the Conference of Federated Missions (which in turn reflects the Edinburgh Conference) that they undoubtedly trace back to the initiative of Dr. Mott and the missionary planners of the West. They certainly did not spring out of the soil in Japan. But, once called to the attention of the Japanese leaders, these proposals had much to commend them. Also the Japanese leaders knew that they belonged in the world currents moving Protestant Christendom toward closer cooperative organization.

For eight years the Continuation Committee pursued its work, in general doing the things that called for joint action with the missionaries, and it maintained relations with the world movements. But the matters that pulled at the heart and conscience of Christians,—the adjustments with their cultural past, the confrontation with government, the stance toward public affairs, and the over-all witness to their own people,—were the issues that engaged the attention of the Federation of Churches.

One nationwide activity, however, did come from the Mott meetings, and was clearly a contribution made by the Japanese members. That was the launching of another evangelistic campaign. It was officially entitled "Cooperative Campaign of Evangelism" but in common usage it came to be called the "Taisho Evangelistic Campaign" after the name of the new ruler and epoch. It proved to be by far the most determined and comprehensive witness hitherto made by the Christians to their nation. Organized in two regional commissions with Tsuneteru Miyagawa the dean of pastors as chairman of the Western section, and the veteran Uemura chairman of the Eastern one, its list of committee members is a "Who's Who" of Protestant Christianity of that time. Over a hundred well-known speakers, ministers and laymen, were assigned to speaking tours all over the country. Local committees everywhere made the preliminary preparations, and did the follow-up work. Twenty different tracts on various Christian themes were prepared and distributed in large numbers. Fifteen hundred volunteers in Tokyo alone distributed millions of pieces of literature.

For three years, from 1914 to 1916, the campaign continued unabated. D. R. Mackenzie, Canadian missionary leader who was in the thick of it estimated that ninety percent of the entire Protestant movement was in active participation. The reported figures are: 5,000 meetings held: 800,000 people in attendance; 27,000 cards of inquiry and decision signed. As in the earlier campaigns, substantially increased church membership was not realized although there was some growth. The total impact on the non-Christian world of Japan, however, was pronounced. And among the Christians, high and low, a new sense of unity and of courage was the result.

World War I was not primarily Japan's war. Her participation was at long range, and involved almost no combat at all. The public felt only the effects of the industrial boom and the exhilaration of their nation's new place in the world. Christians, therefore, were not faced by any critical decisions relating to the conflict. The rough edges of difference with their neighbors and with government were steadily being planed off, and ever smoother adjustments for living were being found. Little if any war work was done, for there were few casualties; and no dangers were close enough to call for even civilian defense. The German prisoners of war formed about the only outlet of compassion for Japanese Christians.

The Siberian expedition of 1918 did offer a field for Christian service. The National Committee of the YMCA in Japan was permitted to organize welfare work for the Japanese troops. Over a score of Japanese secretaries and several foreign colleagues were on active duty in the huts and railway canteens maintained across Siberia. The International Committee of the "Y" also served the total Allied expedition. Under the direction of Sidney Phelps, senior secretary in Japan, the work on an international scale was set up, with over a hundred secretaries pushing a program of recreation, morale-building and religious work. Of these a dozen were Japan missionaries loaned for the special assignment. The American Red-Cross, directed by Dr. Rudolph Teusler of St. Luke's Hospital, Tokyo, recruited a number of missionaries from Japan and cared for refugees and victims of the revolution in Siberia. A team of YWCA secretaries and women missionaries also volunteered for this service.

When the war was over the churches issued a Manifesto in celebration of the victory. After asserting that it was due to the same principles of justice and righteousness for which Christians had always stood, they pleaded for moderation in victory, and for the observance of democratic measures in the settlement. Then came a review of basic Christian beliefs for the citizen: the Fatherhood of God, the authority of conscience, peace and international goodwill, the promotion of the National Mission; a high place for women and the home, and the elevation of the standards of national life. The list seems to be a safe and sane statement of obvious truths until one's eye rests on the third item relating to promotion of the National Mission.

Close observers of the many statements issued later by the churches throughout Japan's accumulating crises, learned to look among the genuinely Christian affirmations for the one or two pivotal clauses that to Japanese citizens carried a weight of meaning. They occur in the constitutions of schools and in the confessions of the churches. They are the cruicial words spoken in support of the "National Structure" (*Kokutai*), of the Emperor-status, of the imperial expansion, of the dealings with Korea, with China, then with America, and of the destiny of the empire of Japan in the world.

The phrases employed are stock terms in official use at the time, and the Western observer is tempted to assume that they were dictated. But this is by no means certain. The national mission, to any citizen in any nation, is a serious challenge. Its validity is always plausible or else it would never be followed. An outcaste group or those of alien affiliation may reject it, and may go underground, but responsible citizens seldom do this. Instead, they take it at its highest interpretation, seek to invest it with spiritual meaning, bring it into line with conscience, and loyally support it by work and word.

The main body of Japanese Christians may not have gone through this process deliberately, nor can one be sure how many individuals may have signed these statements under protest of conscience. It is doubtful that even the persons most concerned really knew precisely what their attitudes were; and surely it is not given to an outsider, decades later, to guess. It is sufficient to note that the Christian movement had swung into the main orbit of Japan's essential life. It was no longer irresponsible and free. Accepted as one of the spiritual forces of the nation, its members now expressed the rectitude of their character as Christians by taking on the yoke of common citizenship with their neighbors. As with their brethren of other nations of today,—and perhaps this will be still more true of tomorrow,—they faced the agonizing spiritual strains of living loyally both in the national state and in the Kingdom of Heaven.

The differing attitudes of several of the leaders, however, should be noted. By this time Kanzo Uchimura had buried himself in his Bible studies, exercising his influence both through his publications and by his weekly meetings with the highly-honored small group of young men selected by him for intensive training. Holding himself aloof from public affairs he ceased making even homiletical application of Scriptural truths to current events and gave himself completely to the spread of the Christian faith. He did this not in support of a strong church organization, but solely on the basis of individual Biblical interpretation and personal Christian experience. So extreme was he in opposition to the institutionalizing of Christianity that with the first evidence of a tendency to organize among his circle he would simply discontinue his teaching and dissolve the group.

Thus it was that the so-called "Churchless" Christianity movement came to life. Even its founder could not keep it completely formless, nor could he finally resist the demand for systematic teaching to wider numbers. In his later years he opened a large lecture hall in downtown Tokyo where nearly a thousand would come from all over the city to receive his teaching.

Uchimura used to say; "the truly Christian temple has God's earth for a floor, and His sky for the ceiling; its altar is in the heart of the believer; its law is God's Word, and His

154

Holy Spirit is its only pastor." The Christian universality and dynamism of this movement has not spent itself. Nearly all the young men who at this time joined the charmed circle came into national prominence, and most of them made their mark as educators. In every later period the members of this group tended to maintain an independent spirit, and often held a critical attitude toward national expansion and war.

The other Christian leader of first magnitude, Masahisa Uemura, in three years had also detached himself from active participation in public affairs. His withdrawal, while not so dramatic as that of Uchimura, was scarcely less complete. As the pastor of a really great church in Tokyo, ministering to people of every sort from students to Cabinet members he must have been dealing with current issues in his weekly sermons and lectures. Nevertheless, he took no public stand on national problems, and his name seldom occurs with those of the other church and school leaders in cooperative Christian undertakings. In the conference of 1909 he urged pastors to preach to their times, and not "like a time-table ten years old." Yet, he went on, caustically: "Some pastors get absorbed in social reform of one sort or another... neglecting spiritual things and fussing over matters of food and drink...Let the dead bury their own dead."

Dr. Uemura's conviction was that the life of God and the life of man come into full union only in the Christian church. Therefore, he gave himself to the church with every ounce of his strength. He plainly said that finally the church would swallow society, absorbing every rebellious element, in the fulfillment of God's purpose for the race. The tendency to a dialectic view of Christian truth, which was later to become dominant in Japanese Christianity, had its incipient beginnings in the example of this influential leader of the church at the time of the First World War. He neither resisted the government, nor would he compromise with it.

155

He gave his witness within the life of the church, and waited for history to unfold the will of God.

It was the leaders in the social action wing of the churches whom Uemura castigated as fussing over matters of food and drink, in their concern for human welfare and the improvement of society. At the time of the Russo-Japanese conflict their position in regard to war had been the burning issue, but with the remoteness of the scene in World War I the challenge to their Christian idealism came not as a call to pacifism, but rather through the swift accumulation of industrial and social problems at home, as a summons to social thinking and action. Whether Kotoku was really guilty of a conspiracy against the emperor's life will never be known, but the shock of the trial and execution was so great that the public gave moral support to the drastic laws and police measures then put into operation.

This ruthless treatment of all unconventional thinking as crime split the ranks of the socially-concerned leaders, including those who were Christians. Sen Katayama fled to America, and later moved on to Moscow where he died. Sakae Osugi left the Christian church, became a Communist, for years led a hunted life, and finally was strangled to death by a prison guard. The few remaining Christian advocates of gradual social change lapsed into silence. No middle ground seemed possible. Even a suspicion of left-wing sympathies meant unemployment, recurring arrests, and possible conviction of crime.

In this unfavorable situation, however, one noteworthy social movement by a Christian did develop. Bunji Suzuki, in connection with a social relief agency in Tokyo was allowed to organize a Friendly Aid Association (*Yu-Ai-Kwai*) patterned after the mutual benefit societies of England. Isoo Abe and others of the Christian humanitarian group supported him in it, and it grew rapidly. Started in

156

1912, by 1916 it had 20,000 paying members with branches widely scattered throughout industrial communities.

These various groups became agents of agitation for universal suffrage,—as were the women of the WCTU—but their main objective was some degree of regulation of labor conditions by law. It was time something was done. The sudden burgeoning of industry had almost overnight created a class of factory workers numbering nearly a million. Of these one half were women, and of them over half were under twenty years of age. A hundred thousand young children tended looms in the cotton mills. Conditions in heavy industry were extremely bad, and in the mines, they were the worst of all. In 1916 the agitation bore fruit in the first factory law which gave at least some protection to workers.

When the Osaka regional Aid Association met in 1916 it took action forming itself into the first unit of Japan's first federation of labor; and labor organization at the national level was on its way. An era of strikes began. The earlier labor unrest had been summarily suppressed, but increasingly it was seen that modern Japan dare not weaken its own foundations by allowing intolerable labor conditions to continue. Concessions were made, and the unions consolidated their strength.

In the midst of this renewed labor movement appeared a new, youthful figure who was to be Christianity's chief bridge into a world almost unknown to its other leaders. Toyohiko Kagawa, an impassioned advocate of humane dealing with any and all underprivileged people, had taken to heart the plight of the workers, and during his days as a student in the Kobe Theological Seminary had often crossed the "deathline" that separated respectable Kobe from the indescribable slums of the Shinkawa section. In 1909 at Christmas he shouldered his few belongings and moved in. He rented two tiny six foot cubicles in one of the long huts.

Darkened by the overhanging roof of the hut opposite, and approached along the alley on the three-feet wide boards that covered the half-open drains between the two rows of sheds, it was literally living in an obscure tunnel.

He was soon joined by three or four pitiable creatures who had no home nor livelihood. Beaten and robbed by bullies, infected by the diseases of his flock, suspected and shunned by his neighbors he nevertheless survived, and eventually became the trusted shepherd of the community.

Kagawa traced the desperate condition of the slum-dwellers to the fact that they had no corporate voice or strength in dealing with employers. He stepped into the vanguard of the social struggle when in 1919 the workers of the Kawasaki Dockyards went on strike. He was imprisoned, and thereafter marked by the police. In the ensuing labor and rural movements on a national scale Kagawa continued to take an active part. Almost alone among the Christians he consistently remained free from extremes; never surrendering his position of active resistance to social injustice, and never giving up hope of the church or leaving it for more radical programs.

Although the pastors and church members generally did not appear at this time to feel much immediate concern for social betterment, the missionaries certainly did. The editor of the *Christian Movement* reported in 1916 that of forty-eight missions in Japan forty-two were carrying on some form of social work. One notes, too, the large number of women missionaries directly engaged in it. Miss Alice Adams of Okayama, Miss Charlie Holland in Osaka, Miss Sarah Bauernfiend in Tokyo, Miss E. R. Gillett, of the railway Mission, Miss Patton of Tokushima come to mind, though there were many more. Their reports show an intimate knowledge of working people, as well as a deep concern for their welfare.

The Misaki Kaikan, the first city institutional church in Japan, was founded in downtown Tokyo by the Baptists, encouraged by the University of Chicago. This "busiest beehive of religious industry in Japan", was directed by William Axling and his colleagues in its manifold program of service, and was the model for others in later years. The secretaries of both the YMCA and YWCA made exhaustive social studies, and their reports, especially those of Galen Fisher, Merle Davis and Helen Topping, awakened the consciences of the missionaries to this area of unmet need.

At the same time the needs of rural people were voiced emphatically by Merrill Vories. Under an arrangement which the YMCA had made with the Ministry of Education for selecting and bringing out young men college graduates under a two-year contract to teach English, Vories had been appointed to a public high school in Hachiman, in Omi Province, near Kyoto. The town was a hotbed of traditional Buddhist zeal. His school principal felt that it was no place for a Christian, much less a Christian such as Vories. His personal magnetism, with his versatile gifts and skills, made him a dangerous element to put among students, for his faith was as zealous as that of the Buddhists. Soon there was a clash, and he was told that he must either cease his Christian witness or leave the school. He chose the latter. He then took lodgings in the town, where he continued his Christian work. Out of this grew the Omi Mission, with several hundred staff members in its architectural and industrial departments, and with the founding of scores of churches throughout the province. Vories in later years was greatly aided by his talented wife, Maki Hitotsuyanagi, into whose family of court nobility he received adoption as a Japanese citizen. In 1959 they were as busy as ever in their many-sided Christian enterprise.

Although fully conscious of the needs of city industrial

159

Christian work, Vories' major emphasis has been directed toward stimulating the churches to enter more deeply into village and rural life. Not all of the two hundred young teachers of English who came out under the YMCA auspices rendered service as conspicuous as did Vories, but in the aggregate their influence was widely permeating and lasting.

The life and work of the Christian schools was greatly fortified by the formation in 1909 of the Japan Christian Educational Association. It never presumed to exercise authority over any school, but it was an excellent instrument for mutual acquaintance and support among the schoolmen and women. It conducted numerous studies and surveys, and many useful suggestions were passed on to the affiliated schools.

A great boon came to the Christian schools when the national law was changed to make larger provision for special schools (*Semmon Gakko*), for vocational and professional training at the secondary and college levels. The law was at the same time liberalized to admit qualified private institutions to the privileges of the government schools. Although the regulations did not come into effect until 1919, the effect was felt for several years in advance, with greatly increased enrollments and in a heightened prestige for the Christian schools. From this time on the Christian colleges began to develop toward university status.

Along with the 1913 surge of missionary impulse flowing from the Mott meetings a special commission was set up to work on a plan for a union Christian university. David B. Schneder of Sendai and Arthur Berry of Aoyama Gakuin, with A. K. Reischauer of Meiji Gakuin took particular interest in the project and made earnest efforts to obtain agreement on a plan to submit to Dr. John F. Goucher who was in Japan. In China, Dr. Goucher had collaborated with the various missions in the formation of several splendid union university projects. But nothing eventuated from the efforts of 1913 in Tokyo.

A great educational accomplishment, however, was successfully completed in 1918 when the Tokyo Women's Christian College was formed by the union of the work of the American Presbyterian and Methodist, and the Canadian missions. Dr. and Mrs. Reischauer were among the moving spirits in this undertaking. Dr. Inazo Nitobe was the honorary president, and Dr. (Miss) Tetsuko Yasui the efficient administrative head.

Women's education in Japan has owed a debt to the Christian movement; and even as late as 1918 the Christian schools carried the torch of progress. As yet there were but two colleges for women in the entire national system. Women were just beginning to be admitted to the national universities, and then only to those of second-rank. In these, moreover, they were chiefly in the schools of medicine, for work of research. Thus, for a full generation the Christian schools of higher grade sent out a steady stream of graduates who were able to take their place, in public life as well as in the churches, as recognized leaders.

Another aspect of education thus far neglected in Japan was that of modern physical education. As a result of the wide activities of Frank Brown of the YMCA its various branches took the lead in developing both individual and team athletics. The old type of contests and skills, such as archery, wrestling, fencing, and horsemanship were practiced as competition of individuals. Japanese young people had litle experience in teamwork or group play. The "Y"s and the Christian schools initiated this almost in its entirety. Soon every form of western sport had taken root, particularly baseball, which became the national game. Some years later Paul Rusch of St. Paul's College, introduced American football, and made other contributions to the collegiate athletic world in Japan.

In the literary field some noteworthy Japanese books were published. Professor M. Takagi compiled a sixteen hundred page *Encyclopedia of Christianity*, and the Keiseisha published it in 1911 at a profit. H. Yamamoto's two-volume *History of Christianity in Japan* was issued in 1918, to take its place alongside E. Kashiwai's monumental *History of Christianity* which had been published in 1914. In 1910 the permanent committee on Bible translation started on the revision of the New Testament. Dr. D. C. Greene was chairman until his death in 1912. The work was finished in 1917, and was received with general approbation. Professor Y. Sacon put out his own excellent translation of parts of the Bible. The changed attitude of the Ministry of Education toward religion quickly affected the demand for Christian literature, and particularly for the Scriptures. The Bible societies reported ballooning sales.

With general recognition by the public the Christian community extended its activities into the wider ranges of influence. The peace movement enlisted the active support of public men, such as Premier Okuma, who became president of the Japan Peace Society, and Yukio Ozaki, the liberal political leader. The Japan National Sunday School Association invited the world organization to come to Tokyo for its next meeting in 1920, and Baron Shibusawa, the industrial magnate accepted the chairmanship of the planning committee. Japan-American relations were unfortunately moving in the wrong direction at this time. Anti-Japanese demonstrations had broken out on the west coast of the United States, and a strong sense of grievance swept over Japan. A strong Committee on Japan-American Friendship was set up, and Count Kabayama gave much time to it. Prince Tokugawa could be counted on for support in all these activities. In every instance, too, there were prominent missionaries at the center of the planning and program.

In 1911 the Seventh Day Adventist Mission started operations, with its threefold stress on medical, industrial (printing and publishing), and direct evangelistic work. Forestalling the familiar criticism that they might draw converts from the other Christian bodies they reported that of the accessions to their churches "80% have come straight from heathenism". H. Clay Macauley, speaking on the twenty-fifth anniversary of Unitarian work disavowed any approach different from that of the other Christian bodies, and said that he and his group were engaged in the "usual mission work". The Oriental Missionary Society of Los Angeles was pushing its house-to-house evangelism. Between 1911 and 1915 this group had direct contact with twenty-one million people in their homes in nineteen prefectures, and had distributed forty million books and tracts.

Although our focus must of necessity be chiefly upon the Protestant work, yet throughout every period we are conscious that the fellow-workers of the other Christian bodies were marching abreast. In 1911 the great Archbishop Nicolai died; in the fiftieth year of his service to Japan. The Japan Orthodox Church which he bequeathed to the care of his worthy successor Bishop Sergius was said in 1916 to have 226 churches with 32,000 members. Everything was placid, the reports said. "Conditions favorable... a general spiritual hunger...government favor (Russian) ...smooth sailing, and a calm wind." More explicit financial statistics showed that four-fifths of the annual cost of eighty thousand yen for maintenance came from the Russian government subsidy. The very next year, with the Russian revolution in 1917, the grants ceased, and the chuch had to meet buffeting storms such as harassed no other part of the Christian movement in Japan.

The Roman Catholic Church was moving toward maturity. Its first Japanese prelate, Father Hisanosuke Hayasaka was made Bishop in Nagasaki. Sophia (*Jochi*) University in Tokyo was setting a high standard of academic work with a distinguished faculty. A chain of orphanages and homes, and of schools for girls and for boys as well as the parish churches and the houses of religious orders were being served by a body of devoted men and women, Western and Japanese, who for consecration, ability and effectiveness were a challenge to the best the Protestant movement could offer.

THE INTERNATIONAL INTERLUDE

The Widening Christian Activities

1919–1929

Modern Japan's progress and expansion, impressive as they were in the first six decades, were made possible because of the limited stage on which she was playing her part. On her own isolated islands and in dealing with nearby neighbors in Eastern Asia she was able to maintain the initiative at every crisis. Her confrontations with an expiring dynastic China, a helpless Korea, and an unawakened Asian Russia were all successful at little cost, and with immense gains. Even World War I appeared to be of the same stuff. Indeed, her services to the Allies seemed to have confirmed her hold on the northern Asian mainland and the South Sea Islands, and to have given her a free hand in world expansion.

But events proved differently. Japan now had to deal with those same Allies in their post-war mood and policies. Included in the counsels though she was, she found herself enmeshed in the web of mutual ties and hostilities of the

Western council table which made this new experience more awesome and baffling than that of battle in the open field. Yet she found a congenial mood in the currents of feeling that were sweeping Europe and Asia in 1919 and 1920. Compounded of the war-weariness of the European peoples, and the high-spirited optimism of the North Americans, it offered promise of a new world order soon to be born.

President Woodrow Wilson gave direction to the hopes of the minority peoples, of whom the Japanese considered themselves one. Government and people moved into the stream, full of hope and expectation. They supported every measure in behalf of the League of Nations, and were gratified when Dr. Nitobe was chosen to become a member of the secretariat in 1921. Through its delegates Japan offered numerous far-sighted measures for human welfare and justice. Yet when Japan attempted to make this body an instrument for implementing its own national interests, it made little headway.

Thus the decade to follow proved to be a disconcerting period of cross-currents and unpredictable winds through which Japan steered a zig-zag course. The events show no logical sequence, but are chiefly domestic reactions to the movements of the world power struggle. In the midst of them all the Christian movement had to find its way as best it could. Increasingly, Christians were becoming accepted members of their own world, and increasingly they were gaining recognition in the Christian world outside Japan. So they, like the Japanese nation, responded to the two poles of tension,—in their own society and in the western affiliations,—swinging first one way and then the other.

Disarmament, unrealistic as it may now appear, filled the horizon with the hope of a quick short-cut to world peace through voluntary national restraint of the power to fight. In this hope the United States called a conference which met at Washington in 1921 and 1922. The same hope for relief from the relentless military and naval pressures, the excessive taxes, and the unendurable tempo of heavy industry, gave a popular mandate for the Japanese government to join the conference. The impossible happened. By agreement, armaments were not only limited, they were actually reduced. Capital ships were scrapped to bring the naval strength of the major powers within an accepted formula. Japan paid a heavy price for her participation. Her allotted tonnage ratio of three as against five each for Great Britain and the United States, limited her range to the Pacific. They, operating from Pearl Harbor and Singapore respectively, as well as from their home waters, had the full sweep of the world.

Furthermore, in the treaties following the Washington Conference, Japan signed a relinquishment of her alliance with Great Britain, a momentous shift in world power, as it meant the inevitable partnership of the two Western naval giants in case of war. Most startling of all she consented to the withdrawal of her troops from Shantung, and signed the agreement guaranteeing the integrity of China under the terms of the Open Door. These costly measures were sincerely undertaken, and some of them were carried out. They must, therefore, be viewed as a genuine effort to apply the brakes to expanding empire and continuous wars, and to abide by the canons of good international relations in pursuing national policy. The nation was near the brink, and this was a real attempt to move back from the abyss. Indeed, it was the last serious attempt.

Two events in which Japan played a passive role quickly followed this deliberate shift of course. In September of 1923 the Great Earthquake and its conflagration levelled and burned to ashes much of Tokyo, all of Yokohama, and parts of other adjacent cities and towns. Half a million homes were destroyed, and over a hundred thousand persons were incinerated. For days, life in the capital region was at a standstill; the entire nation was almost too shocked to move. But within hours assistance was brought in by American ships, and soon a full stream of sympathy found tangible expression in supplies and money gifts from overseas. Premier Yamamoto broadcast the thanks of the nation saying "it is the first time that our people have been the recipients of such cordial compassion and sympathy from all parts of the world, and it is but natural that they have been indelibly impressed thereby."

The next year this "intensity of the feeling of thankfulness" suddenly was cooled by action of the United States Congress in the passing of an immigration law denying Orientals admission to the country. The story is a long one, but this chapter in it dated from 1900, in San Francisco. It is loaded with complicating factors; local racial fears and prejudice, ward and city politics, inept diplomatic language, misunderstood motives, intentional misinterpretations, national party politics, and Congressional hysteria. The final act by the American Congress was an indefensible affront to an unoffending neighbor-people. Against all the standards of personal relations in the East it offered a national insult based on race, a point at which Japan could not defend herself. Henceforth she could scarcely take her place in any international gathering without a sense of embarrassment.

Relations with China fluttered back and forth like the needle of a compass. Chiang Kai-shek was drawing the nation into unity under arms; an entirely new phase to the revolution. By promoting widespread emigration from China proper into Manchuria the nation was frustrating the Japanese expansionists, while Chinese diplomats were skillfully checkmating Japan in every country abroad. Japanese government policies varied. For much of the period

167

the figure of Kijuro Shidehara, the liberal Foreign Minister, moved on and off the stage. In 1922 he managed to liquidate the Siberian expedition, and made friendly overtures to China. His policies of moderation, however, had come too late.

By 1924 the entire Chinese nation was aroused. Students were marching the streets in protest, and merchants and common people used the deadly boycott with terrible effectiveness. When General Giichi Tanaka became premier he announced a "positive" policy toward China, and proceeded to make inflexible demands, which were ignored. Incensed at the way things were going and at the imminent danger of the junction of north China forces with those of Manchuria, a group of officers of the Japanese Kwantung Army in 1928 effected the murder of the Manchurian war lord Chang Tso-ling by the explosion of his train as it crossed under the tracks of the South Manchurian Railway, which was guarded by Japanese troops.

We date the close of this period in Japanese history at the year 1928–9 for two reasons. It proved to be the point of no return for Japanese expansion on the mainland, and the national challenge to China. Within Japan it marked the first of many times that the army acted in complete indifference to the civil government, the Diet, the Cabinet, and the Premier. It ignored its own General Staff and even the Emperor's will; though it always took action in his name. The public clamor for punishment of the perpetrators of the crime was so great that Premier Tanaka resigned. This in itself was a tribute to the continuing strength of public opinion, but the dark shadow of coming events had fallen on the scene.

The domestic situation throughout the early 20's registered a great upsurge of resistance to the regimentations of empire. The common people demanded their turn. Agitation for universal suffrage for both men and women resulted in 1925 in the extension of this right from the limited three million voters, to include all the thirteen million men of voting age. The women had to wait, but they had made their voices heard in this brief period of genuine party government. In 1922 both Yamagata and Okuma had died. The original Oligarchs were gone. Prince Kimmochi Saionji remained as the only surviving Elder Statesman, and he was committed to civilian government.

In the Diet, liberals made devastating speeches against militarism and undemocratic measures of policy. New left-wing political parties were formed; notably the Social Mass and the Farmer-Labor parties. In 1922 the Communist party appeared; organized under direct Soviet influence and led by Fukumoto of the most radical wing. Every group that felt it had a common cause, especially any with disabilities, was being organized. The two million so-called "Eta," or depressed class of persons in Japan who suffer in an equivocal position of veiled discrimination, combined and rallied under the name "Water Level Society." They met with government officials to demand equality of opportunity in jobs, social recognition, and marriage. The lepers, too, were calling for more government assistance.

The desire for peace took the form of emotional revulsion against the domination of the military. It was partly unreasonable, for it was along a path of wars that the nation had emerged into a life more ample and meaningful for most of the citizens than any they had known in feudal or tribal times. But it had been too long a pull without any let-up, and the people would not be denied. They wanted to go back to "normalcy." The national budget was revamped and defense expenditures cut to less than thirty percent of the total. The army was ordered to reduce its numbers by four divisions. For a time it became difficult for the military colleges to fill their quotas with first-rate students. In the Imperial Poem Convocation of 1922 the poem published over the Emperor's name was:

The bright sun rising o'er the tranquil sea
Appears to us a cheering sign of peace
Now coming to the nations of the earth."

There were other national trends, however, which were not so reassuring as these peace-loving tendencies. The movement toward individual expression went to extremes. Newspapers, given more freedom of opinion, became carping gossip-sheets, or irrational inciters to discontent. The government, always fearful of left-wing activities, took sterner measures of control than ever before. As the price of granting manhood suffrage, it enacted a rigorous Peace Preservation Law which was used to justify extreme police activities for years to come.

A rash of cheap Westernism seized the young people. The terms "modern boy" and "modern girl" became synonymous with juvenile delinquency. Crime waves swept the larger cities. At one time one half the members of the Tokyo City Council were in jail for corruption. Daikichiro Tagawa a prominent Christian layman and Diet member complained that the extension of the suffrage had merely meant adding ten million more venal and uninformed voters, and had widened the field for repressive interference by the police.

Japan was by now a modern nation, with good roads, complete educational facilities, highly developed industry and a network of cities. But like other modern nations she had her troubles. The farmers were badly exploited; laborers as yet had little consideration; women were under traditional exploitation or discrimination in most fields; the health of the public was not keeping up with the theoretical medical knowledge of the schools; family life was being shaken, with a mounting divorce rate; vice and drinking were said to claim a larger percentage of the national earnings than in any nation in the world, and the suicide rate was alarming. This was the complex Japan of the 1920's which challenged the religious forces of the nation to action.

There occurred at this time a religious awakening among the old faiths. Shinto is a many-sided religious world with enormous vitality. It has seemed primitive and unsuited to any role in the contemporary world. Yet it has been the driving force for Japanese patriotism all through the modern period. At the rudimentary level of the innumerable village shrines with their local deities and year-round festival ceremonies, it was the all-pervasive neighborhood religion of old Japan. Never to the present day has it ceased to be "the national faith of Japan," as the little shelf-shrine in almost every household attests.

In 1926 Professor Genchi Kato of the Imperial University published for the Meiji Japan Society, in English, his comprehensive *Study of Shinto*. In this he elaborated the thesis that the original primitive nature cult had developed, become purified and spiritualized, and now qualified as a world faith, unique in message and worthy to march forever with Buddhism and Christianity. Its central principle was Uprightness, as that of Buddhism was Benevolence; and that of Christianity, Universal Love. Each needed the others; all were universal. Also, he pointed out, Shinto was alone in this, that it lived in its constant re-incarnation of deity in the line of Japanese "Mikados," renewing its original strength, generation by generation, through the indestructible Japanese nation. Professors in the philosophy of religion at Tokyo Imperial University supported Kato's views.

The shrine system was officially given its keystone in the national arch by the erection of the Meiji Shrine in Tokyo. Set in vast acres of transplanted lofty pine trees, with its gravelled walks through the wooden gateways leading up

171

to the impressive central buildings, it was to become the Mecca for the spiritual aspirations and commitment of millions of Japanese in the stormy days ahead. The ancient shrine at Ise in Central Japan continued to be revered as the traditional heart of the nation, the goal of unending pilgrimages. But when, in Tokyo, the spirit of the Emperor Meiji was solemnly inducted into the holy of holies of the new shrine, with the blessing of his august ancestors, a new force was felt surging through the country reaching from the capital to the farthest outlying school-house or military installation.

The fortunes of the Imperial House during this period gave particular emphasis to Shinto. In view of the increased feebleness of the Emperor, there was a hurried recall of the Crown Prince from England where he was on a visit, and his installation as Regent. The Prince's marriage followed. In 1926 came the death of the Emperor Taisho and the funeral, replete with Shinto ceremonies. A long period of mourning ensued. The nation's observance of each of these Court events was regulated in every detail by government instructions through radio and press.

The supreme emotional stimulation of Shinto came in 1928 when the Prince Regent Hirohito was enthroned as the Emperor Showa. All the ancient pageantry of state was revived. For a year the nation prepared for these forty-nine stated ceremonies leading up to the actual assumption of the throne by the new Emperor. Every step of the four hundred mile procession from Tokyo to Kyoto, with the ruler and the high altar of the court, was on roads sanded, raked and prayed over by thousands, under Shinto direction. The final three days of ceremonies, culminating in an all-night vigil in a crude hut, silent and alone with the Imperial Ancestors, established a mystic bond of loyalty with the people of the nation which almost justified Lafcadio

172

Hearn's observation that the central spirit of Shinto makes the word "patriotism" utterly inadequate.

By this time Shinto ceremonies had been placed under the jurisdiction of the Home Ministry, and the official position taken was that they had nothing to do with religion, but belonged only to true citizenship. This, of course, did not satisfy Professor Kato and his school, but even he noted with satisfaction that by this administrative device Shinto was given "an asylum in which under the protective aegis of the secular government, it is safe from interference by its two religious rivals" (*A Study of Shinto*. p. 210) Religions were under the authority of the Ministry of Education, which in this period was adopting the official position that the shrine observances, whatever their true nature, might be construed as non-religious by those who desired to do so. This was the loop-hole for Christians in the years ahead, when, increasingly, attendance at the shrines for students of all schools became coercive.

Another form of Shinto burst into new strength at this time. Numerous voluntary sects, each deriving from the visions of a religious leader, and usually centering in the worship of some one of the ancient deities, came to life and drew crowds of adherents. Of these, Tenrikyo, or the Heavenly Wisdom sect was one of the most aggressive. It had its headquarters in Tambaichi of central Japan, where, they believed, the pillar of the universe was located. A modern university gradually developed, overseas missions were undertaken, and a magnificent temple was erected to which some four or five million of the faithful turned in thought, and multitudes came on pilgrimage. Faith-healing, voluntary service assignments for good causes, family counselling, and, most of all, the inner seizure by the spirit of Wisdom giving enlightenment, were the main characteristics of this religion which in 1958 was described as

"Japan's most vigorous voluntary faith." There came to be many more of these Shinto sects, and in 1926 the thirteen officially recognized ones were organized into their first national federation.

A Buddhist revival also was gathering strong force in this decade. Current Christian observers viewed it with varying judgments, some calling it "galvanized Buddhism," and discounting its genuineness. But the fact was that among the priests at the upper levels a new spirit was stirring. Self-examination was in the air. Buddhist studies of the Scriptures were taking on new life. Professor Masaharu Anezaki at the Imperial University was commending the theology of Buddhism to modern minds. Notices of preaching services could be seen on the gate-posts of some temples. A half-million children were enrolled in "Sunday Schools" in the temple precincts. Hymns were written in praise of Buddha and in them some Christian words and tunes were appropriated with few changes. On the radio Entai Tomomatsu was attracting national attention by bringing a re-interpreted Buddhism to grips with modern thought and the current industrial revolution.

On sacred Mt. Koya headquarters of the Shingon sects the temples welcomed believers for devotional retreats. Many pilgrims underwent deep mystical experiences, remaining at prayer all night long in a state of rapture. One abbot gave his witness: "Ah, to me Amida (Buddha) is my very life. I could not live without Amida." S.Imai, a Christian minister, formerly a Buddhist priest, said that in this revival Buddhism owed much to Christianity. Even the words: Eternal life, Character, Personality, Love, and Creative Power, were those which Christians had coined for their use, and which now were being taken over with a Buddhist interpretation. He believed Buddhism was steadily drawing nearer to Christianity which was destined to absorb it.

The most pronounced evidence of the new vitality of Buddhism was in its social outreach. Institutions for the relief of the poor, for the protection of children, for the training of defectives and delinquents, for adult education of underprivileged classes, for rural welfare, and for the improvement of living conditions were reported by the one sect of Shingon alone. High schools and colleges were increasing, though most of the students were prospective Buddhist priests. It was generally noted that the quality of the social work left much to be desired, and that many of the institutions appeared and disappeared as though without much rootage. This was an indication of the lag between the ideals of the leaders and the practice of the local believers of which the Buddhists themselves were well aware.

An interesting sign of the times was an article written in 1923 by Daisetzu Suzuki, world-known exponent of Zen Buddhism, criticising Shinto as being neither a respectable religion nor a proper source for national patriotism. Without thought content or ethical insight,—he said,—supported throughout history by clinging to Confucianism or Buddhism, or now to Christian elements, it had nothing to offer the nation. The Government was stultifying itself both by construing it as not a religion, and at the same time by promoting it as a national cult. Shinto was even debasing the other religions, by placing war memorials in the precincts of places of worship; "filling temples with war booty." For anyone to have put such ideas as these into print indicates that the 20's were indeed a liberal interlude before mounting national tensions again returned.

The Christian movement meanwhile had wide activities and many vicissitudes. In 1920 the World Sunday School Convention was held in Tokyo; an altogether bright and happy event for Christians. While the committee in conjunction with influential Japanese businessmen was obtain-

175

ing liberal contributions to its budget and thus carrying a new interest into wider circles than ever before, the churches were preparing for the meeting. With S. Kawasumi and E. C. Colemen as secretaries, the National Sunday School Association redoubled its energies in the systematic development of religious education in the local churches. Under district organizations teachers' training conferences were held, curriculum materials were painstakingly prepared, Sunday School enrollments went toward the two hundred thousand mark,—well beyond the number of church members. Music was given a special place. A union Sunday School hymnal was published.

In preparation for the conference choirs were in training in the various cities, to make up the fifteen hundred singers that were to lead in the services. A pageant "From Jerusalem to Tokyo" was written, and Professor H. Augustine Smith of Boston came in advance to bring the preparations to completion. A large area in front of the central railway station in Tokyo facing the palace entrance, was allotted for the temporary building. A heroic-sized statue of Christ holding a child, and with the legend: "The Light of the World" arrested the attention of the city.

An accident resulted in a vastly enlarged influence for this convention. On the day of the opening as the huge choir was holding its last rehearsal, fire flickered from an exposed wire and in a matter of minutes the entire building was in flames. The committee went into action, arranged for sectional meetings that night, and by the next day had obtained a cleared schedule from the Imperial Theater, where for the ensuing days the sessions were held. This effort enlisted great numbers of non-Christians in changed programs, cooperative planning, and through it all in a new sympathy and friendliness toward Christians.

This world convention was centered where no other faith

176

in Japan had ever put the emphasis—on the child. Around this small being all the addresses, all the seminar studies, all the reports, and all future planning revolved. It was completely novel and intriguing to the Japanese people. The response to the call for funds to meet the doubled costs of the meeting was so abundant that when the last delegate had returned home a sizeable sum was turned over to the National Sunday School Association for future work. This fund was the nest egg for the erection of a national Christian headquarters building in Kanda, Tokyo, the first in Japan.

The activities of the FEDERATION OF CHURCHES give a perspective on the broad concerns of the churches. The annual meeting in 1920 issued a manifesto dealing with current issues. It noted that the alleged tortures of the Koreans accused of a conspiracy in Seoul called for alert watchfulness on the part of Japanese Christians. Kameji Ishizaka was despatched to Seoul to make a study of conditions on the spot.

Anti-Japanese sentiment in China and the United States, the manifesto continued, was a grievous strain on Japanese feelings. And yet it was admitted, Japan had not dealt justly with China. The idea that Japan was a second Germany committed to militarism was considered an unfair judgment. "It is our aim to lead our people to the absolute rejection of militarism..." Joy was expressed over the League of Nations and its promise of future peace, and delegations of Christian speakers had been sent all over the country to inform the churches and commend the international point of view.

A sobering fact elsewhere reported was that in 1922 a deputation of Japanese churchmen was officially sent as fraternal delegates to the annual meeting of the China National Christian Council, and sat throughout its sessions without being introduced or received. Two China missionaries, Rowland Cross and Henry Leiper, came to Tokyo as messengers of good will, but could not commit the Chinese churches to fraternal relations.

As the Washington Conference on Disarmament approached, Kakichi Tsunajima, Congregational pastor in Tokyo, was sent to join Bishop Uzaki of the Methodist Church and Dr. Kozaki as observers, while in Japan, prayer meetings for the success of the conference were set up among the churches. Madame Yajima presented to President Harding a widely signed petition regarding world peace. Other concerns nearer to the inner life of the church also appeared. Sabbath observance was slipping, although for some reason it has never been a sharply distinguishing mark in the lives of Christians in Japan. The difficulty of maintaining good church attendance, especially of young people, was troubling the churches. It was a time when the youth of Japan were especially in evidence. The government promoted Young Men's Societies *(Seinendan)* which enrolled them by millions. In sports, amusements, and in the frequenting of the cabarets, the young people were attracting attention. But too few, it seems, were joining the church.

The recurring phenomenon of a wide constituency of persuaded or partly committed persons, but of a slowly growing, tiny minority church membership was puzzling the hearts and minds of church leaders, both Japanese and foreign missionaries. Various analyses were made, and the causes were sought; but the stubborn facts have remained until the present day. Prince Tokugawa, in speaking before the Washington Conference referred to the Christian population as being one million. If this was an accurate estimate it meant that there were two Christians outside the church for every one in it. If we add the fact that of those enrolled, perhaps two thirds had faded away from active participation in church life we can see how formidable has been the task of the small working core in the local churches.

A study made at about this time described the average Christian group and its work. Of the twelve hundred churches and eighteen hundred preaching places surveyed, the average was scarcely more than fifty in membership; though it was estimated that of these the churches averaged one hundred each. Applying the three to one rule, only a score and a half of members could be depended on for the work of the local church. A few more than that usually attended morning services, but about that number came to the evening service, usually evangelistic in nature; and for the mid-week prayer meeting, it was about the same.

Each church had a Sunday School, averaging two rooms and two teachers, and with possibly fifty children in attendance. These were all from the first eight grades, at which point they disappeared, as they left primary school. A Woman's Society was faithfully at work, much of its efforts being given to devotional meetings and church support, but with some outreach into the neighborhood. One out of three churches was operating a kindergarten, usually with good results. As a rule, these were conducted by the pastor and his wife; though many were under the supervision of women missionaries. Young Peoples Societies were to be found in most of the churches, and the young people helped the pastor with the mimeograph, taught in the Sunday School, put on festival celebration preparations, and sometimes participated in street meetings before the evening service in the church. In one out of four or five churches the pastor was assisted by a woman evangelist, trained by missionaries, and usually competent and devoted. There were a few strong churches, such as Uemura's Fujimi-cho Church in Tokyo with sixteen hundred members, and the even larger Presbyterian church in Kochi. But for the most part the local churches were small. The pattern, though varying with the changing conditions of war, of surrender and of recovery is today not greatly altered.

The open and relentless attack on vice and intemperance was an announcement to the world of the high moral standards of the church. The campaigns went on with increased energy and, as a result, one after another of the prefectures passed anti-brothel laws. There were three thousand branches of the temperance movement throughout the country. Observers noted a certain apathy among the Church members themselves and a kind of public allergy toward the traditional evangelistic approach. Seimatsu Kimura nevertheless was having great crowds in his special meetings; and Paul Kanamori, too, was packing in the multitudes with his "Three Hour Sermon." Kagawa was building up lists of the names of tens of thousands of "Friends of Jesus" who were brought to a decision of discipleship to Jesus in his lecture meetings, but were not ready to join a church.

In the schools some conspicuous spiritual movements took place. Doshisha celebrated its fiftieth anniversary in 1927 with two weeks of meetings led by M. Hori, a Congregational pastor. At the close three hundred students made decisions. Under the leadership of President Ebina they went to Dr. Niishima's grave and there took an oath of fealty to Christ, and to the Doshisha tradition. The Baika Girls School in nearby Osaka then invited Hori to come there, with the result that three hundred and fifty received baptism. Professor Antei Hiyane writing of this many years later recalled that "each girl came away from the platform with a look in her face that made your heart leap for joy; and some of them were crying for joy themselves." Yet the membership of the churches showed comparatively little result from all these movements.

In government schools Christian work was advancing. Professor Roy Smith who in 1959 was still teaching after fifty-five years of service at the University of Commerce in Kobe, was then exerting a deep Christian influence on the students. P. A. Smith of the Episcopal church was doing similar work. T. D. Walser established near the campus of Keio University in Tokyo the "House of the Open Door" where he maintained a schedule of a score of voluntary classes every week, emphasizing Christian faith and world peace. In Tokyo a Methodist Student Center was being set up under the quickening influence of Thoburn T. Brumbaugh. H. B. Benninghoff was expanding the work of the "Garden of Service" for Waseda University students, in Tokyo.

The one evangelistic movement which poured directly into the church was that led by Jyuji Nakada. A product of the Methodist Church, the Moody Bible Institute and the Pentecostal movement, and with a genius all his own, he was indefatigable in his evangelistic journeyings and meetings. He moved his hearers emotionally, called for their immediate decisions, led them to baptism speedily, trained them in a few basic doctrines, with special emphasis on Holiness and on the Second Coming of Christ, and organized them into a church, often under lay leadership. Establishing the Holiness Church with the blessing of the sponsoring Oriental Missionary Society, he became its first bishop, and soon was expanding its membership into a class with the four major Japanese denominations. It was by all measurements the most dynamic group among the churches at this time.

Nakada and Kimura in their stress upon the imminent return of Christ had an unexpected ally in Uchimura, who by this time had come to concentrate his Bible studies on the Prophets and the Book of Revelation. He had entirely given up any attempt to deal with the present world and its tensions. For several years these three leaders, reaching quite different classes of people, gave an other-worldly tone to the Christian emphasis.

181

Dr. Uemura left the scene in 1925, and the whole Christian movement felt the loss of his going. In his own person he had held in balance the various stresses of the Christian witness. Among his many disciples the varied aspects of his influence found expression during the following years. Among the most influential was Tokutaro Takakura, his successor as head of the Japan Theological Seminary, and the pastor of the Shinanomachi Church in Tokyo. For nearly ten years he maintained an exceptional ministry to intellectuals, drawing off from Fujimi-cho Church almost half its membership. His interests were primarily theological, and his orientation was toward the European dialectic school then being vigorously propounded by Karl Barth and Emil Brunner. His sermons, editorials and classroom lectures deeply implanted that theological outlook in the minds of a generation of young ministers; and today it still continues. It has been said of him: "For genuine Reformation fidelity and zeal in faith no one excelled him." Since Uemura's time the crisis theology has had little to feed on except crisis in Japan.

At the other pole of Uemura's influence was Hozo Tedzuka, a layman, a schoolteacher in the mountain district of Shinshu. He never aspired to prominence, but all his life he drew people into the Christian circle by his radiant faith. Over two hundred individuals were led by him into the Christian church, and of these thirty were principals of country public schools,—a truly astonishing record.

Thus, both within the churches and without, Christian influence was spreading. Although the picture of the local church seems not too inspiring, some vital spark was always there, quickening into warm life and awakened conscience the numerous individuals who went out into Japan's larger world to help the needy, to strive for a better social order, to cleanse the springs of public life, and to carry the banners of a regnant Christian discipleship along the frontiers of modern Japan.

In 1922, the National Christian Council was organized, following the dissolution of the Federation of Churches and the Continuation Committee. The first meeting was held in 1923. The Federation of Christian Missions soon began to devolve its functions upon the Council. This body included mission representation as well as that of the Japanese denominations, and also of the national Christian service agencies. It was the most comprehensive and responsible organ of united planning and work hitherto achieved in the Christian movement in Japan; the life-centre for organic Protestant work on the national scale.

Its first work in 1923 was that of relief for the Tokyo-Yokohama earthquake sufferers. Large sums of aid came in, surveys of losses were made, and the ideal plans for future readjustments of churches and schools were drawn. Actually little came of these plans. Those who hoped for the combining of adjacent schools, or of some of the thirty theological seminaries, were disappointed, nor did the proposal for relocating the city churches more cooperatively and more efficiently ever see accomplishment.

This experience of loss of physical plant was a preview of the war destruction of twenty years later, and it offered clear evidence of certain facts. In reconstruction, the institutions aided by overseas churches, boards and missions were planned and rebuilt almost solely in relation to the continuing loyalty of their related denomination, and not by any united effort. Moreover, in the case of churches and other local institutions on Japanese support, the roots of the enterprise that seemed to have been destroyed remained alive, so that it sprouted in the same places and according to the same pattern, and in an incredibly short time was functioning again, much as before.

183

There were various new social projects that grew out of the earthquake reconstruction. Kagawa was called up from Kobe by the Tokyo city authorities to serve as Counsellor, and he managed to get numerous undertakings under way. He himself at this time established several city settlements which became permanent institutions, supported by the royalties from his unceasing stream of books. He also started cooperatives. Other social work was being developed by several of the missions, notably that of the United Church of Canada. Under the gifted leadership of Percy Price, and later ably supported by Ernest Bott, the East Tokyo Mission, a chain of four Christian service centers, was established. Later, Miss Mildred Paine of the Methodist Church with a staff of consecrated young women, mostly graduates of the Tokyo Women's Christian College, planted a new Christian center, the Ai-Kei Gakuen, in the slums-in-the-fields of a ragpickers community in the outskirts of Tokyo. Enlisting the support of concerned Japanese businessmen she still continues to carry on a ministry of exceptional quality among these people, and has seen the establishment among them of a vigorous church.

Several of the denominations at about this period organized departments of social work. In this emphasis the churches were moving with the government which had just established a social section in its Home Ministry. It quickly became a department, and soon widened into the separate Ministry of Welfare, one of the most humane and cooperative of all the Japanese organs of state. It was a time of great social need. Before the decade was over the labor population in the large cities had leaped from one million to ten million. The long hours and bad working conditions that had once been unquestioned, now were an offence to enlightened consciences. Christian leaders were pointing out the urgent need of a whole-hearted ministry to working people

184

through industrial evangelism. The climate seemed favorable, for surveys showed that nearly one third of factory workers were friendly toward Christianity, and four percent reported themselves as Christian, though probably not church members.

Rural needs were equally great, and they rested heavily upon the Christian conscience. In the attempt to meet them the versatile Kagawa was at the center. With a new youthful personality, Motojiro Sugiyama, and backed by the social leader Bunji Suzuki, the first Farmer's Union was organized. The first cooperatives for consumers' purchasing, and for obtaining credit, were exactly suited to deal with the worst exploitation of tenant farmers. Sugiyama made studies of the abject poverty of these rural classes which showed that a land rent of over half the crop was customary, the tenant in addition having to provide the costs of tools and fertilizers—a major expenditure in Japan's cramped land situation. The average debt among farmers was equivalent to the earnings of five long years; and they were going in deeper each year. Yet these people, self-respecting, literate, hardy, and loyal were the backbone of the nation. It was Christian aid and encouragement which set many on their way to betterment of living.

Along with these economic measures Kagawa carried a ministry of Christian witness through the Rural Gospel Schools. Modelled after the Danish pattern, they were really institutes of a week or two with a score or so of selected young farmers who lived together, studied, discussed and planned a better rural life. The Christian permeation of these schools was thorough, and much direct religious teaching was given.

For the third time, in 1924, the government called a conference of representatives of the Three Religions, and Christians felt that the days of discrimination and suspicion

185

were over. Dr. Kozaki was active in the meeting, and in his reminiscences recorded his impressions. The first meeting in 1912, he noted, had grown out of a concern for deepening the spiritual foundations of national life by religious faith. In 1914 the hope was to carry a stream of religious motivation through the educational system. The purpose of the 1924 conference was "to guide the thought of the people, and arouse a right spirit." He, perhaps unwittingly, pointed up the narrowing purposes of the authorities in the utilization of religious forces, assumed by them to be conservative, in the control of any deviation movements or "dangerous thoughts." Again the observer is prompted to ask: What price recognition for a Christian institution in a modern nation-state in crisis? This question rings like a bell during every year of the next decade.

In 1926 the government made another attempt to pass a bill regulating religions. Former efforts had broken on the rock of stubborn Buddhist resistance, but the authorities decided to try again. They set up a study commission, on which Bishop Hayazaka of the Catholic Church, and Bishop Kyugoro Uzaki of the Japan Methodist Church and chairman of the National Christian Council, were the Christian representatives. This participation had the effect of making the Council a continuous debating society over the issues of church and state, of patriotism and of religious liberty in all their aspects.

In the Christian press many articles appeared rejecting the idea of government control, and pleading in support the provisions of the national Constitution for religious freedom. Unquestionably the purpose of the government was to curb the sprouting sects, mostly listed as Shinto, of which there came to be over four hundred by 1935. Their teachings were often bizarre, and in some cases their leaders were assuming to themselves as oracular prophets a role that edged too close to the place of authority of the Emperor. A blanket law would have been a great convenience to the police. But it was not passed. Soon the government fell, the next Diet had other interests, and in 1927 the matter was dropped. From one point of view the experience was an education in resistance for the church leaders; but from another angle it can be seen as a gradual conditioning toward total acceptance of government dictation in the next war period.

During the 1920's the churches moved on toward full maturity. The adverse effect of the American Asiatic Exclusion law of 1924 was to quicken the speed of growing financial independence. One denomination trebled the number of its self-supporting local churches within one year. The National Christian Council spoke for the Christian movement in a moderate statement deploring the American legislation, but noting that it was the Christian churches in the United States that had most vigorously resisted it, and then bespeaking for the foreign missionaries in Japan consideration and kind treatment. This irenic position was repudiated by a group of Japanese Christian leaders, many of them laymen, who met in the Reinanzaka Church and issued a mainfesto burning with anger, and pledging themselves to make every possible effort to undo the unchristian wrong. They appealed to all churches to decline any financial aid from the offending country.

Even without this unfortunate stimulus, however, the churches were taking up their own loads. In the Episcopal church, S. Motoda in Tokyo was its first Japanese clergyman to be chosen bishop, followed by Y. Naide in Osaka. The Congregational Churches had taken over all the church work of the mission, supervising it by a committee of fifteen of whom three were missionaries. The Presbyterian-Reformed church was taking similar action with some of the affiliated missions. The Home Missionary Society of the Japan Methodist Church had become the clearing-house for all church work of the missions. The Disciples Mission was in the process of shifting all such administration to the Japanese church. In contrast to some of the speeches made at the conference of 1900 by missionaries who insisted that mission and church must be separate, each free and "without any semblance of control, open or veiled", the mood of the missions at this time was well expressed by Dr. Mackenzie: "The ark of the Lord is safe in the care of the Japanese Church".

By the formation of the NCC in 1922, Japanese Protestant Christianity for the first time had achieved a firm, nationwide integration. The annual meeting, too, was used, every second or third year, as the occasion for an enlarged national conference of ministers and laymen and women, at which the current issues facing the church were discussed. Many of these issues were related to the world church, and were channelled to Japan through the new International Missionary Council, of which the NCC was a constituent member. Frequent visits of Dr. Mott, the chairman, as well as Japanese memberships on the inner committees of the I.M.C. made the Christian movement fully aware of its new place in the Christian world.

With the approach of the second world missionary conference, held in Jerusalem in 1928, the staff of the NCC was enlarged, and exhaustive preparatory studies were undertaken. The delegation of five Japanese and three missionaries was chosen almost a year in advance, so that ample time could be given to their assigned preparatory studies and findings. Many meetings were held. Thirteen hundred questionnaires were sent out, and the results were made the basis of the Japan report carried to the Conference. Daily meetings on the ship enroute were enlarged to include the delegations from the other Asian countries as they came aboard. Thus the spiritual and mental preparation for the three weeks spent in tents on the Mount of Olives, and the conference sessions in association with their fellow-Christians of the entire world, provided the Japan representatives with a newly inspired vision of the task of the churches.

On their return the delegates visited the larger cities, holding echo meetings, and preparing the local churches for the national report conference in Tokyo in the autumn of 1928. At this conference the major issues were again clarified, and recommendations were agreed upon, for the guidance of Christians. They do reflect the optimistic mood of the middle 1920s. The message is simply stated, and in terms of a liberal theological outlook: the Fatherhood of God, the human personality of Jesus Christ, the Savior, and the reality in society of the Kingdom of God. As to the attitude toward other faiths, a position of great cordiality and appreciation is taken. A patriotic note is struck in the exhortation that Christians should conjoin the spirit of the *samurai* with that of Christianity in a new Japanese contribution to church life.

Large parts of the report are of contemporary outlook. The section on the Younger and Older Churches outlines mission-church relationships in terms which still are in advance of most of the missionary work in the world. They call for missionaries, not more in number, but of advanced quality, training and equipment, to serve within and under Japanese institutional and church administration, and to be recruited and placed in consultation with the indigenous Church. The sections on Christian education, on race relations, on the industrial and social tasks of Christians and on Christian cooperative undertakings might have been written in 1959.

ASIAN EXPANSION IN EMPIRE

Christianity Under Social Compulsion

1929–1937

The lull of the 1920's was not simply a democratic interlude forced by all the common people upon their military
masters. It was rather the temporary control of policy by
one of the two contending forces in the society of modern
Japan. Broadly speaking it represented the city people and
the business interests, linked to the political parties. In
many ways they were conservatives. They wanted an orderly world, and they heartily believed in a greater Japan.
They had no quarrel with the expansionists, but only with
their too radical speed. They believed in gains achieved by
adjustment to the world situation in politics and in trade.
Prosperity at home and abroad was the common goal of
the big business combines and of the industrial workers.

The huge mercantile and manufacturing aggregations of
power, the Mitsui, Iwasaki, Sumitomo, Yasuda, Asano, and
a half dozen other family groupings, controlled the economic
life of the nation. They were internationalists, friendly to
the West, and particularly, to many Christian enterprises.
The "stewards" who actually were the operating leaders
in all of these concerns were in many cases Christians, or
at least supporters of the churches. U. Yoneyama, of the
Mitsui firm was for years chairman of the Board of Trustees
of Aoyama Gakuin, and his associate M. Fukui was closely
related to the Christian world.

Japan's recent wars had also created another younger
group of financiers and industrialists, called the "newly
rich." One of them, Katsuta, gave to Aoyama Gakuin a build-

ing costing a half-million yen. Other similar large gifts to schools were common at this time. As an instance of the freedom Christians were coming to feel in relation both to government and to the big families of business, we may note from Dr. Kozaki's *Recollections* that the expenses of the Japanese delegation to Jerusalem were borne, one half by a government grant, "after long and difficult negotiations," and the other half by gifts from the five families named above. Christianity in the 1920's was feeling quite at home in the relaxed, civilian, international world of Japan.

But there was another more powerful grouping, which soon took the helm. The navy was incensed at the disarmament policies. Likewise, the reduction of the army embittered the military authorities. Instead of retiring the reduced personnel they managed to place most of the officers as disciplinary instructors and drill-masters in the high schools and colleges. This was done first in boys schools, but later in girls schools as well. It gave the army unparalleled opportunities for indoctrination. Sixty thousand teachers of elementary schools were a supporting force for the promotion of orthodox nationalism in terms of the ancient traditions of feudal loyalties and military prowess. The teachers became cadres of convinced patriotism and expansion.

The farmer youth were taken into the army by conscription in far greater numbers than were their less vigorous city cousins. In the new army the officers themselves were mostly country-bred men. The *samurai* were a thing of the past. From top to bottom the military force was a people's body. Inasmuch as it had been the farmers who were consistently neglected, exploited and disfavored by legislation in the new Japan, they were by this time a center of discontent. It did not take much urging to convince them of the venality of the city people, the politicians, the diplomats, and even of the Cabinet and government. Direct action had been a traditional instrument resorted to by the oppressed throughout Japan's history. Matters were now ripe for change, and for violent change.

Ironically, it was the thoroughness of Premier Hamaguchi's retrenchment policies that precipitated the reversal of trends. He was called "The Lion", for his integrity and strength. He encouraged financial counter-measures to the current inflation at home. And in China he undertook conciliatory policies. Both failed. It was a time of accumulating world depression with the United States in financial panic, and then turning to tariff restrictions to crush Japanese competition. Soon business in Japan was slowing down, and unemployment had reached record heights. In China no progress was being made.

Finally, by an act of courage uprecedented in parliamentary history in modern Japan, the premier forced through a ratification of the decisions of the London Conference on naval reduction. Against all opposition he obtained the Emperor's authority and had the treaty signed. The Kellog Pact providing for outlawry of war also was given sanction. This was too much. Premier Hamaguchi was shot by an assassin, and a new period of reaction was ushered in.

Thereafter no government stood for long, nor was any Cabinet sure of itself. The initiative inexorably moved to the military groups, and their actions were generally supported by the will of millions of the plain people of the country. What the army did, no matter how lawless, was always in the name of patriotism, always in fealty to the divine Emperor, and in furtherance of Japan's god-given destiny. So the nation went through crisis after crisis. It must suffice merely to mention them, since they intensified the trends we have sketched, but did not seriously change their direction.

On September 18, 1931 the Japanese army in Manchuria precipitated a crisis. Within ten days by carefully planned deploying of teams of young men trained for the purpose, a tight administrative control of all of the Manchurian provinces was laid down. The soldiers were disposed along the railways and in all strategic centers. This successful venture was offered to the people and government at home as an accomplished fact, and in 1932 the State of Manchukuo was recognized. Except for some political interpellations in the Diet, there are no records of any serious criticism of this policy. Common opinion favored Japan's implementing the actual authority she had exercised over the region since the Sino-Japanese war of 1894. It attributed the welfare of the thirty million Chinese who had trekked there during that time, to Japan's enlightened policies of development. The common view was that Japan had not seized Manchuria from anyone, for she, herself, had created the State and its economy.

Business in Japan immediately picked up, there were jobs for all, wages soared in new inflation. Self support in the churches came on rapidly, though growth in numbers was slowing down. Overseas, the members of the League of Nations in alarm at the tipping of the uneasy world balance sent out the Lytton Commission, which returned a report of censure for Japan. Thereupon Japan withdrew from membership in the League. At home the blood baths continued. First, the great financier Junnosuke Inoue, then his second in national service Takuma Dan were shot by youths under a patriotic vow. Then the aged Seiyukwai head and premier, Tsuyoshi Inukai followed, in the "5–15 incident" of May 15, 1932. Party Cabinets came to an end.

The lines were being drawn. Mussolini and Hitler by

1933 were taking action independent of the League. Russia and China had made an agreement, soon to be followed by one between Russia and the United States. The American fleet was now based in the Pacific. In Japan, compromise Cabinets with some of the moderates in front were following one another, but throughout these years it was General Sadao Araki who, first as War Minister and then as Minister of Education, assumed the place of instructor and spiritual mentor of the nation. An impassioned orator and a brilliant writer of pamphlets he flooded the country with his interpretation of the heavenly empire, under a heavenly lord, toward a heavenly future. With such tinder a smoldering fire might burst into flame at any time.

By 1935 resistance to the national course had been silenced. Even the extreme left-wing agitators, and many of the members of the Communist party then in prison, were experiencing a change of heart and returning penitently to the patriotic fold. A group of moderate thinkers, professors in the Tokyo Imperial University, closely related to the Unitarians and Uchimura's "Churchless Christians" were driven from their posts. Professor T. Minobe, the legal authority who had trained most of Japan's public servants for twenty-five years was set upon, wounded, and thrown into dishonorable retirement. His crime was that he taught that the Emperor was ruler instrumentally for the people. The new orthodoxy required that it be from the Emperor that all rights proceeded to the people.

The pressure was put on several of the voluntary religious groups. With the various legal charges of tax evasion, of infringement of health laws by faith healing, and of immorality the three powerful new Shinto sects—O-Moto-kyo, Hito-no Michi and Seicho-no-Ie—were dissolved, and their leaders imprisoned. All three sects reappeared with new names but in lusty vigor, after the Second World War.

194

Christians did not escape the pressures. The national government was friendly, and continued the custom of calling conferences of the three religions. The one held in connection with the enthronement ceremonies in 1928 had made a record for size with twelve hundred in attendance, including nearly two hundred Christians. Even Professor Genchi Kato announced that although Buddhism and Sect Shinto were incompatible with Japan's inner genius, Christianity had a dynamic force which might well join with pure Shinto in the spiritual guidance of the nation.

On local levels, however, things were not so smooth. At Mino in Central Japan some missionaries of an independent group instructed the children of their Sunday Schools to refuse to attend the local shrine celebration when the schools went to participate. This created a wide disturbance at a time when anti-American feeling was high. The Catholic University in Tokyo suspended consent to the participation of its students, and was soundly criticised throughout the country. Subsequently the necessary Vatican authority was given, and thereafter matters moved for the Catholics more smoothly than for some of the Protestant bodies.

Kyoto always had been a center for national loyalties, and Doshisha campus often had its struggles. In connection with a competition in fencing under the rules of which some Shinto rites were customarily held, a "godshelf" or Shinto interior shrine was placed in the gymnasium where school assemblies were also held. It was removed—presumably by Christian students. Then the trouble began. Neighborhood associations, non-Christian graduates and the public at large joined in the hue and cry. Finally some adjustment was made, but the affair was so intolerable for the President Dr. Hachiro Yuasa that he later resigned his office.

There were a few compromise aberrations within the Christian circles. One young leader commended as the common faith for all Japanese a kind of "Theocratic Mikado-ism", since this would approach the Old Testament idea of God.

One notable example of inspired Christian nationalism was that of Bishop Nakada, of the rapidly-growing Christian people's movement, the Holiness Church. He extended his earlier "four principles" into five. Those who attended his funeral in 1936 were handed a printed sheet for reference when, during the service, the creed was chanted by the great congregation. Roughly rendered, it was: I believe in God, Maker of Heaven and Earth; in Jesus Christ the atoning Savior and Judge, soon to return; in the Japanese, as God's Chosen People; and in Jyuji Nakada, God's Prophet of the coming Messianic Kindgom.

In general, the position of the Christians was that they were, at one and the same time, loyal Japanese subjects and Christians standing in the classic tradition of faith. It was an extremely difficult position to maintain, as Christian citizens the world over are discovering today; but it testifies to the maturity of experience of the Japanese Christians that so early in their history they were able to find this balance, precarious though it was.

The violent forces in Japan's struggle broke out again when in 1935, the army authorities took disciplinary action removing General Masaki from his post where he was secretly encouraging the younger officers to active conspiracy. In retaliation a young officer Aizawa brutally murdered General Nagata; then at his public trial he used the occasion as a sounding-board for his patriotic exhortations to the public. At this time, moreover, many Fascist organizations were springing up, under the tacit protection of the police. The Black Dragon Society was especially active. On the streets one often saw the sinister figure of Mitsuru Toyama the arch-fomenter of violence, in his Japanese attire and surrounded by a clump of rowdies for protection. He seemed to have a charmed life, for he typified the "Japanese Spirit" which was sweeping the country like a typhoon.

The elections of 1936 returned over twenty proletarians to the Diet. In fact, though no one effectively resisted the national military trends, yet every general election still registered a considerable mandate for civil government. This further inflamed the young army agitators. A group of junior officers of the First Imperial Guards Regiment in Tokyo led platoons of soldiers to the home of Premier Saito, Finance Minister Takahashi and General Watanabe, all moderates, and cut them down. Marquis Saionji, the last of the Elder Statesmen barely escaped death. The murderers set up headquarters in the Sanin Hotel, near the Diet buildings, and awaited the military revolution they hoped their superior officers would carry out. But no such thing happened. By radio and in pamphlets dropped from the air the mutineers were commanded by the Emperor to disband and return to their barracks. After three days they obeyed. They, too, at their prolonged trial posed as the spiritual saviors of their country. The public largely took them at their own valuation. The judges knew that assassination might be their fate if they put an end to the daily eloquence and diatribes against law and government. These young men became martyr-heroes, though some of them were finally punished.

The life and work of the churches during this period stemmed from the studies and actions of the National Christian Conference of 1928, and from the 1929 Conferences with Dr. Mott in Kamakura and Nara. Some of these activities were derived from the wider world Christian fellowship, and some were reactions to the Japan situation. The first was the launching of another evangelistic campaign. It was a sound impulse for the church recurringly to stir up its mind and heart by a fresh witness to the public. This campaign, however, differed from the previous ones. Although nearly two hundred speakers shared in the platform presentations, the movement centered in one evangelist, Kagawa. For some time he had been busy with his Million Souls Movement; born in his mind during prayer on Easter Day of 1928. He would often say that so long as Christians were fewer than one million in number they would be unable to move a nation the size of Japan, and that they must quickly reach that minimum in strength if they were to survive. The Conference in proposing a forward movement requested him to merge his campaign with that of all the churches, and to continue as the central speaker.

The other distinctive feature of the campaign was that its emphasis was centered not solely upon individual conversion, but was also upon the social outreach of the Gospel. It was named the Kingdom of God Movement in the hope that the motto: "Thy Kingdom Come: in My Heart, in the World" would lead to renewed social action by the churches. For the first year there were no unusual results, though the churches which actively participated numbered over one half of all in the nation. In the second year the movement gained momentum with two-thirds of all churches in action, and after the third year it was decided to extend the movement for a further period.

From this time one began to hear about "occupational evangelism", directed at the five million factory workers, the half million fishing folk, the half million miners, and the million transport workers. Nurses, teachers, carpenters and clerks were also targets of Kagawa's concern. All these belonged to the "unoccupied-fields" reported at the Jerusalem Meeting. The thirty million farming people stood at the head of the list. In their thirteen thousand villages there were said to be but thirteen small chapels and only a sprinkling of churches-in-the-household. Training conferences were held for a corps of five thousand volunteer lay workers. A new organ, the *Kingdom of God Weekly* was published in large numbers, and an inexpensive edition of the New Testament was supplied by the Bible Societies.

How can such a movement be appraised? It was definitely aimed at classes of people whom the church had never succeeded in reaching, if indeed it had ever seriously tried. The chief new resource was the vision of one man. It was reported that some two thousand decisions a month were being made in the meetings. The number of baptisms during the first three years of the movement did rise noticeably. But the same old problem remained unsolved; no exceptional increase in church membership. After two years more, in 1934 the movement quietly ended, without any public report. The times certainly were unpropitious for a purely Christian witness, and especially for one of a mildly left-of-center outlook upon social and industrial problems. It may be that there was official pressure, for increasingly the emphasis came to be placed upon meetings in public schools with the blessing of the Ministry of Education, and as a part of the government-inspired Spiritual Awakening Movement.

In spite of its difficulties the Kingdom of God Movement wrote something significant on the page of Japanese Christian history. It held before the eyes of the entire church for five years the goal of witnessing among the unreached classes. Numbers of impressionable young people, both ministers and laymen were inspired by it to a sense of vocation on the frontiers of society, and a good many of them are to this day carrying on such a ministry. Although the main body of the churches did not alter their middle-class orientation yet the vision of a Christian movement equally at home in all social classes shone brightly, and it will yet, one dares to believe, come to realization.

Under the leadership of Mrs. O. Kubushiro of the WCTU, the Conference of 1928 issued a Social Creed, which became the moving goal of social effort for the churches. It opened boldly: "We maintain that making the life of Christ a living force within organized society is the only salvation for the present distress;" and went on through fourteen items dealing with problems relating to women, children, public and private morals, labor, taxation, cooperatives, and Sabbath observance. The fourteenth statement was a pledge to support the limitation of armaments, to strengthen the World Court of Justice, and to work for the realization of a warless world. As the national situation tightened it was felt that a modification of the creed was in order, and in 1936 it was revised. But even in that explosive year the churches speaking publicly still declared for implementing the Paris Pact, and for the promotion of world peace.

Christian social work was greatly stimulated by the example of the British COPEC movement of Christian social action, and by the visit to Japan in 1930 of Kirby Page and Sherwood Eddy. Two national Conferences were held with them; the first ones ever called to deal exclusively with the social application of Christianity. Peace and international affairs were the specialty of the two men, but the conferences kept closely to Japan's urgent industrial plight and the Christian's responsibility. The National Christian Council sponsored conferences with the employers and managers of factories, regardless of their faith; in order, it was said "to fill their hearts with real parental love for their employees." This has a quaint sound of ancient paternalism, but it must be remembered that more than one half such employees were girls in their teens and were unorganized, so that the attitude of the management had a great deal to do with their welfare.

In a similar conference with Christian managers looking toward opening systematic religious work in the factories a much more fundamental depth of understanding was reached in a pledge to "pray and strive for the Christianizing of industry through the spirit of Christ as expressed in the Christian Social Creed." That creed was ahead of even today's level of laws. The Christian employers had really tried to make a beginning.

A number of Christian industrialists were putting forth sincere efforts to carry their faith into action in business and industry. S. Homma head of a well-known construction firm employed only ex-prisoners, for moral rehabilitation. The Ishikawa family of a generation before had founded a silk manufacturing company which the father divided into eight plants, one for each of his sons. Clustered in the town of Toyooka near Tokyo they operated on a Christian basis, with hundreds of the employees belonging to the church and with regular services held on company time in the factories. More instances than can be mentioned come to mind, of owners who at the time welcomed factory evangelism. It was then, of course, recognized that such amelioration of harsh conditions by voluntary act of the owners did not get at the root of matters. Kagawa was continually encouraging labor organization, and was vigorously promoting cooperatives for working people. His cooperative pawnshops in Tokyo and Osaka were famous. He also developed a large cooperative enterprise for preparing and distributing cooked meals costing only a few cents, for working parents.

The radical labor movement became less violent as the national crisis deepened, but in 1930 when the Kingdom of God Movement undertook social activities it was not too safe to move closely into the circles of working people.

At that time, the Communists, raided again and again, had gone underground. They infiltrated schools, labor unions, factories, and even the national arsenal. Without any means of livelihood, much less of promoting their propaganda, they were reduced to actual crime for subsistence. Calling themselves Tigers they went about in threes, one with a gun, one with a dagger and one with a pamphlet. Many police were killed, banks were robbed, fellow workmen were held up, and labor in general was in terror. It was the first time Christians had been closely introduced to this rough world.

Almost equally venturesome was Christian work among the Koreans in Japan. They had left Korea because of lack of opportunity under the Japanese administration there. Once in Japan they found conditions still worse, as they joined the camps of unskilled laborers on the outskirts of cities, mines and public works sites. Underpaid even by the standards of that time, discriminated against, and practically outcastes they were a pitiable group. Among them were many criminals and large numbers of anarchists and communists. The Korean Christian Council sent a pastor into the Osaka region, and soon some thirty churches were started among them. For years the Japan missionaries by individual contributions helped carry on this work, which was under the direction of H. H. Young, a missionary of the Presbyterian Church of Canada. Later, the Korean Church of Christ in Japan was organized, and joined the National Christian Council in Japan.

The upsurge of social consciousness among the churches led them more generally to turn to the rural regions. This, too, had been an emphasis of the Jerusalem Meeting; and under the auspices of the IMC Dr. Kenyon Butterfield was sent to Asia to help promote the work. It was a time of many conferences in Japan, and among them two of the most productive were those held around this experienced visitor. He first moved quietly about Japan, visiting the several local enterprises undertaken by the few awakened Japanese and missionary rural workers; then he met ministers and laymen in conference. Their surprised judgment was that he already knew more about Japan's agrarian world than they did. The discussions and findings were down to earth, and were taken seriously by the church.

Over a hundred Rural Gospel Schools a year were being held. Several Japanese had studied in Denmark and were introducing measures for rural betterment. A Rural Department with a full-time secretary, K. Kurihara, was set up in the National Christian Council. A manifesto was issued, largely under the inspiration of Kagawa, and its burden was: "Love God; Love Neighbor; Love the Soil; Overcome Death." The omission of any "Love the Nation" is significant.

The Butterfield formula of "comprehensive evangelism" called for the planting of rural Christian parishes, with a central church and diversified ministry to the adjacent villages. This, while it caught the imagination of missionaries and pastors, never did come to fruition in Japan. But the training of a rural ministry did take hold. The Kobe Theological Seminary developed such work, and later a separate training center for rural workers was established in the Musashino plain, near Tokyo.

Christian Medical service, both in city and country, received fresh attention from the churches. The buildings of St. Luke's Medical Center in Tokyo were completed by the prodigious efforts of Dr. Rudolf Teusler of the Episcopal Church. Its designation by the Kyobashi Ward as the official guardian of the plysical well-being of the entire population opened a new world of opportunity for the Christian ministry of health. In the neglected rural areas, where there were fewer physicians, and where the people were too poor to call them, the extension of medical cooperatives, and of charity clinics by Christian doctors, were an attempt to help meet an urgent need.

The early 1930s were a time of financial recession, in the Western countries. A mood of pessimism and anxiety was replacing the exhuberance of the 1920s. With reduced income the churches began to review their commitments to the overseas missions. A Laymen's Inquiry was set up, and an exhaustive factual study of Protestant work in Eastern Asia was launched. In 1932 a group of American laymen and clergymen visited Japan, and, with the data of the professional "fact-finders" who had preceded them, added their own report. It was published as *Re-Thinking Missions*. The facts adduced and the insights brought to bear on Japanese Christian work by this somewhat neutral group may prove a valuable permanent deposit for future reference. Since the initiative was from the West, however, and since the conclusions were somewhat negatively critical, the Japanese Christian movement was not very deeply inspired by it to self-examination, nor to more effective service.

Another study was that of Christian educational work, which took place in 1932. By recommendation of the IMC, a commission of four persons from the United States met for several weeks of concentrated joint study with a representative group of Japanese educators. The Japanese section had prepared detailed studies of all the Christian institutions, and by considerable mutual conference had arrived at a consensus of judgment as to desirable future policies. Their great concerns were the development of a union Christian university, and more adequate support of the present schools. On the initiative of the Western members the final conference report was a series of recommendations for academic improvement, the uniting of present institutions, and a voluntary renunciation of university status by the several Christian colleges in the interests of a central university. No suggestions were made for financial strengthening of present schools. This conference, too, left things about where they were. Twenty years had to pass before the vision of the new university was to be realized.

The schools were having their troubles in the developing national situation. The old rule prohibiting direct religious teaching still held, although the National Educational Association again made an appeal to the Ministry of Education to have it repealed. In practice, however, the rule was often left unenforced. Another kind of religious influence was introduced with the increasing ceremonial use of the Imperial Rescript on Education, the obeisance before the Portraits, the teaching of the ancient classics with current interpretations, and the new military indoctrination introduced by the retired army officers. One by one the Christian schools were brought into line.

The student bodies on all campuses were reflecting the uncertain condition of society. A spirit of depression was common. The current literature fed this mood of self-pity. Although the students were overwhelmingly rightwing in sentiment, yet they were harassed by the few radicals to be found in all the schools. Strikes for every imagined or real wrong were the order of the day. For all this, in the Christian schools the religious witness was maintained. Some spectacular awakenings still were taking place, Kimura held meetings in Kwansei Gakuin, and six hundred students flocked forward when the call was given. Over two hundred received baptism. On many campuses Christian student activities were reported to have better standing among the non-Christian students than ever before. In government schools the Christian group organizations outnumbered those of the Buddhists and all other faiths combined. During the decade student registration in Christian schools doubled.

The YMCA and YWCA were going at full speed, with a wide-range program for youth. Many activities, such as those for boys and girls, the physical education department, industrial work, the camp movement, and some rural work were being developed. But among students the impact was most clearly seen. The Gotemba summer conferences registered the concern of young people for a socialized Christianity. Stirred by Professor Enkichi Kan of St. Paul's University they devoted the entire session of 1930 to the view of the Christian faith as a societal matter. If the emphasis had been practical, some program of action might have eventuated from this so-called Social Christianity Movement. But as it was presented from the theoretical angle from the start, it never got off the ground of discussion. Leftwing opinion became so vociferous in 1931 that the YMCA authorities dismissed the conference. For some five years in the early 30's this social emphasis engaged the thoughts of the student world, but in the end it left few tangible results.

Christian student hostels were increasing. Amherst in memory of Dr. Niishima set one up at Doshisha. In Kyoto, too, the Presbyterians established Fellowship Houses. Although the programs in these places included more than direct evangelism, they did actually bring into Christian membership almost ten percent of those who used their facilities.

Japan's first school for deaf-mutes was started by Mrs. A. K. Reischauer, and soon obtained the recognition of the government. Here was another instance of Christians first seeing a need and meeting it, and then passing on the vision to the constituted authorities for wider extension.

Christian women were never more active than at this time, Madame Hirooka, of the Mitsui family was infusing women's work in the churches of the Osaka area with a new energy. Mrs. Edward Gauntlett, with her colleagues of the

206

Japanese WCTU was out on the front line organizing women in their agitation for the vote. They also were pushing a national organization of women for peace, which was quite different from the furiously expanding Women's Patriotic Associations everywhere sponsored by the government. Christian women had their courage with them when in a national appeal they called on the people to oppose "big budgets for the army and navy, and the publication of books or articles which excite war sentiments."

The other organizations for the promotion of peace continued their work, but it was uphill going, as the patient and indefatigable peace-lover Gilbert Bowles sadly commented. The Institute of Pacific Relations was a new organization in which J. Merle Davis, and Arthur Jorgensen of the YMCA and internationally-minded Japanese associates were active. As a forum for friendly exchange of views with persons from all over the Pacific Basin it served its purpose of international understanding for a few precious years. The final solutions for international tensions, however, more and more were sought in the field of the power struggle.

The output of Christian literature flowed in a full stream, with about two hundred new titles a year, as well as many translated books—by far the major number were published entirely without subsidy. The Scriptures—a million copies and portions a year—were in a class by themselves. Their distribution was looked on as an evangelistic effort, and was financially assisted. But Christian periodicals, nearly two hundred of them, and numbers of Christian books stood on their own feet. Some were formidable projects, such as Uchimura's works in fifteen volumes, and Uemura's in eight volumes, Calvin's Institutes, and Luther's works. Augustine's City of God was becoming a center of deep study, and there were many books of interpretation of it. Barth, Heidigger, Troeltsche, and Kierkegaard,—some of whose works were translated into Japanese before they had been rendered into English—all had their reader followings.

Willis Lamott, looking over the scene in 1933 commented: "Japan's Christian output is unmatched by any younger church in the world.....it stands up, person for person, with any of the older church constituencies, mostly way ahead."

At this time the use of paid space in the columns of Japan's large newspapers for the promotion of Christian influence—Newspaper Evangelism—was at its height, through the Japan Christian News Agency, directed by H. Murray Walton, and S. Murao. It was carried through numerous branches in the various parts of Japan, where missionaries and some Japanese pastors followed up the results by correspondence with thousands of inquirers.

In general, the theological or religious outlook of the time agreed with the analysis made by Professor H. Kuwada. Three major trends were seen. One was that of Fundamentalism, with its apocalyptic overtones, held by the extreme evangelical wing of the churches, and by some independent missionaries. Another was the pietistic and mystical emphasis, traditionally attributed to the Methodists, but also diffused among other groups. It had a recent development, at first called Buchmanism, from the name of the founder who had twice come to Japan. Renamed the Oxford Group Movement, and later to become Moral Rearmament, it was enlisting the interest of many in the Japan Christian world. At least a hundred pastors were said to be attending the weekend house-parties, the majority of whose members were missionaries. A member of the Mitsui family came to be the center of the Tokyo group.

A third school of thought and faith was that of the Barth-Brunner re-interpretation of the Reformed theology in Neo-Orthodox terms. Always congenial to the strong intellectual

208

leaders of the Presbyterian-Reformed Church it was becoming dominant as the prevailing theology in Japan. In Kyoto the veteran philosopher Ashida was fascinated by this dialectic world-view, and attracted a strong student following. Among his disciples at Doshisha University were Tetsutaro Ariga, later of Kyoto National University, Tetsuji Otsuka, later Chancellor of Doshisha University who published numerous works, and T. Uoki historian of Christian doctrine at Doshisha. One of the main streams of the dialectic theology came from members of the faculty of the Japan Theological Seminary. President Takakura was supported by Toshitaka Kumano, rated at the time as perhaps the most influential philosophical mind among the Protestants. Professor Kuwada belonged to the same Neo-Orthodox school of thought. Professor Kan swung into the camp of Neo-Orthodoxy, but with an emphasis on Christianity and culture.

Professor Kuwada did not mention the continuing modified liberalism of many missionaries and ministers in the Congregational, Baptist, Disciple and Methodist bodies, and in some others. Their conviction was that this theological outlook was better suited to a sound, prophetic dealing with the oncoming national crises than any of the other three, and that this would best furnish the driving power for a dynamic Christian effort to redeem a society in crisis. It was the pressure of these same issues of crisis that had sent Uchimura into the Book of Revelation, driven Uemura within the walls of his church and pulpit, and repeatedly drawn Christian gatherings into "spiritual retreats" when what was called for was forthright dealing with the live problems of their day in the name of a living Christ.

In this context the figure who comes to mind is Kagawa. For the period of the 30's, he was the driving spirit in the prevailing trend toward social action, as well as toward enlarged evangelism. It is a noticeable fact that he did not receive early or ready acceptance from his own denomination. He was an ordained clergyman, for years the pastor of a church in Tokyo, yet seldom if ever was he elected to any representative church assembly. He later became an indispensable member of every important Christian gathering, but his inclusion was almost invariably by being coopted. The missionaries found light and leading in him, and were inspired to undertake new ventures of faith.

Kagawa's social program for the church, to be sure, did not bear directly on the knotty problem of religion and state. But at least it was the way of Jesus in a world mad with the claims of Moloch, Mammon and Mars, and it commended Christianity to multitudes to whom when they once saw it in action it was, as he said "common-sense!" Christ's way of suffering love, the way of the Cross, written about, preached and lived, was held by Kagawa at the center of the witness of the Christian church in Japan as it approached its greatest crisis.

A glance at the missionaries at this time shows that the old giants had all gone. The middle-period group, too, were thinning out. The collapse of the grandiose Interchurch World Movement of 1919 before it was launched had carried the thirty-seven million dollar askings for Japan into oblivion, and had brought the mission organizations sharply to earth. The big maps of planned expansion were folded up and put away. Missionaries who read the signs of the times were leading their missions into the new cooperative relationships with their affiliated churches, which were now coming to full maturity. An actual dissolution of the mission was accomplished by the Congregationalists, the Disciples, and the Baptists. In some others of the larger missions the agenda became increasingly one of implementing the plans of the Japanese associates, for the institutions and churches.

The Federation of Christian Missions in 1936 resolved itself into an informal Fellowship of Christian Missionaries and transferred its work to the National Christian Council. This was done before any official pressure was put upon any group to reduce foreign missionary influence. It was a natural, inevitable adjustment to a Japanese Christian movement that was trusted and loved. C.B. Olds had well expressed it when he wrote: "We put everything into your hands; our churches, our money, ourselves. Now use us as you will."

Not that all missionaries were mild and placid. Among the missions which were most fully committed to Japanese initiative in church life there were some "angry young men" who openly protested against the national trend toward authoritarianism and war. Calling themselves the "Christian Internationale," they issued the periodical "Our Graph" in parallel columns of Japanese, Chinese and English text. It was dangerous ground for foreigners, and some of them suffered reprisals and penalties, but it was clear that at least some of their Japanese colleagues admired them for their courageous witness. As modern Japan came to her three-quarter century mark she stood in dire peril, even though her size and wealth and power were unparalleled in her history. Her expansion in Asia had embittered her neighbors, and had frightened into determined hostility the Western powers. At home, civil government was capitulating to irresponsible military forces. The pursuit of empire was proving a gamble, with national survival in the next throw of the dice.

Christians shared in the general sense of crisis, they felt deeply at one with their own nation both in pride at its marvellous achievements, and also in solicitude for its future. They would have far preferred a peaceful way ahead if one could be found, but in any event they belonged to their people and must give their witness from within the ranks.

211

In the summer of 1937 a Japanese troop of soldiers clashed with Chinese forces on the Marco Polo bridge near Peking, and the Asian conflagration burst into flame.

CHAPTER FIVE

TOTAL WAR, DEFEAT, OCCUPATION

1937—1952

The Church Under the Cross

THE WAR IN ASIA
1937–1941

Christian Adjustments

Nations seldom intend to become involved in a war, though they may be unyielding in national policies that can have no other issue. It was so with Japan. Her unswerving objective was the consolidation of strength on the Asian mainland for the sustenance of her life. This was called her "immutable policy." She hoped to pursue it in the simple terms of the development of Manchuria, but it was not to be. The fires lighted along expanding frontiers by the Japanese military were caught by the mounting winds of Chinese nationalism and carried far and wide. Within a few weeks in 1937 they had leaped from Peking to Shanghai, and soon were sweeping up the Yangtse River basin and on down the China coast.

Everywhere there was fierce fighting. The capture of

Chiang Kai-shek by a Chinese warlord at Sian and his communist-negotiated release marked a turning-point in China policy toward Japan. If he did not actually promise the Communist forces a more determined resistance, at least his helpness in accepting their good offices was a public placarding of their strength. Their opposition to Japan was never in doubt. From the summer of 1937 on, every inch of Japanese progress had to be gained by stubborn fighting. Every mile won meant a deeper penetration into hostile territory, longer lines of communication, and an ever receding hope of a peaceful settlement of Japan's claims on the mainland. In December the capital Nanking fell, but there was no slightest weakening of resistance.

In the meantime the European powers had been quick to register their attitudes. In November Italy joined the German-Japanese pact. President Roosevelt made his "moral quarantine" address branding Japan as a moral pariah. By this time the polarization of the nations into the two orbits was quite clear.

At home the Japanese people were bewildered and shocked by the rapid movement of events. In the general election of 1937 they registered their dissatisfaction with the harsh government of General Hayashi by electing thirty-seven of the Social Mass Party to the Diet. The police arrested three hundred conspirators in another plot of assassination. Prince Konoye, a scion of the ancient Fujiwara court family, blood relative of the Emperor, and supposedly a representative of civil administration took over as premier. But the real power remained with the expansionists and the military.

Konoye at once announced a refusal to deal with Chiang Kai-shek, and ordered general mobilization. In November of 1938 the government solemnly announced to the world a "New Order in Asia," and the "Co-Prosperity Sphere" was proclaimed with Japan as the paramount power. Russia

214

reacted by massing troops along the thousand mile border of Mongolia and engaging the Japanese forces in an undeclared series of battles that resulted in 18,000 Japanese casualties in a year. Neither side dared allow the matter to come to full-dress war, but it was a serious preview.

Life in Japan came under more and more strict control. The Spiritual Mobilization Movement was set in motion immediately upon the outbreak of the trouble with China. This featured the high aims of Japan and proclaimed her complete moral justification. It encouraged thrift in spending, savings, contributions to the war effort, diligence in work, strict observance of all wartime regulations, a strong family morale, and disciplined personal conduct.

The handling of all news was brought under the Bureau of Information which was soon raised to the rank of a separate Cabinet organ. Whatever it authorized was distributed to newspapers, radio and the foreign press by the new government Domei News Agency. By the witholding or distortion of information, and by official interpretation of news releases the public was guided into a unity of outlook hitherto unknown. Month by month the emergency was made clear to all citizens, and their places of responsibility were indicated for them. This was an accelerating process which went on until the end of the war, but the trends were clearly evident from the beginning.

Work was plentiful. By a new system of national laws all industry was re-organized. Under government sponsorship "economic bodies" were set up, including the major concerns in each industry in a federation. Bonds were sold to the public, to obtain their savings. Subsidies were given to industry from public funds. The government took most of the industrial output, distributing some for rationing to the public, and using the rest for defense.

Labor unions gave way to a new "Industrial Harmonization Movement" in which the factories joined, enrolling all their employees with them. The cooperatives with their seven million members were dissolved, and the government took over. Some farm products were beginning to be brought under rationing, along with those of industry. The men at the front had to be kept warm and well-fed. At home the people were rationed a cloth mixed with staple fibre which was far from warm. The tuberculosis rate soon began to mount. Food, while not scarce in quantity, was often almost completely vegetable in content. Malnutrition was general.

Amusements were strictly censored, foreign films were banned, and Western music was under stern disapproval. Although there was no objection to the licensed prostitution quarters on the part of government, Western style dancing was held up to moral execration. Wherever Romanized writing of Japanese was officially used the generally adopted system of the American pioneer Dr. Hepburn was displaced by one devised by a Japanese scholar.

To all these moves the people responded with a firm spirit of cooperation. They were by now convinced of the necessity for unusual devotion, and they rendered it. The first year of war cost seven billion Yen (about $2 billion) and it was met by the savings deposits of the people. When week-long black-outs came, everyone was at the assigned post. At the railway stations almost every departing train carried some conscripted youth being given a rousing send-off with flag-waving and cheers. It was only as the crowd broke up and one looked into the faces of the silent relatives that the truly human expression of sadness and uncertainty could be seen. Occasionally, too, a student would call on a missionary to report his coming induction to the services, and in the privacy of personal conversation would unburden his heart. But on the surface there was no break in the solid loyalty of all.

The government was well aware of the need for a deeper moral stability than the ordinary circumstances of life required, and it turned to the religious forces of the nation. Official Shinto was the obvious channel for this reinforcement. While Hayashi was premier there was serious talk of actually dissolving all Buddhist and Christian organizations and of making the ancient rites and their modern interpretations the one religion of the land. The formula of primitive Shinto, "Ceremonies and Government; One" was revived as the practical working principle for the state. If this had ever been enforced it would have meant the registration of every individual of whatever faith as a member of some local Shinto shrine, with obligation of constant attendance at rites of worship. Fortunately Christians were spared this ordeal.

At this time, too a treatise was prepared which was intended to be the New Testament of modern Japan. *Basic Principles of the National Structure"* was issued by the Ministry of Education, put into every school, and made the standard of citizenship for all the people. Trained commentators and lecturers travelled the country, and filled columns of periodicals with its teachings of the divinity of the Emperor, the people and the land.

In 1937, the authorities called another meeting of the major religions. As a result there was formed the Great Unity League of Religions, embracing the Buddhist sects, the voluntary Shinto groups and the Christian denominations. For winning the cooperation of the ten million Moslems in Mongolia some attention to that faith was seen to be of importance. Several mosques were built in Tokyo. The term "Holy War" now came into general use among religious people.

Japanese Buddhists, following their basic principle of "accommodation," have found little difficulty in making adjustments to their surroundings. In the national emergency they promptly offered a complete official acceptance of all government directives. The "Mei-Wa-Kwai" was formed for patriotic service. By alternative readings of the ideographs it could mean either "Glorious Peace Society," or the "Society of Meiji Japan;"—a Buddhist-Shinto formula well suited to meet changing situations. Professor Takakusu, a recognized Buddhist scholar wrote: "From the very beginning Buddhism has devoted its entire self to the safeguarding of the nation." The lodestone in the heart drew even the peace-loving Buddhists into the armed camp with their kinsmen.

In the Christian circles the first year or two of the emergency showed a mixed pattern. The Roman Catholics in 1937 formed the National Committee of Catholics for Foreign Propaganda, "for enlightening Catholics of other countries in regard to the nation's true aims and motives." They sent priests to Manchuria and China "so that the authorities in the newly occupied areas might know what were the needs of the Catholic Missions in their districts." These came back reporting the deep impression which the strong missionary work on the mainland had made upon the Japanese military authorities. It was claimed that this had led to a new interest in Catholicism and had brought heightened prestige to the church. In the midst of the uncertainties of 1937 and 1938 the Roman Church was sending additional personnel, even from America, and was reporting work as making good progress. Later it was the German and Italian priests who were most in evidence. The supranational character of the church made it possible to adjust its position to go with the stream of national policy.

In contrast, the Protestants had some trouble getting into line. They had their overseas affiliations not with the Axis powers, but with the potential enemies in the West. They were thus under close scrutiny as to the propriety of their conduct; and they were natural targets for over-heated patriots. Several incidents attracted public notice. At a Christian rally in Osaka in 1938, K. Nishio, executive head of the Congregational churches, was so disturbed by the systematic heckling of a gang in the rear of the assembly that when he attempted to quote from memory a poem of the Emperor Meiji he lost the line and had to consult his notes. This was all that was needed to prove his disloyalty, and he was forced into retirement.

A foretaste of what local police authorities later did to some Christians came when in 1938 the head of the Osaka gendarmes circulated a questionnaire to all Christian pastors in the city, demanding categorical replies to questions regarding their faith. This he had no right to do, but at the time no one felt disposed to resist the pressure. Christian circles were immediately alerted to the possibility that any one might be called up for such an inquisition. In their blunt way, too, the thought-police had laid their hands on precisely the moot questions that had been raised against Christians ever since the opening of the Meiji era, so the matter could not easily be brushed off.

Plain questions were asked; What is the Christian's idea of deity (referring to the Shinto gods)? What view of the Emperor do Christians hold (Christ or Emperor)? What are the views of Christians regarding Imperial Rescripts and Pronouncements (Authority of the Bible)? What is Christianity's attitude toward worship of the Japanese national gods (Attendance at Shrines)? This public challenge drew fire from the NCC which issued a statement appealing to the national government to clarify the issue of shrine attendance. If it be religious, they said, then let attendance be voluntary; if not religious, let every element of worship, sacrifice, ritual and prayer be removed. Daikichiro Tagawa, Diet-member and one of the clearest thinkers in this field, wrote stressing the necessity of making a clear line between religious faith and a legitimate patriotism.

After many consultations the Osaka pastors made a corporate reply and thought the matter was dropped, but after a few months the gendarme authorities came back with their report. Upon investigation, it said, it had been found that after all Christians were not disloyal subjects of the Emperor. And inasmuch as they had satisfactorily established their position, it was now expected that in every home the tablets issued by the central shrine at Isé would be placed upon a suitable shelf for the appropriate Shinto rites.

The required use of the shrine tablets in the homes never ceased to threaten the Christians. It was nationally urged in 1938, and in 1940 it was actually ordered by the Home Ministry. It may be that in some households Christians did make the adjustment and introduced Shinto charms. But it is certain that the main body of Christian reaction at this point was one of resistance. This issue was considered by the leaders of the churches in the NCC as a head-on collision with unbridled statism, and they stood up to oppose it whenever it gave evidence of pressure. If, during the war, the line of persecution and martyrdom had ever been drawn, it would probably have been at this point, but the government never took the final step of enforcement. It is true that in the later days of feverish patriotism officials of the Christian churches did visit the Isé Shrine, and offered there before the altar to the Sun Goddess petitions for the well-being of the Emperor, and for success in the nation's conflict. They said that their prayers were of course addressed to the Christian God. The act, however, seemed to meet with general disapproval among the main body of Christians.

In the schools there were some cases of trouble in connection with the Imperial Portraits or the Rescript on Education. In the Tohoku Gakuin College in Sendai, nationalists made a disturbance because a figure of Christ in the large colored glass window of the Chapel stood above the officer who read the rescript. Also in St. Paul's College, Tokyo, an official of the school was said to have mispronounced one of the words in reading the Rescript during a public ceremony. For this he was made the object of a bitter attack, and finally was forced to resign. In 1939 the authorities of the Salvation Army were warned that they must cut their overseas ties and become a completely Japanese organization. Such were typical of the pressures put upon the Christians even as early as 1937 and 1938.

Officially the churches moved quite promptly with the government directions. At its July, 1937 Executive Committee meeting the NCC issued an announcement saying: "We expect to support with all our strength the statements of purpose of our government in this crisis." In September it repeated its "utmost loyalty to Imperial aims, and to accomplishing the unity and peace of the Far East, in reverential loyalty to the Imperial Will." It pledged the churches to throw themselves into the Spiritual Mobilization Movement, and also into the movement for Spiritual Awakening—the indoctrinating of students in public schools.

Most of the separate denominations in 1937 passed resolutions of patriotic support. The one adopted in 1938 by the Episcopal Church promised to "clarify the ideas of our national structure, serve the Emperor with loyalty, help the people reinterpret this as God's Holy War, save souls, and strengthen the church." Along with the official celebration of the Tripartite Pact against Communism in 1938 a great wave of pro-Hitler and pro-Mussolini sentiment was stimulated. Bands of Hitler Jugend came to Japan and fraternized with Japanese students.

The program of action expected of the churches was clearly summarized in one of the pamphlets for the times issued in 1938 by the NCC, under the title *The People's Spiritual Mobilization and Christianity*. It laid before all church leaders their basic duties: 1. To pursue with increased vigor the service to the troops and society in the emergency, and to help correct public opinion toward Japan overseas. 2. To this end to intensify unity in cooperation with other organizations. 3. To utilize all national assemblies of churches, and especially summer conferences in the re-education of ministers and laity regarding the national goals. 4. To make use of the materials sent out in the several Christian periodicals for patriotic action. 5. Through the experience of Japanese ministers working overseas in the Manchukuo and China fields, to integrate with the Christian work of British and Americans there. 6. To support and advance the Spiritual Mobilization and Awakening movements."

In a further directive the local churches and pastors were cautioned to take special care in the following details: In every sermon or address they were to make clear the true meanings of the conflict, and to instruct the people as to their duties, and particularly, to train Christians so that they should be models of conduct before the rest of society. They were to stir up the public to moral improvement. Ministers and people were to join all local, neighborhood or official organizations and to take a full part in their work. They were to offer the church buildings for every possible public need.

These injunctions closely followed the requirements of the government, and were intended by the Christian authorities to do double duty—as a spur to performance of the Government's instructions, and also as precautions against inadvertent failures that might get Christians into trouble. They cover the major activities carried on by the churches during the long war years. Such a minimum of support from religious bodies seemed quite reasonable to the officials who at this time always attended representative Christian meetings and constantly exhorted the leaders to "do what people of religious faith alone can do."

During those war years the church leaders and the co-operative organizations were intensely preoccupied with the tasks just outlined. The regular work of the churches, though it did not stop, was increasingly encroached upon by these wartime duties. It can readily be seen that if the National Council's directives as to the duties of pastors and people were to be taken literally there would be little time left for regular church work or life. Even the church buildings would be put to other uses. Sunday was appropriated for all sorts of activities, mostly centering in the public schools. Church attendance fell off sharply. Evangelistic campaigns were fruitless in attracting newcomers to the churches. The number of baptisms steadily dwindled to a low of less than seven thousand in a year. Christian work from 1937 on suffered under grievous handicaps.

While the churches generally were moving into the main stream of national effort, some individuals held out. At the Imperial University Professor Tadao Yanaihara, a true disciple of Kanzo Uchimura criticized the Manchurian policy in his *People and Peace:* "To a Christian, it is not a matter of advantage, but of conscience and of honorable international dealings." In the October, 1937 issue of the *Central Review* he wrote: "O Japanese nationalism die! and in dying you will come to a new life." This caused such a storm that his superior officer, Dr. Shigeru Nambara was compelled to let him resign from the Faculty.

A little later Nambara himself risked his own professional life by openly combating Professor Tanabe, the famous philosopher. Tanabe was espousing nationalism as the supplanter of earlier religious ideas, and arguing that a perfect

223

State was the natural expression of the Kingdom of God on earth. Dr. Nambara supported the outright Christian thesis against this. For this he too was virtually ostracised. After the war, however, both he and Yanaihara were restored by their colleagues to their professorial posts, and each in turn became chancellor of the university. Takeru Fujii, a leader of Churchless Christianity wrote that a false patriotism could be exorcised only by a true patriotism, and that this was best found among those who knew the overall authority of the God who gives all men their own homeland and folk.

In 1938 the second decennial meeting of the International Missionary Council was held in Madras, India. A delegation of twenty-two was chosen, and with some preparatory studies they went to the world conference. It was a tragic time, with Europe just about to take fire, and with Asia already raging. No Korean delegation was there, for the Japanese government would not recognize the existence of an independent Korea National Christian council, and the Korean Christians would not go under the aegis of the Japan council. The policies of Japan were under general condemnation except among the German delegates. Attempts were made to get the Chinese and Japanese delegation together, but in the one meeting that was held there was little to be said on either side. Personal friendships did continue in some instances, but officially nothing could be done by way of mutual understanding.

On returning to Japan the group brought back their reports on the work of the various sections. These deal with almost the entire range of Christian concerns, and in reporting, each delegate revealed his own attitudes and interpretation. They indicate a wide range of feeling and conviction. Dr. Chiba in commenting on the Message adopted by the conference took pains to write: "When an intense form of nationalism of a self-satisfied and self-aggressive type

224

with blind contempt for other nations is sweeping over all the world, it is very important to warn the people not to fall into a narrow-minded patriotism." Professor Takuo Matsumoto, concerning the work of missionaries, pleaded for increased forces of workers, since "We do not care who does it, our only concern is that Christ be enthroned in the hearts and minds of the people. We are utterly unable to accomplish it. Come over and help us." Miss Michi Kawai writing of the work of Christian education observed: "Materialistic education is like fire-arms in the hands of children; and the world today has too many concrete examples of that."

Others of the reports were quite conventional, and some distinctly reflected the orthodox interpretation of the national policies. These glimpses of attitudes on the part of individual Christians reveal a wide range of personal opinion concerning their country and its situation. They furnish a needed corrective to the impression of the entire Christian movement given by the official pronouncements of its officers at headquarters. Those pronouncements, almost of necessity, were the echo of the government directives. But beneath the surface the persons who made up these groups found unobtrusive ways of expressing varying Christian judgments of their own.

The Christian schools, though often interrupted in their academic work by patriotic duties and demonstrations, nevertheless went ahead with regular schedules. For the first two or three years of the war the authorities discouraged any student enlistments, and commanded young men to remain at their studies. The policy then was to postpone conscription until after a student's graduation from middle school or college. Under the strain of the crisis numerous students turned to religion. There continued to be spiritual movements among them.

During 1939 and 1940 all the trends of the preceding years were intensified as the war in China assumed an ever-enlarging scale with no indication of victory. Japan had occupied the major eastern cities and the Yangtse Valley a thousand miles inland to the gorges. But still there was no sign of yielding. The roads belonged to the invaders, but not the country-side. By day every Chinese was an innocent farming householder; by night he was a prowling, armed commando.

In 1939 the European war broke out, and at once the moderate premier General Abe announced that Japan would maintain a position of strict neutrality. But the waves of German invasion were so swift and so irresistible that soon Japan was taking sides, with a rising hope that her two partners might be ushering in the dawn of a new day in the Western world. German and Italian visitors were much in evidence.

Official Shinto was everywhere visible. The shrines were repaired and beautified. Especially was this true in Kashiwabara, the traditional site of the domain of the semi-legendary Jimmu Tenno, the reputed human founder of the Imperial Line. Daniel C. Holtom, Baptist missionary and Shinto scholar, some years previously had made a visit to the old shrine, and only with the greatest difficulty was he able to find it or surely to identify it, as it lay unmarked and untended. In 1940, the 2,600th anniversary of the official date of the empire's founding in 660 B.C., the nation was planning to celebrate with a great new outburst of Imperial glory.

By 1939 social controls had become more detailed. Heavy industry had reached a magnitude three times that of all other manufactures. Two-thirds of the workers in all industries were women, as able-bodied men were being called into service. Individual labor conscription had begun, even to the point of specific assignments in Manchuria or Korea. The cities were teeming with factory and office workers. The number of city commuters increased five times in three years. The evidences of a free, civilian society were steadily disappearing in the general regimentation. Each morning, when the six o'clock bugle sounded over the radio every household snapped into action. A low bow toward the Palace in Tokyo was followed by physical exercises, listening to government notices and instructions, and sometimes to long lectures and harangues, before the family went to work. Elaborate fire-drills, training for black-out duties, and standing in rationing lines took innumberable hours of the ordinary citizen. Yet no complaint was heard. Although there was said to be some hoarding and black market dealing, the compliance with the emergency regulations was astonishingly complete.

In January, 1940, Admiral Yonai became premier. He was known as a friend of America. The attitude of the Emperor toward the crisis is indicated by the fact that it was he who designated Yonai and ordered the intransigent General Hata to serve in his Cabinet as War Minister. Hata sullenly obeyed, but within six months had catapulted Yonai out of office. Again Prince Konoye, the pliant gentleman, was called back to the premiership. The military "Old-Guard" with Generals Koiso and Hata in the lead now took firm control, with American-trained but bitterly anti-American Matsuoka as Foreign Minister.

An all-out military pact with Germany and Italy was signed. As Britain was thrust off the continent at Dunkirk, and as Paris fell, Japan moved southward. This was done with the clear knowledge of America's opposition, for Ambassador Grew in his famous address to the American-Japanese Association in Tokyo "from the horse's mouth" had warned that the declared New Order for Asia had no existence in American eyes. Konoye announced the next step, a New Order for the World. In Nanking, Wang Ching-wei was placed at the head of a "National Government of China," and that phantom state was given recognition by Japan.

The United States had turned from words to deeds when in July 1939, it gave notice that it would not renew the Treaty of Commerce and Navigation, the basis of all its trade relationships with Japan since 1911. The expiration went into effect in January, 1940, and from then on the issues of life or death between the two nations were joined. If the policies of both proved to be "immutable," nothing but war could ensue. An embargo on oil, steel, rubber and other war materials essential to Japan at this juncture would mean strangulation. The government saw no alternative to total withdrawal from China except an irresistible advance through all restraints to the southern countries of Asia, where supplies could be had. The terrible choice had to be made.

The year 1940, then, proved to be a year of decision for Japan. The air was filled with forebodings of change. Konoye announced a "New Structure" for the nation, to meet the new crisis. Each day's newspapers were scanned for news of the next developments. Some sort of authoritarian pattern was in the making, but Konoye either could not or did not wish to take the final step toward dictatorship. What he finally produced was the Imperial Rule Assistance Association, a system clumsily named and cumbrous in action. Political parties were abolished, the Diet was set aside, and in one totalitarian organization every sector of Japan's life was to be represented. The Association had no power of government; that belonged solely to the premier, and the military chiefs, acting in the name of the Emperor. It was intended through this association to keep the people informed of public policy and enlist their support, and conversely to give them an opportunity to express their views for the benefit of the rulers.

The crisis struck the churches in August, 1940. In 1939 a national law had been passed regulating the life of all religious organizations. This was to go into effect in 1940, and in preparation for the change all the churches were busy studying the law and making plans for necessary alterations in their structures. The government had never yielded the principle of its right to control religious bodies. Over three hundred regulations already were in effect. It was something of a satisfaction to know what the national law was and to fit in with it. Once done that would guarantee legal security, some tax benefits, and, most valuable of all, immunity from unwarranted interference by local police or petty official trouble-makers. From the government side it offered dependable controls over the religious systems; one of the last fields of society to come under regimentation in the emergency.

As negotiations went on, the government set a lower limit of fifty churches and 5,000 members for any denomination to qualify for registration. This was reasonable enough, since the Shinto and Buddhist sects numbered millions in a single body, while some of the Christian denominations were microscopic in size. By the new standard of size only five or six of the larger denominations would qualify. The smaller ones had no recourse but to unite with one another or join a larger one. This necessary reorganization of church structures inevitably opened anew the old question of a general unification of all denominations in a single body.

Over the years, ever since the founding of the Yokohama Church in 1872, union had been the dream of many Protestant Christians. But every plan had failed of accomplishment. In recent years there had been a Commission on

Church Union representing most of the Protestant churches. It too had come to a standstill. One group only had kept up the agitation. A score or so of ministers and laymen calling themselves the Christian Brotherhood had set as their goal a continuous agitation until the churches should come to union. They were active also in wartime service; but from 1938 they decided to confine their work to Church unification efforts. Some of them were close to influential government leaders, and thus were kept informed as to probable future official policies.

As late as the National Christian Conference of 1939, called especially to deal with church union, the denominations had turned down any immediate action. Matters were, therefore, in the stage of partial consolidation of the smaller denominations for conformity with the new national law when the storm broke upon the churches. In July, 1940 a second plot on the part of the "Heaven-sent Troops" against the life of the Emperor, was discovered. The first, in 1933, had been averted by sheer accident. The air was full of spy scares. Suddenly on August 9th, Colonel Uemura, head of the Salvation Army, and his six next ranking associates were arrested for espionage, and taken to prison for examination. The charge was that with their direct subordination to the London General Headquarters they were, in the process of furnishing even routine reports, constantly violating the National Defense laws and releasing essential information abroad.

There followed in rapid succession a series of conferences among the church leaders. Strong efforts were made for the release of the arrested persons, and plans were formulated for the guidance of all denominations. No doubt, too, behind the scenes the Christian Brotherhood and others were working out with friendly officials a *modus operandi* which might bring the churches through the crisis in safety. On August

15th the Episcopal Church called a meeting of its General Assembly, and requested all foreign personnel to resign their offices. It was feared that this church would be next on the blacklist, on account of its large number of foreign bishops, as well as because of its integration with the Anglican Church and the Lambeth Conference.

The many informal meetings led to a common course of action which was adopted in a conference in Tokyo on August 26th, with similar action taken in a conference in Central Japan on August 30th. On September 2nd this was codified into a specific statement of policy, and on September 6th, it was adopted at a meeting of the National Christian Council. On September 2nd the Japan Christian Educational Association, speaking for the schools, came to a decision implementing similar policies. The measures generally decided on were simple, but radical in their abruptness. They corrected the two features of the Christian movement which troubled the government authorities: the intertwining of church life with the West, and the atomization of denominations into tiny units too small to handle.

The items relating to Western Christian contacts were several in number. There were the recurring gifts of money for maintenance of work. These involved, it was felt, obligations as well as continuous confidential correspondence and Western influence in policy-making. The ownership and control of the properties was also a problem. Although by this time most of the institutions had boards of trustees chartered under Japanese law this was not true of all. Even those that did usually included some foreign members who voted on matters of policy and administration. In some missions, where pioneer church work was still being done under direct control, the properties of local churches were held in the name of the mission.

231

Another issue was that of the posts occupied by missionaries. A number, especially of women missionaries, still served as heads of schools and kindergartens. In other cases missionaries as deans and department heads were included in the inner circles of school administration. And finally, the question was raised of the need for missionaries at all. In no other area of Japan's life was there any reminder of the early days of her tutelage when she looked to the West for counsellors and advisors. Nowhere but in the Christian church did there seem to be any felt need for assistance from overseas in working out Japan's domestic enterprises. The government authorities asked why the Christian church did not grow up and handle its own affairs.

This last matter of the missionaries was so personal that it was dealt with in a separate conference on September 14th at which only Japanese were present. Their conclusions were a dignified, friendly and loyal affirmation: "If any missionaries feel that they must return home they will go with our blessing and our hearty efforts to help find permanent work for them in their homelands. If any desire to stay we shall welcome their services, and we pledge them our best efforts toward protection and necessary assistance."

The action of the National Christian Council on September 6th committed the churches to: total financial self-support: complete autonomy in matters of ownership and administration, and: a union of all churches in a single ecclesiastical body. These measures were recommended to all the constituent organizations for action. During the following weeks the denominations held their assemblies, and one by one they voted acquiescence in the policy. Some took the hurdle smoothly and quickly while others struggled and wrestled with qualifying provisos as to creed and structure. In the end all differences were dissolved in the

232

national current of events. When the last church body had finished its work on October 16, 1940 there was still a margin of twenty-four hours before the public announcement had to be made.

The dramatic culmination of this series of events came as planned on Jimmu Tenno Day, October 17, 1940, in all-day ceremonies on the broad grounds of Aoyama Gaku-in, in Tokyo. Thousands of persons gathered for the morning and afternoon meetings, seated on straw matting spread upon the hard ground, for the long hours of addresses and sermons. The climax came in the reading of the manifesto pledging the churches to still greater efforts in the national emergency, and mutually agreeing to come together into a single church. In this declaration, except for the Seventh Day Adventists, every one of the more than thirty denominations joined. It was the most inclusive action ever taken by Protestants in Japan.

On the following day the Commission met and organized for the creation of this new body. With Methodist Bishop Y. Abe as chairman and with four major sub-committees; on organization, finance, creed and order, respectively, they went to work. By the Spring of 1941 they had produced the final draft of the constitution of the Church of Christ in Japan, (Nihon Kirisuto Kyodan—often briefly called "The Kyodan"). On June 24, and 25, 1941 the Founding General Assembly of the church was held, the constitution was adopted, and application was made to the government for registration. Along the way the Episcopal Church as such had withdrawn from the planning, although the Bishops and churches of two dioceses whose members comprised one third of the denomination, did join.

The thirty-four bodies that went into the union had irrevocably dissolved themselves as autonomous entities, yet they hoped for a considerable degree of separate life within the unitary wartime structure. The original plan provided for this by the "bloc system." The various denominational families grouped themselves into eleven such units. Each of these chose its representative. These eleven were to form a Board of Councillors for the church. In the absence of some such plan, it would have been extremely difficult to have obtained the consent of all the uniting denominations. Before the charter was granted in November, 1941 the various groups had wound up their affairs, and had formed sub-organizations to look after their own traditional interests within the structure of the Kyodan.

The two Episcopalian bishops who entered the united church proceeded to consecrate seven others, so as to provide general episcopal supervision. The Lutherans, Baptists and others continued with adherence to their traditional creeds, and their own forms of worship. The eleven groups put into the hands of their respective leaders the matter of pensions, placement of ministers, counselling with local churches, and virtually everything except public relationships and activities. It seemed a most workable plan for united, yet autonomous church life, and it received the approval of the authorities.

Along with this somewhat flexible feature, however, the over-all structure prescribed by the government for the Kyodan was of quite a different sort. It was monolithic and totalitarian in pattern, hung from the top where a single person, the Director, ultimately held all authority. He had to be approved by the Minister of Education, and all his actions were reviewable by the Ministry. Within that limit, he had autocratic ecclesiastical powers, extending to every minister, every lay officer, and even the members of every local church. It was taken for granted that these extreme powers would never need to be exercised. They were patterned only for a crisis situation. The lines of integration for normal church life were well balanced between the autonomy of the congregational pattern for the local church, a series of representative assemblies of the Presby-terain-Reformed tradition at the various regional levels, and the administrative authority of the Episcopal or Methodist type, at the summit.

A strong central office with staff, various commissions for work, and a government-approved recording, financial and auditing system were a part of the plan. The government set standards of accuracy in finance, of qualifications of ministerial training, and even of faithfulness in individual membership which were a challenge to some of the churches. Yet the church constitution with its nearly two hundred articles was a burdensome strait-jacket for a Protestant Christianity with a heritage of freedom. It was a typical product of government bureaucracy.

The crisis which drew the denominations together in 1940 effectively dislocated the missionaries and their work. For a time some of them reported no alteration in the attitudes of their Japanese colleagues, nor of the public. They continued with work much as before. As the autumn of 1940 wore on, however, a change of climate was clearly felt. Visits of police for inspection of missionaries' homes became more common. Administrators of schools where they taught had to answer for their movements and activities. Travel into the country from the cities had come increasingly under surveillance. The presence of a foreigner was now an embarrassment to the pastors of churches in towns or villages where he visited. Whereas in former days a missionary often heard the word *"Yaso"* (Jesus) passed from mouth to mouth of the people about him, in 1940 and 1941 on the streets and buses the word commonly heard was *spai* (spy).

In January, 1941 the Methodist Church in the United

States sent Bishop James C. Baker and Ralph E. Diffendorfer, secretary of the Board of Missions, to attend the annual mission meeting in Tokyo, and to take counsel regarding missionary policy. On the basis of their observations, they sent back from shipboard a radio message instructing the mission to evacuate and return home. It is now known that this forthright action startled not only Japanese Christians, but also wider circles of informed Japanese persons, who jumped to the conclusion that these eminent churchmen brought reliable advance information of the hostile intentions of the American Government.

The actual fact is that while in the process of weighing the probabilities of peace or war they had had an interview with Foreign Minister Matsuoka. Although he was at first fairly courteous, as the conversation went on he gradually became excited, and then rising from his chair he stood over the visitors in a threatening posture and shouted: "If America does not change her attitude and accept Japan's position in Asia, we shall draw on our weapons of last resort, the nature of which you well know, and in three months the war will be over." Sobered into silence the American visitors withdrew, but they needed no more to convince them that the scales were going to tip toward war.

In contrast, the Foreign Board of the Presbyterian Church, U.S.A. adopted a policy of encouraging individual missionaries, so far as possible, to decide to remain. Thus for several months the missionary body had the two patterns of action between which to choose. As March and April came on, however, the swift-moving tide of events swept away all freedom of choice, and by June, 1941 out of about one thousand missionaries in Japan, scarcely a hundred were left. Of those Americans who remained few intended to stay throughout a war with the West, but they still hoped that this eventuality might be avoided. Hoping even slightly to help stabilize the perilous situation, and bravely casting in their lot with their Japanese Christian colleagues, they remained.

The last communication between Japanese Protestant Christians and the Western world came in the spring of 1941. It was proposed that a Christian deputation be sent to America in a last attempt at gaining a mutual understanding between the two countries. The Christians took this opportunity with extreme seriousness, and chose some of their very most able and internationally-minded leaders: Bishop Yoshimune Abe, Soichi Saito, of the Y.M.C.A., Dr. Michio Kozaki, Congregational Pastor, Dr. Hachiro Yuasa, former President of Doshisha University, Miss Michi Kawai, Principal of Keisen Girls School and Dr. Toyohiko Kagawa. These persons were known and loved all over America, where time after time they had attracted large audiences with their addresses. Most of them had studied in America. To them no tragedy could have been graver than a war between their native and their foster-homelands. With them went Hon. Tsunejiro Matsuyama, Diet-member and Congregational layman and Dr. William Axling, noted internationalist, peace-lover and from its founding the honorary general secretary of the Japan National Christian Council.

In April, 1941 they met in what came to be called the "Riverside Fellowship" at Riverside, California, with representatives of the Federal Council of Churches of North America and of the Foreign Missions Conference. Days of conference and prayer knit them together in a deep experience of unity and common concern. They then moved to Atlantic City, where in a conference with representatives of over thirty mission boards and agencies they faced the possibilities of a separation of years duration ahead.

From this conference two important decisions emerged,

both of which were validated when the war came to an end. One arose from the awareness of the American missionary administrators that if war did come it would mean the end of an era of missionary-church relationships. They determined to face new thinking and changed procedures. A committee was set up to study every side of this matter. It was at work throughout the war years. The other decision was to receive and as soon as possible to act on the invitation of the Japanese delegation, for a return visit of representatives from the American churches to Japan. The Japanese delegation returned on one of the last ships to leave an American port for Japan.

The impasse between Japan and America remained. In April, 1941, the Secretary of State, Cordell Hull laid down the principles on which his government stood. They included the total withdrawal of Japan from China:—a complete reversal of direction in national policy. By this time Japan's Asian involvement was no longer a reckless adventure of a distant army nor the conspiracy of a hidden clique in Tokyo. It was the desperate momentum of eighty million people already four years deep in a full war with an unconquerable neighbor, and inextricably bound in with the tumultuous events on the European stage.

Admiral Kichisaburo Nomura, Ambassador in Washington was instructed to continue negotiations, though his government offered no concessions to give hope of a settlement. Mr. Hull, too, never yielded an inch. When September came the new Foreign Minister Shigenori Togo obtained one more delay, sent Saburo Kurusu, a pro-American accomplished diplomat to assist Nomura, and waited, hoping for some result. None came. In October, Konoye in despair yielded the premiership to General Hideki Tojo, architect of Japan's war plans. All hopes of a peaceful or civilian adjustment now faded.

The Japanese government sent a final note to its representatives, indicating a date in November as the dead line for continuing the negotiations, after which it warned: "things will take their course." That in itself was a declaration of war. The American State Department had broken the code and read these instructions. Mr. Hull's reply was the reiteration of the April ultimatum. When Nomura's cable was received in Tokyo the fleet, with its airplane carriers moved to the attack, and Pearl Harbor, December 7, 1941 ushered in the Pacific War.

Christians on both shores of the ocean heard the news with a sense of shock and sorrow. In Tokyo, Japanese leaders and friends of the missionaries in deep solicitude mediated with the police, as the round-ups for detention took place. In Los Angeles, San Francisco and New York missionaries spent much of the night calling, comforting, and reassuring Japanese residents who were awaiting in terror the visit of the federal agents. The tides of war swept away all communications, and the Christian communities of Japan and of the West went on their separated ways, with their people.

THE PACIFIC WAR YEARS
Christians in Suffering

1941–1945

Simultaneously with the attack on Pearl Harbor the Japanese swept along the Asian coast, and spread across the South Pacific. Within a few weeks the lines of the perimeter had been drawn. A vast rectangle, it ran from the Aleutians to the Gilbert Islands and from Sakhalin almost to Australia. Troops made landings, new military regimes were set up, and the Japanese net was thrown over Hong Kong,

Indo-China, Malaya, Singapore, Burma, Thailand, the Netherlands Indies, the Philippines, and the islands of the western Pacific. The first six months of 1942 saw one dazzling Japanese victory after another. The people believed the "New World Order" was about to take shape.

Then the swift currents of conquest slowed down. The battles of the Coral Sea and of Midway set the limits to naval expansion. On New Guinea the land thrust was stopped. The Western allies were now organized, harnessing a mighty industrial potential to the war effort, and digging in along the extended borders of Japan's power world. The Japanese people did not know of the change, though the leaders did. After long months of silence, in the spring of 1943 news of the Japanese evacuation of the Solomon Islands filtered through. At home a new organization of life quickly followed. For the civil administration of the occupied countries, the Greater East Asia Affairs Bureau had been set up. Japan itself was now divided into nine large regional districts, each with a single head who was answerable directly to the premier, or in fact, to the army. "Awake Asia" became the national slogan, in an attempt to enlist enthusiasm for the new regime on the part of the millions in Asia, who were to be "liberated" from the yoke of Western colonialism.

More months of silence followed; then in the spring of 1944 the deadening news came that Saipan in the Marianna Islands had fallen. This provided the enemy with air-bases within striking distance of Japan. No amount of manipulating or repressing of the news could keep discerning persons from reading between the lines that the war was irretrievably slipping toward defeat. The home front was re-organized again, this time by the setting up of a Munitions Ministry with sumptuary powers over goods and manpower. The arrogant Premier Tojo had to give way to a more moderate

Cabinet, with General Koiso as head, and the moderate Admiral Yonai as Vice-Premier.

It was the hope of many that some kind of peace might be negotiated, but matters had gone too far. The enemy was storming from island to island. Iwojima fell, and the way was open to Okinawa. By the spring of 1945 the German power in Europe was collapsing, and in May the European War ended. In the Pacific, Okinawa had become the base for direct air attacks on the Japan home islands. The nation was entirely cut off from all overseas contacts. Food was low, fuel was gone, industries were reduced to a creeping pace. Men called to the colors were given a sharpened bamboo stick for equipment. The country was struggling to keep on its feet.

In March, 1945, the invasion by air struck the capital. Much of downtown Tokyo was reduced to ashes by incendiary bombs dropped from the B-29's. Again the government changed. Admiral Kantaro Suzuki a balanced and honorable statesman of constructive international attitude, became Premier. In May a second wave of bombing brought ruin to residential Tokyo, and the systematic destruction of Japan's cities began. A final decision was faced. A new Supreme Imperial Conference had been established over which the Emperor presided; the six members being the Premier, the Foreign, Navy and Army ministers, and the chiefs of staff of the army and navy. For the first time in recent history the Emperor took decisive action—twice breaking a tie in favor of ending the war. To the bitter end the Army minister and the two chiefs of staff held out for death on the beaches.

Week by week—and then as June wore into July, day by day—the issues were weighed and attempts were made for a negotiated peace. It was of no avail. The Allies in a long series of conferences from that of the Atlantic Charter

241

to Yalta, had been shaping the pattern of "unconditional surrender," and they refused any discussion of peace terms. Japan ignored the Potsdam Declaration of July 26 with its demands for immediate surrender, and on August 6 the atom bomb destroyed Hiroshima. Before the dazed statesmen in Tokyo could recover their senses Russia on August 8 entered the war, and on August 9 another atom bomb was dropped on Nagasaki.

That day the emperor called the Supreme Conference, and after hours of deadlock, at 3'oclock in the morning of the 10, he made the tie-breaking decision to capitulate. As the Allies still waited for unconditional surrender, the Emperor on August 13 for the second time forced the recalcitrant military leaders to yield. He recorded his address to the nation, to be delivered the following morning, announcing the end of the war by the defeat of the Japanese Imperial Forces. The army, defiant to the last, sent a posse to block the announcement. They murdered the palace guards, for hours searched the premises of the Imperial Household, and were still unable to locate the recorded message when the voice of the Emperor on the air sounded the death-knell of their world. They committed suicide. Japan's chapter of world empire by force of arms had come to an end.

Along this kaleidoscopic journey of three or four years the Christian community had moved with the nation. Two weeks before Pearl Harbor the united Church of Christ had been granted its charter, and its tentative organization, officers and actions then became official. On December 9, 1941 Mitsuru Tomita, former Presbyterian pastor, and now Director of the Kyodan made a public address to the constituency urging them to go beyond the range of duty in "reverently promoting the Great Endeavor"..."In prayer is victory. Let us all turn to prayer." That was the official

242

pronouncement of the church. In the meantime quite another mood had been expressed by the individual Christians when, from December 1 to 8 in the Ginza Church, Tokyo, representatives of the Protestant churches of the city met around the clock in a Prayer Vigil for Peace. In turn, they came by assignment, and kneeling at the altar, they kept their hourly watch, never allowing the flame of intercession to cease till the tragic news of Pearl Harbor sent them sadly to their homes. This clear distinction between the unofficial, human reactions of ordinary Christians and the dictated formal actions of the official Christian bodies must be kept in mind. Throughout the war years both continued. One side of the Christian life was lived quietly, and for the most part without public expression, while for the other, every event of the war furnished an official sounding-board for echoing the national themes.

Most of the Protestant American missionaries were placed in internment in December, 1941. The majority were repatriated and returned by the S.S. "Gripsholm" in 1942, the remainder coming a year later in a second exchange. Less than a dozen remained throughout the war. Of these one or two women missionaries sought Japanese citizenship.

Wartime changes took place in the structure of the Kyodan. The First General Assembly was held in Tokyo in November, 1942, one year after the granting of the charter. At that time the Director announced that the bloc system was being discontinued, and he called for a vote by acclamation. Thus were dismantled all the partitions within which the different denominational families had proposed to live in privacy under the one roof. The unchanging intention of the authorities that there should be a monolithic unity in Protestantism was to be carried out. Actually, however, a great deal of informal autonomy under the eleven bloc leaders continued throughout the war.

When the government set up its army-dominated Greater East Asia Ministry, the church was geared into it. Under the vigorous leadership of General Hibiki, a retired army officer who had given the enterprise his whole strength from 1932 on, there had been developed a Japanese Christian mission for work in Manchuria. This and all other overseas activities were now merged in the wartime church organization, the Greater East Asia Bureau and everything done outside Japan came under its direction. Another new development was the changing of the Department of Education in the church to one of "Indoctrination," charged with the promotion of studies in Japanese past culture and present ideology. A third major change was the linking up of the various religions in the Great Japan Wartime Religious Patriotic Association. Within this framework the Japan Christian Patriotic Association had its own organization. These changes were all necessitated by the new wartime structure of the nation.

A gradual but decisive series of emergency changes took place in the actual administration of the church, as conditions called for more and more centralization, while travel and appointed meetings became increasingly difficult. The Second General Assembly was held in November, 1943. It was then decided that there should be no more national gatherings. Even the holding of district meetings became an extremely difficult problem. In Tokyo the Executive Committee was given authority to act on internal matters for the whole church, while the Patriotic Association under the leadership of Yoriichi Manabe, a former Methodist pastor, was made responsible for all public wartime activities. By 1945 committee meetings became impracticable, and the Director of the Kyodan alone had to make all decisions and supervise the work of the central office. It is to his credit that he carried these heavy responsibilities with integrity and fairness to all groups in the church. He also met the obligation of the church to the nation, as he conceived it, by undeviating obedience to every government directive.

The wartime work of the church followed closely the pattern of the preceding war years, the difference being chiefly one of intensity and degree of sacrifice. Through the General Affairs Board the church promoted all the objectives of Spiritual Mobilization at home. The first task was to take a share in the Patriotic Airplane Fund-raising. It did not meet its allotted goal of ten planes, but it did proudly provide for six, and for this effort it received public approval. The general aims of Spiritual Mobilization were morally commendable, and could be heartily supported by the churches.

As casualties began to multiply, hospital visitation and work for the wounded were expanded. It was routine service to make calls on the families of men at the front, and to care for their needs. The neighborhood meeting of ancient Japan, whereby five households joined for essential services, was revived in the wartime structure to become one of the most potent institutions for national patriotic unity. Church members were instructed to take an active part in these small group activities, thus establishing the loyalty of Christians while at the same time helping the war effort.

Participation in all public celebrations was systematized. For years Christians by special permission had gathered at the Double Bridge of the moat surrounding the inner palace in Tokyo, and there had celebrated a watch-night service with prayers for the Emperor and the nation. Upon every indicated occasion during the war, they were expected to join the throngs who with lighted lanterns would march to the Yasukuni Shrine in Tokyo, where 160,000 spirits of departed heroes were enshrined. After obeisance, the march would continue to the Imperial Army Headquarters, then into the wide expanse of the Meiji Shrine park to the great shrine itself, where every young Japanese did his best to go and bow in dedication before reporting for military service. Another period of reverent silence, and the line would go on to the palace precincts for prostration on the gravelled ground, after which at a given signal the final "Banzai," would be shouted. Following that, would come the weary trudge for miles to the home in the suburbs.

Under the Greater East Asia Bureau, the church extended its influence onto the Asian mainland in a systematic visitation. The task was no longer simply one of evangelism among Japanese residents, but rather the "harmonization" or pacification of the native people. It was carried out largely through contacts with the Christians of each country, and under Japanese military authority. The chairman was Michio Kozaki, the popular successor to his father as pastor of Reinanzaka, Tokyo's strongest former Congregational Church.

As the work became more demanding Akira Ebisawa, long-time secretary of the National Christian Council, transferred his full efforts to it as secretary. He and the chairman made visits to the various parts of Asia, usually accompanied by T. Matsuyama, member of the Diet and of the Riverside Fellowship and an ardently active supporter of Japanese expansion. In Korea the integrating of the denominations with the United Church was officially completed. North China set up a church federation of its own pattern which was accepted by the Japanese authorities in lieu of one more like the church in Japan. In Central China, former Bishop Yoshimune Abe took up residence as liaison between the military authorities and the Chinese churches. He lived in Shanghai till after the war.

In the farther regions of the invasion, groups of young

ministers were sent, in uniform and under conscription, usually by the navy. Roman Catholic groups went to the Philippines, as well as two teams from the Protestant churches. Most of them were students in theological seminaries. Their work was to maintain touch with the Christian movement and with the Japanese occupation authorities. It can be easily seen that this middleman position might vary according to the spirit of the individual, as well as of his commanding officer. Some of these young men came to be respected and their work appreciated by the people of the occupied countries. They softened harsh blows, modified stiff regulations, prepared the people for sudden shocks and sometimes became spokesmen at headquarters in presenting the case of the native Christians. Others, as was bound to be the case, conducted themselves quite differently, and left behind them an unenviable record of over-zealous enforcement of the military regime.

A member of the Christian Brotherhood, impassioned patriot and strong leader, Hachiro Shirato, pastor of a church in Tokyo was put in charge of the team who were sent to Indonesia. He travelled widely, stationing the Japanese contact men in various centers, and holding religious meetings in the churches. His report in 1944 was most enthusiastic, indicating a warm welcome everywhere. A very different impression is gained from another report by a Roman Catholic emissary who said that everywhere there was hostility, and that only the authority of the church and his vestments protected him from the rage of the crowds. Whatever the facts of its reception, something of the range of outreach of the united church can be seen from this overseas program.

The worship and inner life of the Protestant Christians underwent many changes. Sunday worship was a casualty of the war. The weekly Sabbath day had no meaning in

Japanese tradition, and it had small chance in a wartime society. Pastors had to exercise great perseverance and ingenuity to manage a fixed period of public worship week by week, though many did contrive to do so. The introduction of the "people's ceremony"—a moment of silence with bowed head in memory of the war dead—became more and more an instrument of nation-worship as the authorities added to its specifications. It came to be quite a service of its own, with a turning toward the palace in Tokyo, the singing of the national anthem, and the reading of some rescript issued in the name of the emperor.

The atmosphere of awe instilled in students by the ritual use of the Education Rescript carried over into this "people's ceremony" in the churches. It was no longer possible to deal casually with it. At one time the United Church authorities sent out suggestions for a change in the position of pulpit furniture. The inference is that the government wanted some particularly sacred spot set aside for this supreme act of worshipping citizenship. Inasmuch as many of the little churches could not boast of an entire pulpit space of more than a few feet, a divided chancel would have been impossible. Apparently nothing came of the idea.

Special prayers for victory were called for, and the church responded by holding meetings in which prepared prayers were presented, and selected for distribution to the church at large. Some of these prayers are extremely ardent in patriotism, and represent a total acceptance of the holy war for the liberation of Asia. The hymnals underwent changes. First there was the excision of some of the hymns with the most forthright references to God as Creator, Judge and Arbiter of human destiny. References to peace were taboo, as were some of the themes of the Christian witness stressing its universality. In a shortened edition of a hundred selected hymns the churches were given a restricted area in which to praise God in song. Some new special hymnals were issued, such as the Children's Songbook, the "Awake Asia Hymnal", and a Youth Edition of the same title. These new books were reportedly scarcely used at all, since the Christians loved their own old hymns. As their books wore out they still could manage a fairly wide range of congregational singing from memory.

The sermons were expected to be directed toward helping on the war effort, and the headquarters of the church passed along the suggestions. When the nation was in an extremity of danger throughout 1944 and 1945, the government issued monthly a theme for all religious bodies to stress. This furnished the pastor with the subject of the sermon, and the local police knew whether or not he used it. The church calendar was made to conform largely to the national holidays, or else to yield place to them, as did Christmas to the Emperor Taisho's Day on December 25.

Evangelism was carried on, but the term "patriotic evangelism" which was generally used, indicates its divided objectives. It could scarcely have been directed primarily toward the Christian conversion of individuals. It must have aimed at a public presentation of Christianity's place in the national crisis. In November, 1942, in connection with an interfaith patriotic celebration the leaders of the different religions were received in audience at court. Director Mitsuru Tomita, representing Protestant Christianity, made some words of salutation before the Emperor. Thereafter, for a whole year, until the next General Assembly in 1943, he travelled over the country, visiting the churches, holding meetings, and reporting on the honor bestowed on the church through him. These services of thanksgiving must have affected the patriotic feeling and thinking of the church membership.

During the war, the term "established religion" came to

be used by Christians in referring to their faith. Of course, there was no established religion except official Shinto, but as one of the three accredited religions recognized in the national law, Christianity had been given a status which, to its adherents, was so vastly better than any they had ever known that they called it "established." The govern- ment was glad to have it so, for it was a guarantee of complete control in case of need. It was the unregistered, unmanageable sects that caused officials anxiety. They felt at home in dealing with a "recognized" religious system.

In order that Christian ministers might be thoroughly equipped for their national service of morale-building, as well as exemplary in heir own attitudes, a series of "proc- essing meetings" was set up. In the districts and at the national level they were conducted as seminars or work- shops. For long hours the text of the *Basic Principles of the National Structure* would be studied, and lectures upon it listened to. The various rescripts, including the Decla- ration of War on the Allies, would be expounded by govern- ment commentators, and the ministers quizzed. Exercises in writing, over and over again, the lyrical poems of the Emperor Meiji or of the present ruler were carried out. The term "brainwashing" had not then been coined, but it must have been some such processing which the authorities had in mind in putting Christian leaders through this tedious course of indoctrination. The pastors were instruc- ed to conduct similar courses for members in their local churches.

The wartime thinking of the church was not left to chance by the government. When in the organization of the United Church the Bureau of Indoctrination was sub- stituted for that of Education, it was expected that the thinkers of the Protestant denominations would find a way to harmonize the ancient spiritual bases of the Japanese

250

people with the foundation doctrines of Christianity. The choice of director for an Institute of Japanese Studies was President Shiro Murata, of the Japan Theological Seminary with Antei Hiyane, professor of the History of Religions and voluminous author, as full-time secretary. The most obvious link in such a joining of traditions was the work of the great scholar Atsutane Hirata of a century before. In his studies of Chinese Christian books he had come to the conclusion that the Christian God was the same as the deity "Lord God of the Central Heavens," in the ancient chronicle of Japan. Dr. Ebina had quite fully developed the idea. In the 30's D. Tagawa had written on this subject. Kagawa had also noted the possible identification of this ancient deity with the God of the Hebrews. He, however, had gone on to say that faith in such a deity alone would be arid and harsh, and that only as upon this foundation the new structure of the revelation of God in Christ was built could manking find a truly satisfying or universal faith.

During the war the theological argument sometimes became distorted. It appeared that the unique quality of the Christian revelation was to derive from the peculiar genius of the Japanese people, their insights into the nature of deity, and their creative touch in bringing new life to the traditional faiths of others. One scholar wrote that whereas all other peoples had made their interpretations of the Christian faith, then had placed a *comma* for the continued contributions of later generations, with the Japanese Christians, it would not be so. When they had made theirs there would be nothing left to do but place a *period*.

A series of pamphlets was issued over the imprint of the United Church, and the best thinkers in the church were among the authors. In one, written by the very able Professor Uwoki of Doshisha University on *The True*

Nature of Japanese Christianity, the theme of the uniqueness of Japanese Christianity was developed. Christianity,
he explained, always and everywhere has unique worth, in
that it brings God to man and man to God in terms of
forgiven sin and the new life. But Japanese Christianity
does more. By virtue of a quality possessed only by the
Japanese race it enables people of other races actually to
become Japanese Christians. It is destined to make of all
people one nation; but more than that, it will, by a miracle,
be the Japanese nation.

The other theme developed in the Indoctrination Bureau
studies was that of the spiritual virtue of the Asian expansion. During the late 30's other pamphlets published
by the National Christian Council had played upon this
theme. The general secretary in the key pamphlet likened
the fatherly beneficence of the Emperor in Asia and toward
the family life of mankind to its heavenly counterpart in
God the Father and his Kingdom.

Another author described Japan's armed conflict in China
as intended to correct an erring people, by saying: "with
tears in our hearts we have raised aloft the whips of love."
During the war it was repeatedly written that Christians
desired only the emancipation of Asia. This was the "Awake
Asia" theme, so widely used in the churches. The term "the
righteousness of the gods" also was employed to fortify the
claims of a holy war.

There was, nevertheless a core of faith and conviction
on which the Christians did not yield. In the original drafting of the credal basis of the United Church in 1940 the
Ministry of Education recommended a very brief and simple
minimum, leaving leeway for the component groups and
membership to exercise some individual choice. This seemed
wise counsel from the standpoint of the churches, as well.
Thus, instead of one of the historic creeds, a recital of

several of the Christian doctrines was given, and then reference was made to the Apostles Creed and the other confessions of the church. The Bible was also cited as the basis of belief.

It is noteworthy, that even in this simple formula God was described not as "the Father Almighty, Maker of Heaven and Earth," but only as "the Father of Jesus Christ." It was this belief in the universal Creator-God of Christianity which meant head-on collision with revived Shinto and the State. The United Church never did succeed in placing the doctrine squarely in its constitution as its creed. It was a cause of continuous strain all through the war.

A commission worked on Christian doctrine and offered draft after draft to the government authorities, only to have them all rejected. The one which was under negotiation when the war came to an end in August of 1945 was apparently too sub-Christian for the church to be willing to publish it, and too Christian for the Ministry of Education to sanction it. It was never adopted. There stands the record of a brave struggle.

In all this area the church was confronted by one of the most formidable of all the national organs for national conformity, the Bureau of Thought Control—or Indoctrination Bureau—of the Ministry of Education. It had its own powers of punishment for "subversive thought" paralleling those of the secret police of the Home Ministry in the field of subversive action. Some sixteen thousand individuals during the years 1940 to 1945 were imprisoned by it for suspected disloyal sentiments. Through the Bureau of Indoctrination of the Church of Christ it dictated and checked the official thinking of the Christian bodies to the last detail. Where it left some freedom of Christian interpretation, that was gratefully exercised. Where national orthodoxy drew the line freedom of open expression or of published creed by the church had to stop. It was this government bureau which sharpened every facet of the revived wartime Shinto beliefs. It may be conjectured that the reason this fearsome and all-powerful organ of the Ministry of Education tolerated for the entire duration of the war the stalling of the Church authorities in the drafting of its creed, was that some other forces within that same Ministry, more favorable to Christianity, were acting as a counter-power.

What the Bureau of Thought Control did dictate was a second portion of the Constitution of the church which dealt with a Code of Living. This, too, consisted of beliefs, but they related to citizenship, proper understanding of the "National Structure," and the duties of a Japanese subject. They included the pledge of loyalty exacted of every citizen, and they were viewed alike by the government and by Christians with extreme seriousness.

The inclusion of such an addendum to the creed in the constitution of a church was no new thing in Japan. From the time of the Kumamoto Band and of the first church in Yokohama, it had been recurring. Whether or not those early ones were voluntary is not known, but certainly during the war years every phrase of such a code was directed by the government authorities who made explicit in a series of questions and answers in the Constitution of the church just what a Christian must be and do in Japan. He must promote the national welfare according to the "Way of the Subject," under the "Way of the Emperor."

Late in the war, when the authorities were forcing Christian leaders to give their members commentaries on these essentially Shinto phrases, Director Tomita requested of them an official clarification. The reply was that Christians could know their duties by referring to the Imperial Rescript on Education. Upon this Professor Hiyane of the church Indoctrination Bureau wrote in the Bulletin that Christians always had gladly observed the universal moral demands of the Education Rescript and that they were gratified at being encouraged in no wise to confuse their duties with any Shinto syncretism, but to remain staunchly Christian Japanese subjects. Since this was an implied disparagement of the new Shinto orthodoxy, Hiyane was publicly cashiered by the government and forced to retire from all writing activities.

It was in the months of deepening suffering in 1945 that the Christian church gave its finest witness. The frenetic year of the 1942 victories with the messianic sense of destiny of the nation was gone. The "Awake Asia" demands of 1943 were in the past. The "Homeland Become Battlefield" mood of 1944 had darkened into "Resist the Invader Unto Death" of 1945. The sterner issues of life and eternity were being faced. When Premier Koiso was asked in the Diet whether he believed that defeat meant the displeasure of the gods, he replied that he did.

In the widespread debate on religious matters, as to God's will, the national objectives and the facing of death, Christians had beliefs and could express them. The columns of the one periodical remaining to the church, its Bulletin, are filled with deeply spiritual Christian editorials and sermons. They carry a strong tone of moral insight and conviction. There must have been multitudes of Christians in churches throughout the nation who were giving this authentic witness. By 1945 inner tensions between faiths were melted in the common fires of disaster. Christians could forget their defences and give themselves to works of mercy and comfort. This they did in the closing months of war.

The Church of Christ as such conformed in every detail with national laws, but within it there were groups who found themselves in trouble. The ministers of two branches of the Holiness Church, over a hundred and fifty in number, were arrested in the spring of 1942. The issues were those of the Osaka Gendarme questionnaire of 1938. They called for a definition of the respective claims of Caesar and Christ. The chief points of the case were their belief in Christ's second coming in relation to the end of the Japanese Imperial Line and judgment upon the Emperor. Also there was an imputation of belief in a period of Jewish rule over mankind. The investigations dragged on, with court trials, appeals, imprisonment, and finally a stalemate, as the court records were burned. Then the Supreme Court building itself was destroyed in the bombing. The last of these prisoners were released by the Occupation in October, 1945. Several died as a result of the hardships of prison life.

The Seventh Day Adventists had not applied for registration within the Church of Christ. They were ordered dissolved, and all their properties were confiscated. After the war these were restored. The Korean churches in Japan suffered constant interference by the police, and some of their ministers were imprisoned. Other individuals attracted police attention. Dr. Kagawa had been twice arrested and investigated in 1940 for apologizing in China for the invasion of Japan's neighbor. He was not held for trial at that time. During the war years, however, he was again twice arrested for his peace sentiments, and the second time was indicted; but he was released under suspended sentence.

The Episcopal-Anglican Church withdrew from the Church of Christ while this was in process of formation, declaring itself not a Protestant church, but a bridge between that and the Catholic churches and therefore unable to take sides. It was not granted a charter and was ordered to dissolve. The church went through the procedures of dissolution of diocesan organization, revamped its structure and continued. This, of course, was known to the authorities, and they made trouble for the church leaders. The Presiding Bishop, Yashiro was repeatedly harried by the police, and for several months he and two other bishops were imprisoned. The point the police wished clarified was why the church did not join with others. This not only reopened the delicate subject of integral relationships with the enemy Great Britain, and the authority of the Lambeth Bishops, but also it exposed to the suspicious view of police investigators a "high" and mystical doctrine of the church, and its ministerial orders.

The Christian schools suffered varying fortunes and treatment, depending on the attitudes of their responsible heads, as well as on that of local police and education authorities. All to some degree had to curtail Christian witness and work. Indeed, all virtually suspended academic work after the Student Mobilization Law of 1944. The buildings were utilized for war industries. Teachers and students were assigned jobs in factories and on farms. The school life was demoralized. Yet all the Christian schools maintained a continuous existence and some of them gave a valiant Christian witness in the face of difficulties that appeared insurmountable.

The Orthodox Church, deprived of the leadership of Metropolitan Sergius, had continuing trouble to find a suitable Japanese head. It was not accorded a charter. Throughout the war it suffered all the vicissitudes of uncertain treatment by local police. Its numbers shrank to a fourth of the pre-war level.

The Roman Catholic church submitted to the regulations of the National Religions Law. It reorganized under a Japanese archbishop, and was granted a charter as "the Japan Catholic Church," which name it still bears. No serious difficulties with government were reported during the war years. In becoming a totally autonomous Japanese organization as it had to be, some essential canons of the church were violated. Under a special ruling that these might be viewed as civil and not ecclesiastical in nature, the Vatican assisted the church in making its adjustments. With the wisdom born of age the church managed to maintain a fairly normal existence until the war closed, though it suffered the same hardships of wartime in its life and work as did the Protestant churches.

DEFEAT AND ALLIED OCCUPATION
"Love Among the Ruins"
1945–1952

On August 14, 1945 the people were alerted to a special message to be broadcast the following day by the Emperor. It was taken for granted that this unprecedented measure of a direct vocal communication from their ruler was to call forth from them one more supreme effort for final victory. Reverently they awaited his voice. He said: "To our good and loyal subjects:

> After pondering deeply the general trends of the world and the actual conditions obtaining in our Empire today, we have decided to effect a settlement of the present situation by resorting to an extraordinary measure.
>
> We have ordered Our Government to communicate to the Governments of the United States, Great Britain, China and the Soviet Union that Our Empire accepts the provisions of their Joint Declaration. To strive for the common prosperity and happiness of all nations as well as the security and well-being of Our subjects is the solemn obligation which has been handed down by Our Imperial Ancestors and which we lay close to the

heart. "(Translation in *Nippon Times* Aug. 15, 1945)."
This message had the sweeping majesty of style to which
the people had become accustomed in the numerous imperial
rescripts issued throughout the war years. The appeals
made for increased devotion had always stressed the welfare of the nation and the peace of the world. By many of
the common people this Imperial address was listened to as
having the same intent. Father Hildebrand, Catholic missionary in Yokohama, tells of calling his elderly woman
housekeeper in from the kitchen to hear the broadcast.
When the voice of her emperor struck her ears she fell to
the floor in obeisance, and remained with her head down
until the end; then, her eyes streaming with tears, she rose,
looked into the radio set, breathed her renewed commitment
to all the necessary privations of continued war, and went
softly back to her work. So general was this impression,
especially among the country people who scarcely guessed
at the hopeless state of the cities and the nation, that it
became necessary for the government later in the day to
give the facts to the public in plain words which no one
could fail to understand.

To say that the nation was stunned is to put it midly.
For eight long years the people had bent all their energy
toward victory. Concerning the war they knew little. It was
being fought at long range. They trusted their leaders, and
believed whatever news was given them, along with its
official interpretation. Even the devastating bombing of the
cities was rationalized, and the public was assured that soon
new measures of retaliation would put an end to the destruction of the homeland.

Now, by word of the one in whose name all these years of
sacrifice had been spent, the conflict was over. During the
war not even the word "peace", much less "defeat" or "surrender" was permitted by law to be written or spoken.

But now, defeat had come. On September 2, 1945 in Tokyo Bay, where Perry's ships had anchored ninety years before to present Japan with her first modern dilemma, the representatives of the Japanese government boarded the United States "S.S. Missouri" and there signed the instrument of unconditional surrender.

In facing this new world the people had mingled reactions. Loyal though they were, it was but natural that they should feel an immense sense of relief at the end to all these horrors. They could have made their own the words of General Douglas MacArthur: "A great tragedy has ended... the skies no longer rain death—the seas bear only commerce —men everywhere walk upright in the sunlight."

Multitudes of families had lost everything, but they had survived. Their men might still be alive and might someday return from whatever front they were on. Life was going forward. For literally millions of the people the shock of defeat and the wearing years of privation left no capacity for much beyond a dull sense of rescue.

To many others the ending in failure of this holy war meant the crumbling of a world;—a world that was not merely physical, but deeply spiritual. They profoundly believed in the uniqueness of Japan's land and people, of her culture and her faith, and particularly in the Emperor who formed the center of the national life and destiny, the channel for fulfilling the purposes of the ancestral gods in the new age. In the hour of humiliation to whom should they pray? Were the gods, indeed, angry; and if so for what cause? Or were they impotent; and if so, who or what was the greater power to which they had bowed? Many a Japanese paused before the further bleak question: were there, after all, any such ancestral gods, or had their faith been a dream ending in a nightmare of despair? Had they awakened to a world in which only simple old women pray?

As to the ideas of what the occupation by victors would be, there was a stereotyped thought-pattern of savagery, pillage, oppression and hatred which was the stock characterization of the enemy and all his deeds during the war. The people who could do so sent their wives and daughters into remote country places where relatives lived, and braced themselves for the ordeal. Others struggled vainly to find a proper attitude to take toward the invading westerners. Some may have determined to make friends with them, but, probably most of the nation hoped that they would not need to have any direct dealings with the enemy.

If the surrender was bewilderingly strange, the ensuing Occupation proved to be stranger still. Although a dozen nations were involved, in actual fact its structure, personnel, and policies were almost entirely shaped by America, the arch-enemy of the war years. As the organization took form it proved to be a pyramid with one man at the apex, the Supreme Commander of the Allied Powers. So totally did the entire Occupation come to be identified with this individual that throughout the years of its duration it was called SCAP, a word coined from the initials of his title. The man appointed to this task—one that he called the greatest gamble in history—was General Douglas MacArthur. His entire life had been that of a military man, and much of it was spent in the Orient, where presumably there were few informal contacts with the common people. During the war he had had the assignment of defending the Philippines and had suffered the mortification of defeat, retreat, and escape to Australia. During years of relentless fighting, he had recovered the lost territory. Victory had come at last, and the Japanese people assumed that an occupation headed by General MacArthur, the symbol of conquest through defeat, would of all imaginable kinds be the most retaliatory in its enforcement of the terms of surrender.

261

On the contrary, from the first he showed a deep respect for the nation, military and civilian. Personally he had an impressive presence, he held himself aloof from all individual contacts, worked long hours, and travelled fearlessly along the streets in his black limousine. He planned with a comprehensive grasp, in wide ranges of concern for the nation's good, and soon communicated to it his own sense of direction toward recovery. If he had been a Japanese he would have made a perfect Shogun, drastic in dismantling but vigorous in rebuilding, shielding the emperor, and leading the people out of crises to safety.

Actually there had been, before the surrender, a long period of postwar planning within American government departments. Already, on August 29, 1945 SCAP had received by radio its basic directions in "The Initial Post War Policy for Japan." Within a few months there was set up in Washington the Far Eastern Commission of the eleven participating nations, with powers of review over the Occupation. The President of the United States moreover approved policies before they were forwarded to Japan. But this intricate procedure was all invisible. The people of Japan saw only the heroic figure of the great Pro-Consul, in whose mind the chaos of the ruined nation seemed to give way to order, and in whose hands its destiny seemed to rest.

In fact there was much of truth in this view, for early in the Occupation MacArthur had seized the initiative, and he held it so firmly that soon he was being given wide discretionary powers of interpretation and execution of policy. It is not surprising that there should have gathered about the General an aura of mysterious greatness, and that his deeds should have become a popular myth. It was even whispered that he had been born in a far-off village in Japan of a Japanese mother and a great American military chief-

tain, and that the national deities had given an oracle commending him to the people.

The role of Shogun was surely suggested to the public by
this unusual man. Most thoughtful Japanese saw no way
ahead except through cooperation with the Occupation.
They wanted it to succeed, and were grateful for the prestige its leader might gain from Japan's historic past. The
almost total acquiescence in the Occupation by the people at
large was a mark of their intelligence and integrity. They
helped carry it to success as their only hope for the long
future.

General MacArthur not only inspired many Japanese
with something of his confidence and hope, he also managed
within a few months to put the impress of his spirit upon
the entire Occupation forces. Fortunately the original plan
for a thoroughgoing military government of Japan was
abandoned, and a much better one was adopted. It provided
for three wings.

The first one was the occupying army, with headquarters
in Yokohama. There a barracks installation became the
center for all actual movements of troops. These were deployed throughout the country, mostly in the Japanese military
bases which were at a distance from city centers. American
and other foreign soldiers were not too much in evidence.
There was very little for the army forces to do, since there
was no opposition on the part of the Japanese people. This
army might be called the muscular system of the Occupation.

A second wing was made up of small military teams stationed all over Japan to furnish liaison with Japanese
officials and citizens, to explain Occupation directives, pass
judgment on questions of compliance, and in general to keep
open the lines of communication with the Japanese people.
The teams were sometimes embarrassed by a too assiduous

eagerness to obey, as when one officer was asked by a physical director of a school about to hold an athletic competition whether it would be militaristic to use a pistol in starting the races. Another brought a paper-knife and requested permission to use it in a dramatic skit where a dagger was indicated.

One sergeant recounted his agony of soul when he had to go to a remote city where a highly technical electric device for automatic piloting of planes was manufactured. By orders, if this device could have no use other than in warfare, the stock would have to be destroyed, and the factories dismantled.

He conferred with the townspeople and manufacturers, giving them two days to try to make a case for its commercial use, only to have them come disconsolately and admit that they could not utilize it except for a fighting plane. Sadly he stood by while the work of demolition of these beautiful instruments went on. When he left, the town-fathers sent him off with gifts and a vote of thanks for his understanding attitude. These teams were the eyes and hands of the Occupation, usually friendly with the people.

As the third wing, in Tokyo, SCAP built a headquarters staff of military and civilian personnel, organized in twelve major sections, with numerous departments, divisions and bureaus. It was set up to deal with every aspect of national life that would be the responsibility of a central government. The heterogeneous group gradually became a unit interested in the possibilities of reconstruction of Japanese society, and on the whole sharing MacArthur's high estimate of Japanese character and achievements. There, in downtown Tokyo in a score of large office buildings—intentionally spared in the bombings—the plans and blue-prints for the peaceful revolution were worked out. This was the brain and nervous system of the Occupation.

The new policies were carried into effect by a complete
system of liaison with Japanese officials. The position of the
Emperor as ruler was left untouched. Theoretically, every
act or wish of the allies was to be communicated by SCAP
to him. In practice, however, there was a Japanese government as heretofore, with local, prefectural and national
branches, centering in the Diet, the Cabinet, and the Premier. Naturally, there grew up at all these levels a body of
Japanese officials who became practiced in dealing with
their opposite numbers in the Occupation. Where there was
mutual cooperation, as there usually was, each learned much
from the other. SCAP was saved from many blunders of
ignorance, while Japanese governing bodies were given excellent briefing in the constructive purposes of the new order.

Major decisions were announced as "directives," issued
publicly. But, for the minor decisions, the day-by-day administration was " government by nudge." Even a hint given
in an individual interview by the proper Occupation official
usually was all that was necessary to effect its execution as
a voluntary procedure of the Japanese government. This
was the method Japanese Christians had become accustomed
to during the years of pressure, when friendly individuals
in the government would give them informal hints as to
what course would be wise to take in order to avoid more
coercive measures. It is a procedure well-understood in the
Orient, and it has much merit as a flexible way of dealing
with decisions without making a final commitment from
which neither side might be able to withdraw. Many tentative policies were tried out in this way, and some were
allowed to die a natural death.

The Potsdam principles were of two sorts, both to be
carried out by the Occupation. The negative or punitive
aspect was the cutting back of Japan's territory to the four
main islands, and some small ones off the coast; the dis-

arming of all troops and dismantling of military installations, reparations, the criminal trials of the war leaders and, in general, the abolition of militarism. On the other hand there was the mandate to lead Japan to a condition in which she would be able to resume peaceful relations with the world. This too, would involve some measures seemingly destructive, but they would be steps on the way to reconstruction.

MacArthur pre-viewed his work as falling into three periods; first military, next political and then economic. Curiously enough, this order is the exact reverse of the one followed by the Oligarchs in the first decades of Japan's modern life. As events developed, the six-year Occupation went through four phases, each being parts of two years in duration.

THE YEARS 1945 AND 1946 were a time of dismantling and clearing the site for rebuilding. In early October, 1945 the so-called "Bill of Rights" was issued, followed by specific directives for carrying it into effect. It abolished the repressive Religious Bodies Control Law, allowing all religions freedom of organization as well as of belief. SCAP disestablished State Shinto and reduced the shrines to a voluntary status. It established a new, non-militaristic policy for the public school system, though it was too early to implement it by detailed regulations. The schools were ordered to go on, even though some principals and teachers might expect later to undergo purges for their nationalistic attitudes. Textbooks were hastily scanned for undesirable material, and pages containing such passages were pasted together, then the instructor and students were left to do the best they could.

All persons imprisoned for "dangerous thoughts" were freed; the courts were ordered to clear the records of those in process of trial. Freedom of opinion, speech, assembly and publication were established by fiat. The secret "thought"

266

police were done away with, and a curb was placed on the regular police.

This ruthless tearing away of the wartime structure was too much for the Cabinet that had been especially improvised for working with the Westerners. Prince Higashikuni, uncle of the Emperor and a measurably liberal-minded man, was Premier, and Prince Konoye, whose disposition, though ineffective had been toward moderation, was Vice-Premier. When they were told that the Home Ministry itself would eventually have to be abolished, they protested that without it no domestic administration or control would be possible, and they resigned. In October a new Premier, Baron Kijiro Shidehara took office. He made his official call to report to General MacArthur, and upon leaving he was handed an envelope indicating the essential policies to be undertaken by the Japanese government. "I expect you," it read, "to institute the following reforms in the social order of Japan as readily as they can be assimilated." Then followed five brief paragraphs dealing with:

(1) The emancipation of women through their enfranchisement.

(2) The encouragement of the unionization of labor, with the correction of child labor practices.

(3) The opening of the schools to more liberal education, "so that people may understand the system under which government becomes the servant rather than the master of the people."

(4) The abolition of "a system of secret inquisition for one of justice designed to protect people in their rights."

(5) The democratization of Japanese economic institutions, "so as to insure a wide distribution of income and ownership of the means of production and trade."

The Premier immediately called a meeting of the Cabinet and laid before them this revolutionary document. It seemed more like a pronouncement of the Social-Democratic party than the policy-making by an invading army. Coming to Japan's initial postwar responsible government as its first dealing with the Occupation it was seen as a challenge of primary importance. It involved the whole matter of genuine acquiescence with the foreign regime or an alternative of calculated tension and resistance. But still more it called for an immediate reaction of acceptance or rejection of what was to be a bloodless, but an exceedingly radical revolution in social and national life. The Cabinet conscientiously adopted this Magna Charta of the Occupation in all its basic goals, and faithfully went to work to implement its provisions. Throughout the entire period of the Occupation there was no essential deviation from this sincere cooperation.

What was the position of Protestant Christianity during those first months of the post-war period? It was in a state of ruin. The work to be done was one of immediate Relief. Christians, together with their neighbors, had suffered the privations of decreasing rations, increasing hazards of health, with lack of medicines and drugs, general malnutrition, insufficient clothing, dilapidated houses, inadequacy of transportation and the incessant fear of death from the skies. Then the bombings had taken homes, churches, whole neighborhoods in their flaming maw. Industry was halted, and the lay members as well as pastors, dependent on supplementary jobs, were without any dependable source of income.

The spiritual problems of Christians were even more acute than were those of their body and estate. They had had close ties with Westerners, and especially with Americans. Should they renew these or repudiate them? It was not yet known what would be the attitude of the general public toward the invaders. What should theirs be?

While many Christians were pondering this dilemma the women of the WCTU promptly resolved it. They obtained permission to set up a refreshment tent on one corner of the Atsugi Airfield. The first detail of air-borne troops alighted, uncertain of their reception, apprehensive of attack, and without a knowledge of the language or the ways of the people. They were greeted, in the English language, by a group of ladies dressed in their best black, all wearing the white ribbon many a boy had seen on his mother's breast. And they were invited to stop for a sip of tea!

When Prince Higashikuni had accepted the premiership, he called on Dr. Kagawa to assist him, and placed him in a private office next to his own in the government mansion. Undoubtedly he did this because he considered the Christian internationalist to be well-acquainted with American ways, but also he distinctly said that he needed the insights of this moral prophet for guidance in setting a new spiritual course for the nation. Under Kagawa's suggestion the first month after the surrender, September, 1945 was declared to be a Month of Penitence.

The acceptance of this public assignment must have caused Dr. Kagawa some searchings of heart. He was especially vulnerable to charges of disloyalty and friendship with the enemy, for during the war the public had heard over the air from America that Japan was to be defeated and that Kagawa was to be placed in authority over his people by the victors. It was in response to that unfair blow of psychological warfare that he took the microphone to assert to his people that he was a loyal citizen of his own country, totally unassociated with the enemy. His address, monitored in the United States was generally misconstrued to have been in some way a repudiation of his Christian principles. This was utterly untrue, for though he is an ardent lover of his nation, he has never once lowered his Christian banner. Kagawa was glad when released from his semi-political post, to pitch into the work of actual relief and reconstruction. He belongs deep in the rough and tumble of the human scene.

Immediately after the war a radio message from a Christian leader in Japan was picked up and relayed to the Foreign Missions Conference of North America for interpretation and explanation. It was recognized to be from Rev. Tsunetaro Miyakoda, Secretary of the Church of Christ and formerly Secretary of the National Christian Council. What he said was that at the time of the Riverside Fellowship meetings in 1941, an invitation had been extended to American church leaders to reciprocate by a visit to Japan; and that if it was still in their hearts to do so, they would be welcomed. This was all that was needed.

Within a few days arrangements had been made for a deputation of four, representing the Foreign Missions Conference and the Federal Council of Churches, to go to help rebind the ties torn apart by the long years of war. They had all been in the Riverside group, and each was linked to a prayer-partner in Japan. Although they went as individuals they were persons of large influence and responsibility in American and world Christian circles; Dr. Douglas Horton, Bishop James C. Baker, Dr. Walter Van Kirk, and Dr. Luman J. Shafer. Their stated purpose was "to reestablish face-to-face contact with fellow Christians in Japan, to strengthen the living bonds of unity in Christ, and to take counsel regarding the common tasks of the ecumenical Church."

Obtaining passports as the first private individuals to enter Japan, or as a Japanese minister said, the first to come "in praying clothes", they arrived in Tokyo on October 23, 1945. With deep emotion they met their comrades of Riverside, and together celebrated a communion service. Five days of conference with Japan's Christian leaders followed, and the deputation returned bearing affectionate greetings of the Japanese Church to American Christians and a cordial invitation for renewed inter-relationships.

It was too early for systematic planning on the Japanese side. In every direction there was destitution and stark need calling for succor. Emergency measures of relief demanded priority, though even these must be under the severe restrictions of a total embargo of goods, communications, and entrance of civilian personnel. The reports of the Christian ambassadors to their large constituencies in the West released a flood of understanding and affection toward their fellow Christians in Japan. Mission boards began to make specific plans to help; but even before this, individuals and groups had found ways to reach the Christians across the Pacific with parcels sent by military post and in other slightly irregular but morally defensible ways.

During 1945 and for some months in 1946 there was no further direct contact between Japanese Christians and the outside world. But everywhere there were Americans in uniform. Before long the inevitable associations began and developed. SCAP did not prohibit fraternizing, though most Japanese buildings were declared out of bounds. Not so the churches; nor was the rule enforced in the case of the two or three homes in Tokyo where elderly missionaries had sat out the war without interference from the police. In these places American servicemen gathered for companionship and for Christian services.

In west Tokyo near the group of shacks Dr. Kagawa had thrown together as his "compound", stood the home of the Toppings, Baptist Missionaries. Mr. Topping had died during the war, but "Mother Top", far advanced in years, bed-

271

ridden, and not too clear in mind, opened her heart alike to G.I.s and to Japanese young people, with indiscriminate admiration and love. A continuing stream of people of every sort came and went to the house, using the rooms for Christian prayer services, hymn singing, evenings of drama, and parties for neighborhood children. During the war Mrs. Topping, had gone on the air on Radio Tokyo, pleading for peace, and her home was viewed by some journalists as a center of subversion. The Occupation authorities with sound common sense permitted this wholesome project of reconciliation to follow its innocent course. Active in the group was Miss Elizabeth Kilburn, Methodist missionary who spent herself in works of mercy, and of unofficial service between servicemen, chaplains and Japanese Christians.

Downtown in Tokyo the Ginza Church was a beehive of activities. A gaping bomb-wound in the roof let in rain, and every available foot of the parsonage and church was jammed with refugee families, their bedding, impromptu cooking and housekeeping. The main auditorium, at least on clear days and nights was usable. Soon the indefatigable pastor, Isamu Mitsui had rounded up some Christian servicemen and invited them to come to church. They could not understand a word of the service, but they knew the hymns and felt the warm atmosphere of Christian fellowship. A few of the Christian laymen knew English, and little by little the lads were drawn into the life of the church. Several evenings a week were kept open for their own services in English. Saturday evening especially, evangelistic groups among the armed forces conducted services and Bible classes, both for one another and for the many Japanese young men who were brought into the magnetic circle. There were conversions and baptisms of Americans and of Japanese.

Some leaders of the United Church felt a concern for evangelism among the Occupation personnel, and conducted daily meetings in the same Ginza Church. The auditorium was usually filled for the twenty-minute noonday service. Few records were kept at this time of almost complete ruin and prostration, and many church buildings had not survived; but unquestionably in other centers throughout Japan, churches near concentrations of Occupation forces were opened to this same sort of informal association in Christian services. Church papers later reported more than one lonely, or perhaps guilt-laden American serviceman as having been guided by a Japanese pastor into a Christian experience and church membership.

Within the Occupation staff there were former Japan missionaries, both as military men and as civilian employees and advisors. Several of these found it possible to meet all their official duties and still to establish contacts with Christian groups which were of the greatest importance in an early recovery of morale. Russell L. Durgin, secretary of the YMCA, was conspicuously useful in this field. Paul Rusch of St. Paul's University rendered great service to the school and churches of the Episcopal communion. William C. Kerr, Presbyterian, became the trusted counsellor of many Japanese Christians in need. William C. Woodard, Congregationalist, had an outreach beyond Christian groups to those of every faith, and was very much trusted by them. Glen Bruner, former Methodist missionary, and later American Consul, renewed relations with Japanese Christians, as did Boude C. Moore, Dutch Reformed, and his brother Lardner Moore, Southern Presbyterian. Visits of other officers, such as Robert S. Spencer, Methodist, furnished opportunities for informal contacts with Japanese Christians.

At Christmas, 1945, American servicemen joined the all-Tokyo Christian choirs in rendering Handel's "The Mes-

273

siah" in Hibiya Hall, before an audience of 6,000 people. Later, when the Tokyo Chapel Center was built Ugo Nakada, singing evangelist and choir-director, took over the entire ministry of music with his well trained choir. Col. Ivan L. Bennett Chief of Chaplains, was invited to deliver a course of lectures on Christianity in the Tokyo National University, and in preparation flew to Australia for books. Crowds of students attended the lectures, astonished and impressed by this military officer turned Chrstian theologian and university lecturer.

In this general spirit of rapport it was natural that the Chaplains should be interested in the Christians whom they met. Some Japanese who knew English applied and got jobs of interpreting, care of chapels, organ-playing and general assistance to the chaplain. This formed a natural bridge into Christian communities where sometimes a chaplain would be found of an evening teaching an English Bible class. They were invited to preach at worship services, when off duty. Informally they rendered many services that did not go into the reports.

The Division of Religions of the Civil Information and Education Section kept a sharp eye out for any improper discrimination by Occupation personnel in favor of Christians, since policy dictated complete neutrality and freedom for all faiths. Briefings were given the chaplains as to where the borderlines of official and unofficial activities lay; and care was taken that the non-Christian communities might have no cause for complaint of unfair treatment. Thus the chaplains remained within the regulations, but nevertheless rendered much service to the Christians in the first months of the Occupation. This applies equally, or perhaps in even greater degree to the Roman Catholic chaplains and Occupation personnel, who established and maintained contact with their brethren in Japan.

274

In January, 1946, the Emperor addressed the opening session of the Diet with an astonishing affirmation. He said: "The ties between us and our people have always stood upon mutual trust and affection. They do not depend upon mere legend and myths, they are not predicated on the false conception that the Emperor is manifest deity, and that the Japanese people are superior to other races and fated to rule the world." This was, indeed spiritual demolition on a grand scale. The people were utterly unprepared for it. Its implications ran out into every area of the psychic life of the nation. For forty years the doctrine of the Emperor's divinity had been inculcated in explicit detail, and it had become the moral and spiritual central pillar supporting the entire "National Structure."

This belief in less systematized form ran through Japan's two thousand years of history as the "Way of the Gods." It rested on the ancient compilations which were believed to chart the course for Japan from time immemorial. At one stroke the Emperor himself had disavowed all this, and apparently had left the nation to fall apart. Incredible as it must have been to his subjects, their world was already topsy turvy, and they were almost beyond the capacity to react. Furthermore, they assumed that it was dictated by the Occupation, and that in making the statement their Emperor was suffering humiliation with and for his people. Yet it is believed that, radical though it was, it represented the personal views of the Emperor, at least as regards his own nature. Undoubtedly he preferred that his ties with his people should be those of "Mutual trust and affection," as indeed they were.

This sweeping change did not go by without challenge, for within a few months the Minister of Education announced that there had been no change in the "national structure," nor would there be any in the instruction of the young. This was allowed to pass, but the repudiation of the extreme wartime philosophy of the state by the ruler himself had gone into the record, and would stand as a firm basis for individual freedom and for national democracy in the future. It still offers Japanese Christians a platform wide and solid enough to maintain devoted patriotism along with the faith of classic Christianity.

The implementing of the Potsdam Declaration called for the adoption of a new national Constitution. The Supreme Commander in October, 1945 asked Prince Konoye to proceed with the plans for drafting one. A Diet committee was set up. Its work dragged on month after month, and finally there was produced an outline of proposed changes in the national organization. These showed but few and unimportant alterations of the old structure. The Occupation staff, therefore, was instructed to make a draft. This was quickly completed and presented to the country for action. It is scarcely accurate to say that it was done on the initiative of the Japanese Government, though SCAP so announced it. It was agreed to by Cabinet representatives, and an official Japanese text was published, but the entire document bears the stamp of Anglo-Saxon thinking and political tradition. In November, 1945, it was passed by the Diet, and in the spring of 1947 it became law. It can be revised only by a two-thirds vote of both Houses and a referendum by the people.

In the new national structure, sovereignty rests with the citizens, and the Emperor acts in their name. The people enjoy universal suffrage. The laws are made by majority rule of responsible political parties in a national Diet, in which an elective upper House of Councillors is secondary in power to the Lower House. The majority party names a Premier and Cabinet who administer the laws. The Peers, the Privy Council, and the Elder Statesmen are all gone;

and the Imperial Family is cut back to the immediate relatives of the reigning emperor. Of the more than one hundred articles in the Constitution of 1946, the majority deal with the rights of citizens rather than with their duties, as had been the tradition heretofore.

One article in this blueprint for change did meet with immediate and almost universal approbation. Article Nine reads: "Aspiring sincerely to an international peace based on justice and order, the Japanese people forever renounce war as a sovereign right of the nation and the threat or use of force as a means of settling international disputes.

"In order to accomplish the aim of the preceding paragraph, land, sea, and air forces, as well as other war potential, will never be maintained. The right of belligerency of the state will not be recognized."

This article precisely expressed the longing and the intention of the war-weary, war-accursed Japanese people.

In the spring of 1946 a United States Education Mission came on the invitation of SCAP to do the groundwork for an overhauling of the entire system of education in Japan. Its twenty-four members were eminent men and women, experienced in their various fields of education. They remained for a month, meeting at first with a group of about sixty Japanese educationalists, and then later, in conference alone. Their recommendations charted the course of educational change for the years ahead. The new policies aimed at decentralization and the curtailing of the monopolistic powers of the central Ministry of Education. Local boards of education were to be set up, with powers over curriculum, teacher qualifications, textbooks and finance. "National Ethics," or inculcation of the doctrine of the "National Structure" was excised from school instruction, and there was put in its place a subject called "social studies." This was intended to be a training in the principles of democracy.

277

Privately prepared textbooks were to have a free field for adoption by any school. The curricula were to be more flexible, providing elective courses from high school on. Modern methods of teaching, group dynamics, and individual research were to become the practice.

The anatomy of the school system was to be changed from the one long in operation in Japan. Nine years of compulsory and free public education break into six years of primary, and three years of secondary grade, carrying the student through junior high school. Beyond that there are three years of senior high school, and the university. Later, since the gap filled by the old three-year "higher school" needed to be bridged, a two-year junior college was put into the system. Into these new forms the Christian schools have had to reshape their life. Many of the changes, though difficult of adjustment to Japanese tradition and temperament are congenial to Christian educational principles, and in time should work on the side of sound character nurture.

One reform unanimously espoused by the American Educational Mission but which was met with indifference and unconcern on the part of the majority of Japanese people was that of the abandonment of the use of Chinese ideographs in writing the Japanese language. The arguments for pulling up the tightly clinging roots of this ancient tree which spreads through all Japanese culture were cogently presented. Some educators and some newspapers promised to give the matter another trial, for it has often been agitated in the past. The old roots were not even loosened, and soon the whole matter was forgotten. The opinion of Westerners throughout all of Japan's modern century has been that Japan must give up this archaic form of communication and join the rest of the world in the use of phonetic symbols. But still the ancient ideographs, with the brush and ink-stone hold their place.

278

One of the massive undertakings of the immediate post-war period was the calling home of the six and a half million Japanese servicemen from all over Asia. Their rehabilitation was assigned to the Welfare Ministry of the government, which then turned to the YMCA and requested the services of Soichi Saito the talented General Secretary of the Association. He organized a staff sometimes exceeding 20,000 in number, and with rare distinction directed this task, bringing it to completion within three years.

As 1946 moved toward summer the physical plight of the people became alarming. The Occupation had resolved not to interfere in the daily living of the public, and to assume no responsibility for financial assistance. However, in addition to all the dislocations of war and all its privations, there was added the dismantling of the public agencies which, though they had controlled the people, had at the same time provided them with rationed subsistence and jobs.

The 1945 crop had not been turned in to the central government storing agencies, and in the general demoralization there was little power of enforcement. There may have been food in the farmhouses, but in the bombed cities there was small sign of any. People went into neighboring country districts and brought home in rucksacks a few days supply of food, paying for it by selling some family heirloom or prized garment. Even this was illegal and might be punished, for rationing and food control was still the law, though impossible of enforcement. The people were in a state of actual starvation such as they had never known during the war. Their body weight on an average was down one third, and their energy was almost gone. Many employees in the Occupation office buildings could scarcely drag themselves up the stairs.

At this juncture the Occupation came to the rescue. Food

was bought and imported from abroad for supplementing the local rationing. Not always suitable Japanese food, it nevertheless saved millions from starvation in 1946 and the following year when there was a worse crop failure. Permission was given for food parcels from abroad to be addressed to Japanese individuals. In the streets the heaps of debris piled along the curbs were levelled off and soon pathetic little crops of wheat and barley were waving their heads. Every traffic circle had a center of earth where a tiny garden was grown. Amid all the adversities of the defeat and the early disruptive years of the Occupation the Japanese people refused to bow to fate. Bravely and ingeniously they managed to survive.

In the Protestant Christian communities, relief work began, although it was not yet systematized. Individuals here and there shared what few possessions they had, moving over into one-half of a room to take in another family, devising schemes to help the needy, and serving on local bodies for relief-distribution. Dr. Kagawa was spiriting from somewhere the materials to build small barracks shelters for the Japanese servicemen who were coming back from overseas.

Church services were revived. For the most part they were held in the room or two in which a refugee pastor and his family had found space with some household that had escaped the flames. One Tokyo pastor whose church had been razed by government orders as a fire-brake, became an itinerant evangelist, ministering to five different types of people. He held weekly services among students, merchants, professional men, factory workers and government officials in five different parts of the city. He was one of many who did not survive the ordeal of those first years.

There was a dearth of Bibles. Japanese Christians know much Scripture by heart, but it meant a starvation as real as that of the body not to have a Bible or New Testament to carry to church, or to be without any text for daily worship at home. During the war years there had been no censorship of the Bible, but after 1942 no paper was issued nor was permission to print given by the government. Doling out a few thousand copies a year the Japan Bible Society finally had used up its entire stock when, in 1945, it was absorbed in the organizational life of the Kyodan. In the bombings of the Bible House in Tokyo all the paper molds were destroyed. In 1945 after the surrender there were no materials, nor were Japanese firms as yet permitted to publish books.

One of the first concerns laid upon the American Deputation of Four in October was that of trying to get Japanese Scriptures to the Christian people. In a few months, shipment after shipment began to arrive. The American Bible Society had set itself to produce and ship two million copies of the New Testament in two years. Arrangements were made to admit the books under the category of Chaplain's supplies. Distribution and pricing were a problem, for in the extreme demand for them they were almost in a class with American cigarettes as temptations to black-marketing. With care most of the supply found its way into Christian hands and stayed there. The quota was met, and by 1947 two and a half million copies had come to slake the thirst of the Christians.

The next felt need was for copies of the Union Japanese Hymnal (Sambika). It was nearly a year before they began to come. Fresh copies had to be obtained in America, then photographed page by page. Eventually nearly ninety thousand of these large hymnals with music were channelled out to Japan to take their place with the Scriptures.

In April, 1946 the first official link with American Christianity was established. The Boards in North America had decided to renew permanent relations by sending out a commission of six representative and experienced Japan missionaries. This was no easy task. At this time no person outside the employment of the Occupation was permitted to enter Japan. The Supreme Commander was eager for missionaries to return in large numbers, and he justified this position on the basis of the Potsdam Declaration's purpose to restore Japan to the normal society required for resumption of world relationships. But SCAP policy prohibited any religious favoritism (the Bibles and hymnals being among the few infringements of the principle). Missionaries could not avail themselves of army facilities of food, housing or transportation. Yet they must not be allowed to be a charge on an impoverished Japan. There was a stalemate of months as to procedure. Finally it was broken by a special regulation whereby one missionary of any denomination might go ahead and make provision on the field for the maintenance of others who would follow.

Under this arrangement two men were sent out; G. Ernest Bott, a United Church of Canada missionary of wide experience in Christian social work, and Paul S. Mayer, who for nearly forty years in Tokyo as a missionary of the Evangelical Association in church work had been at the center of the Japan Christian movement. They divided the task, Bott to organize relief from overseas Christian sources to meet the emergency, and Mayer to act as contact person with SCAP for the opening of channels for returning missionaries, as well for dealings with the Japanese churches.

By June, 1946 the remaining four of the Commission of Six were cleared and had arrived. They were: Miss Alice Cary, Congregationalist, who was to specialize in the renewal of contacts with Japanese Christian women and their work; Henry G. Bovenkerk, Presbyterian, U.S.A., with responsibility for relations with the Japanese church and evangelistic work; Karl D. Kriete, Reformed, U.S., with an assignment as liaison with Christian schools, and John B. Cobb, Methodist, whose territory was to be Osaka and Central Japan. They all quickly slipped into place and began to establish communication between the Christian movements of Japan and the West.

In June, Miss Esther Rhoads, Quaker, together with a representative of the Catholic Welfare Conference joined Bott to channel into Japanese society the abundant outpouring of Christian compassion coming from the churches of North America. The largest organization was Church World Service, but there were the corresponding relief agencies of the Church of the Brethren, the Friends Service Commission, the Mennonites, the Lutherans, and the Roman Catholics. These all were coordinated in LARA (Licensed Agencies for Relief in Asia).

With the help of the friendly and efficient Public Health and Welfare Section of SCAP, and of the splendid Welfare Ministry of the government they constructed a network of facilities for receiving, and distributing into all the prefectures of the country, the supplies coming from abroad. The administration at every level was tri-lateral, including representatives of the government, of private Japanese agencies for relief, and of LARA. The crisis was so great that denominational concerns were surmounted, and even Christians as such were given no special priorities. People were supplied according to their degree of urgent need, and no other questions were asked.

Ten thousand young waifs, orphaned by the bombings, wandered like wolf-packs among the ruins of the cities. Their wits sharpened by the hazards and thrill of such a wild life, they were on the way to become a major national problem of delinquency and crime. The relief program reached them, and their taming began with the care and

283

attention given them by those who distributed the supplies. Even persons who had some food were unable to get any with much nutriment. The fishing fleets had long since gone the way of the lost war, and there was no meat supply. There was no refrigeration if their had been any milk. LARA Powdered milk preserved the life of a generation of newly born babies. Patients in tuberculosis sanitariums were also rationed this milk. Later, lunches for the younger children in public schools brought up the general health level.

With all the ruin of the early postwar years, with the stop-gap facilities of housing, the lack of central water systems and of proper waste disposal, no major epidemic occurred. This is astonishing in view of the general state of emaciation of the people, and it is a tribute to their cleanliness, as well as to the efficiency of their medical service, and to the constant vigilance and activities of the Occupation section of Public Health.

In June, 1946 the Kyodan met in General Assembly at the Fujimicho Church in Tokyo. Travel was extremely difficult and only 220 of the 300 delegates managed to attend. Signs of poverty were everywhere evident in the nondescript clothing and equipment of the members. Yet there was an air of hope and of fellowship which inspired the few visiting Westerners. Clearly the war experiences had welded the members of the various former denominations into one single body with a spiritual unity that was constantly in evidence. There was no radical revision in the structure of the church, though the war had changed it from the intended semi-federated body composed of denominational blocs to an undivided whole. A few wanted a return to the original plan, but the great majority clung tenaciously to the deep unity already achieved, and made no change.

There was no suggestion of the withdrawal of any group.

The question of the wartime leadership was pressed by some of the younger men who wished a thorough replacement of officers. On the vote, the faithful Director of the church during the gruelling war years, Mitsuru Tomita, was succeeded as Moderator by Michio Kozaki former Chairman of the Board of General Affairs. Tomita was elected to the Executive Committee. No other officers were changed. Apparently the delegates felt that their leaders had done as well as anyone could and should not be set aside in favor of an untried group. No recriminations were made, and no rifts of feeling registered in any of the debates.

The changes from the wartime apparatus of the church were left to the Executive Committee to recommend to the Third General Assembly held in October, 1946 when the office of Director, The Greater East Asia Bureau and the Bureau of Indoctrination disappeared. A group of theologians and intellectuals pressed for a reconsideration of the creed. After a four-year stalemate with the powerful bureau of Thought Control of the Ministry of Education the experienced leaders were in no mood immediately to enter into the intricacies of theological debate and adjustment that would be certain to be required. The matter was referred to committee, not to be brought to a settlement until nearly a decade later.

The church was uncertain as to what attitude to take toward those who had been in trouble with the wartime government over their faith. Finally Onomura, fresh from his battles in the courts in Sapporo, took the rostrum and asked whether no recognition was to be given to those who had suffered for their faith. In response the assembly called to the platform several others who had been under arrest. Yet it seemed more an act of commiseration than one of approbation.

The spring of 1946 had brought other visiting church

representatives from the West. At the close of the war Presiding Bishop Yashiro of the Episcopal Church in Japan had led the church out of the underground and declared the canons reconstituted. It now remained to bring back those clergy and churches which had joined the Kyodan, and to determine the standing of the six persons who had been consecrated Bishops for service within the Kyodan by the two Bishops who had gone into it. The Church of England sent John Mann of the Church Missionary Society, and Samuel Heaslett, of the Society for the Propagation of the Gospel, and the Protestant Episcopal Church Council sent Charles Reifsnider, all three of these having been bishops in the Japan church.

It was the ruling of the Archbishop of Canterbury and of the Lambeth Conference that, while the consecration of the six bishops without the mandate of the church was irregular, yet it had been done by bishops according to the canons of the church, and so was valid. As to the clergy, they were not to be compelled to pass through a penitential process before reinstatement,—as was being planned,—but were ruled never to have been out of communion with the church, and they were therefore to be welcomed back in a simple service of reconciliation. Thus the Episcopal church in Japan was reunited and set on its way with the eventual loss of only one or two of its clergy who remained within the Kyodan.

At the same time Brigadier Charles Davidson came from London Headquarters of the Salvation Army commissioned to help extricate its Japanese division from inclusion in the Kyodan, as necessitated by wartime regulations. After a period of uncertainty this was accomplished, the Kyodan gave its blessing to the withdrawal, an independent leadership was set up, and the Army returned to its specific tasks as social and evangelistic outrider for the Christian movement.

286

The Christian schools came through the war years and their aftermath in varying degrees of dislocation. Some of them, particularly the oldest and those most deeply rooted in Japanese life, had made comparatively large accommodations to non-Christian pressures. These institutions had to carry out changes of leadership and administration. As a rule they were eager to do so, for the adjustments had been made under duress. The wartime officers recognized that their usefulness could not continue into the new regime of democratization. They resigned and were replaced by persons who were for the most part much closer to the life of the churches. Fortunately, only a small number of the schools had to undergo this change of administration.

The physical losses were unevenly distributed. Doshisha enjoyed the immunity granted the city of Kyoto as a cultural center respected by the enemy, and was not bombed. St. Paul's and Meiji Gakuin in Tokyo both strangely escaped the conflagration. Hiroshima Girls' School and most of the students were obliterated by the A-bomb. To-Hoku Gakuin in Sendai was wiped out. On the campus of Aoyama Gakuin in Tokyo ninety-three buildings of wooden construction went up in flames. As the bombs were incendiary and not demolition missiles the heavy concrete buildings still stood, but with all windows shattered and furnishings gone, gaunt ghosts of their former selves. None had any heating system; few even had stoves and there was no fuel.

Under these trying conditions the educators faced the first two years of the postwar period. Their work demanded long hours spent, for many of them, in half-destroyed buildings. Student discipline was gone, and teachers' morale was not much better. The wartime subsidies from government had stopped. Unlike the churches which were being given all the freedom they could use, the schools were under the close scrutiny and the crusading policies of an Occupation determined to make all educational institutions purveyors of the new democracy. To make matters more complicated the release of all thought-prisoners had given the Communists their chance. Persons who registered as students were appearing in every section of every class in the higher departments and universities, busily organizing their fellow-students for obstruction of school rules and policies.

Yet, in spite of difficulties the schools pressed forward. They had more resources than any local church, and they managed earlier than the churches, to get back into operation. Already some missionaries were returning, as Edwin T. Iglehart at Aoyama Gakuin, Tokyo. Others of German citizenship, such as Theodor Jaeckel of the German Evangelical Mission were ready to join the teaching staffs. In their spare time, several members of the Occupation forces were doing some teaching. There was a new freedom for Christian work on the campuses, and the very extremity of need of the students made them amenable to religious counselling and influence.

After all the factors have been viewed, however, the total scene shows a situation of emergency, of shock and of only a moderate capacity to react to the whirlwind of changing events going on. Both in Japan at large and in the Christian circles of Japan it was a time of impromptu planning, and of the need to experiment, but also a time of physical weakness in which original thought or experimentation was almost too much to ask. Yet among the ruins, love was at work in the administration of relief, in the reuniting of pre-war bonds of fellowship, and in the first stages of systematic planning for recovery.

THE YEARS 1947 AND 1948 may be characterized as a time of Rehabilitation. Emergency relief was still going on, but everywhere there were stirrings of initiative among the people which gave promise of recovery. In government, in industry, in education, and in all other areas of life the Japanese people were adjusting to the new regime, little by little absorbing it into the structure of Japanese society.

Shigeru Yoshida the Premier though personally conservative had honestly cooperated in the Occupation reforms. In 1947 his coalition fell, and with the swing toward a more hearty acceptance of the new order the Social Democrats came to power, with a Christian, Tetsu Katayama, as Premier. He was a disciple of Uemura, and a devoted elder in the Fujimicho Church. When the other Christian members of the Diet came to his office to congratulate him they brought their hymnals with them, and with his consent they held a little service of thanksgiving, sending the echoes of a hymn down the corridors of the building. During his year of tenure Katayama brought into law some of the most progressive of the new measures.

The Occupation continued to implement its basic policies. The war trials went on. The reform of the police system was enforced. Purges of individuals began. A record of any aggressive promotion of the philosophy of Japanese national life that had led to the war was considered sufficient cause for disqualifying a person from taking office or even from employment in his particular field. Boards of review were set up, and a total of 700,000 cases were investigated with a resultant purging of 200,000 persons. Many of these were school teachers.

Another negative measure was the breaking up of the network of great industrial and financial concerns of pre-war and wartime Japan. Their stock was sold to the public. Decentralization was carried out in other fields, one of the major aims being to shift responsibility away from the national capital and the central government to the prefectural and the local levels.

The organization of labor unions was encouraged. Two federations, corresponding to the American Federation of Labor and the Congress of Industrial Organizations in America, were formed, and eventually they enrolled over six million members. A drastic law limiting the ownership of farm land to seven acres abolished absentee landlordism, and made landowners of three-fourths of the former tenant farmers of the country. At one stroke this measure plowed under the agrarian unrest which had been such fertile soil for Communist agitation and extreme political action.

With these changes the Occupation staff began to feel that its work was nearing completion. General MacArthur asked Washington to negotiate a peace treaty, believing that the rehabilitation of Japan was sufficiently advanced for its government and people to assume responsibility for its future. In November, 1947, the national flag again appeared above the Diet building.

It was in this situation that the Christian community began to resume its functions. Following the 1946 Assembly of the Kyodan, an All-Japan Christian Convention had been held. It was the first such general Christian gathering since that of 1940 which had declared the intention of all the churches to unite, and it was held in the same place. Surrounded by the ruins of the city, the thousands of Christians assembled there renewed their pledge of loyalty to Christ, and launched a three year national campaign under the motto, "Christ for All-Japan." There were few financial resources in sight, travel was extremely difficult, national organization was almost impossible, yet the pastors and laymen carried this vision back to their homes, and the movement got underway.

The campaign was led by Toyohiko Kagawa who risked his health week after week, holding great meetings in public halls or in the open air, travelling from city to city, standing or sitting on the floor of crowded third-class railway cars. Every one of the major thirteen social settlements he had established was gone. The common people he loved were never in such dire need. Labor circles and rural areas called for his counsel and help. To every call he gave attention, and he extended some sort of help to every case of need. No amount of disaster could dismay him. His vibrant voice still could ring out in laughter. The skill with which he set up temporary measures for emergencies was amazing, but always at the center was his Christian message, burning for utterance.

Crowds of people would gather for any kind of a meeting. There was not much regular employment as yet; and at a time when any new thing might be seen or heard, curiosity led many persons to stop to listen. But deeper than these surface causes was the spiritual perplexity and the sense of inner shock of multitudes of earnest people. They deeply desired to know the truth, to find the way, and to gain strength for living. Japan was ready as never before in its history to give a hearing to Christianity. Kagawa saw this and rushed to the encounter. During the three years of the campaign nearly two hundred thousand cards of inquiry and decision were handed in.

In this period several groups of churches left the Kyodan to resume their own separate organizations. In October, 1946, Edwin Dozier of the Southern Baptist Convention returned. He cleared the way for the arrival of a large number of missionaries, later to reach the goal of one hundred. In April, 1947 the churches related to this mission met in Fukuoka and reconstituted themselves as the Japan Baptist Convention, after withdrawal from the United Church.

Lewis S. G. Miller of the United Lutheran Mission returned and established contact with the former churches and ministers. With their headquarters in Kumamoto these churches reorganized as the Japan Evangelical Lutheran Church. W. A. Eckel reopened the mission work of the Church of the Nazarene, and the churches of that denomination withdrew.

Within the Kyodan there was a group of pastors who wished a more distinct emphasis on the Reformed theology. They left the United Church and founded a separate denomination of their own, called the Japan Reformed Church. Altogether, it was reported, for various reasons about two hundred churches withdrew in the years 1946–1950. The Kyodan, however, more than replaced the losses by the addition of some five hundred new churches. These other denominations, too, with renewed vigor were writing their own chapters of Christian achievement.

In the summer of 1947 a decisive step was taken in mission-church relationships. As early as 1941, when the union had first came about, the North American bodies realized that this marked a new stage in the life of the "younger churches," and that it called for new departures in missionary policy. The East Asia Committee of the Foreign Missions Conference had set up a Japan Committee which met all during the war years anticipating a renewal of relations at their end. Within that committee, those boards willing to pool their interests in common planning and action for cooperation with the Kyodan arrived at a basic harmony of outlook. Then the war had ended.

For a year the Commission of Six in Japan studied the situation and reported. Matters were ready for joint action, and on January 9, 1947 in New York, representatives of the following churches met to establish a new body, as yet without name or form, but with a common purpose. They were: The Congregational Christian Churches, the Disciples of Christ, the Evangelical and Reformed Church, the Evangelical United Brethren Church, the Methodist Church, the

Presbyterian Church in the U.S.A., the Reformed Church in America, and the United Church of Canada. Two of the eight boards had separate Women's Divisions, bringing the total membership to ten.

Representatives of some of these bodies went to Japan, and in the summer of 1947 at Hakone entered into unhurried conference with sixty Japanese leaders of church and schools. Every phase of inter-relationships was explored, and the basic plan for future cooperation was sketched. The Kyodan leaders especially requested that there be no recurring grants for pastors, but that any aid received should go to special evangelistic and pioneer extension projects. Within a few months drafts of a constitution had been made, modified and accepted. The plan went into effect in 1948. In North America the churches and boards named above authorized representatives to constitute an Interboard Committee for Christian Work in Japan. The boards agreed to channel and administer all finances and personnel to Japan through this Interboard Committee. Here was indeed a revolution in missionary strategy, and it was recognized as calling for "fearless realism, dynamic planning, fluid organization and unselfish cooperation."

In Japan the Kyodan set up a Committee on Cooperation to deal with church-mission affairs. It was composed of twenty-four members, eight each as representatives of the Kyodan proper, of the National Christian Educational Association, and of the Interboard Committee. The last group of eight were missionaries, and they comprised a Field Committee of the Interboard for handling purely personal and family matters of the related missionaries. In 1949 when the League of Christian Social Work Agencies was formed, two representatives from that group were added. The moderator of the Kyodan was chairman. As administrative secretary on the missionary side Darley Downs has rendered conspicuous service. All initiative for policies was vested in this Committee on Cooperation, for the associated boards in North America had pledged themselves not to make any moves in Japan except on its request—another revolution in missionary practice.

Reports of the openness of Japan to the Gospel reached the churches in the West, and among the members there was a surge of renewed missionary interest. The Occupation policy, too, gave priority to those bodies which had had work in Japan before the war. But there were circumstances that made it difficult for the Interboard to channel quickly any considerable number of new missionary families. Housing was a problem. More than that, the period before the war had been one of few accessions to foreign mission ranks. Those families which had been evacuated from Japan had been assigned to other fields, or were back in the homeland in Christian work, not easily available for fresh recruitment.

It was of the genius of the Japan church, also, to stress self-reliance and responsibility, so that there was much of recovery of inner strength to be achieved before the leaders would reach the point of asking for reinforcements and assistance of foreign missionaries in large numbers.

The schools, however, were calling loudly for missionary reinforcements. In this situation the Methodist Board and some others went to the college campuses and presented the case for service as "J-3's"—that is, for going out immediately after graduation for a period of three years. In 1948 and 1950 over a hundred such young men and women volunteered. They were assigned to live in student dormitories, to teach English, and in their own natural way to communicate the Christian witness to the young people of their student world in Japan. It was an immense success. The young Western Christians were modest, teachable, devoted, and proved to be exceptionally gifted in their classwork and in personal relations. A number later married and returned for lifetime service.

Thus the early renewal of missionary contacts in the schools was accomplished. In the church life, however, it was 1950 or 1951 before a systematic program of missionary integration on any general scale got into action. This was given real momentum with the formation at that time of a Cooperative Evangelism Committee within the larger Committee of Cooperation, to encourage and supervise the work of Kyodan missionaries in "evangelistic," or church service.

In the meantime some of the smaller prewar missions were being reconstituted. Among these was that of the Swedish Missionary Alliance Church. After the war, its two or three families returned and resumed their work. Presently a stream of reinforcements began to come to join them, sent by churches of like outlook in America who found this organization a natural channel of entrance. The newcomers took over the administration of the mission and its institutions, changed the name to The Evangelical Alliance Mission (TEAM), and introduced a policy of separatism with relation to the older missions. When SCAP modified its regulations in 1948, admitting new postwar missionary bodies, large numbers of the Pentecostal and Fundamentalist groups poured into Japan. TEAM furnished a militant rallying center for the organization of their work.

A new factor within Protestant missionary life became visible when, after the resumption of the annual retreats and conferences of the fifty-year-old Fellowship of Christian Missionaries, another national missionary body, based on a conservative credal test was set up. As the Evangelical Missions Association of Japan (EMAJ) it largely parallelled the work of the other fellowship, with a publication *Japan*

Harvest, summer conferences, and the promotion of various missionary projects.

Among the new missions one of the strongest was that of the Lutheran Church, Missouri Synod. Under very able missionary leadership they established a center in Tokyo with extended work in the northern island of Hokkaido and in Western Japan. They founded a college, set up a separate Japanese language school for the training of their missionaries, and through their "Lutheran Hour" broadcast widely over the country.

After a visit from Charles W. Ransom and J. W. Decker, Secretaries of the International Missionary Council, the Japanese Christian leaders reconstituted the National Christian Council of Japan. It had rendered noteworthy service until the wartime pressures destroyed it. After Christian agencies had all been incorporated into the Kyodan there was no place for a National Christian Council, and it had dissolved. By 1948 several of the churches had separated from the Kyodan, and the schools, social work and other activities of the Christian movement had reorganized in functional groups. The need for an over-all Christian council again had become clear. In that year it was reorganized with Dr. Michio Kozaki as Chairman, and with much the same leadership as before the war. The veteran Akira Ebisawa was redrafted into service as its General Secretary. At once its influence as a coordinator of the Christian bodies and as a voice for Christian sentiment was felt.

In this period of Rehabilitation some rebuilding of physical plant did begin. No permits for private buildings could be obtained, and nothing more than temporary construction material was available, but under those restrictions some schools managed to get repairs done; and here and there a local church was being put into working order. The first assistance in replacing buildings came from abroad in the form of twenty Quonset huts given to the Kyodan for as many church properties. They still, in 1959, stood somewhat incongruously among the modern structures of later years,—a monument to the resourcefulness of Christians, in the first hardest days after the war.

THE YEARS 1949 AND 1950 may be called the period of Reconstruction in the Japanese Christian world. In the general life of Japan they were that, as well. In the Occupation a great change had come.

At the first mention of a peace treaty with Japan, all the slumbering tensions and jealousies within the ranks of the Allies had asserted themselves. It was clear that even among the friendly powers no agreement was in sight and that the Soviet Union stood ready to block any American proposal. When this became plain the Supreme Commander—presumably with the concurrence of the American Government —settled down to a continuance of the Occupation, but on a caretaker basis with relation to Japan. The war trials were brought to their gloomy end. The dismantling policies were left to be enforced or not, largely as the Japanese Government should please. The dismemberment of the great business interests went by default. SCAP turned to the rescue of the slipping economy and to the encouragement of industry. The yellow paint markings on the factory machinery previously assigned to be taken for reparations was brushed off, and the machinery was put to work for Japan.

Economic advisors from America charted a new course, setting aside the system of government subsidies and opening the field for competitive development of industries. A more lenient issuing of permits for foreign trade was adopted. Ship-building was permitted once more. Even the heavier industries began to come back, and the sound of steel construction could be heard. The Yen was pegged, and by a policy of firm control inflation was stopped. The shops began to show color, On the streets people were sometimes seen in Japanese dress, in place of the drab khaki wartime garments worn by men and women.

Yoshida was again Premier, working happily in the sunlight of the friendly Occupation. With the new slant in policy foreign traders were admitted into the country. It is to the credit of the Occupation that it permitted no exploitation of Japan by American business. In the hour of Japan's helplessness there were no "carpet-baggers" to despoil it. Men representing the major American industrial and financial interests were employed by the Occupation, but their firms could not do business in the country. This gave time for the domestic recovery of the economy before foreign trade began. When it did reopen it was under Japanese law which kept all foreign concerns on a level of competition with their Japanese rivals. By what was called "Private Point 4", foreign firms did invest large sums of capital in Japan, but it was to the mutual profit of themselves and of the country.

In the summer of 1950 Korea became a battlefield, with General MacArthur in command. From then on, every American serviceman in Japan was potentially in that war, and every Japanese factory was an arsenal essential to victory. The "Great Reversal" had swing the Occupation from the position of overlord to that of ally. Japan was virtually on its own. A period of unprecedented prosperity followed.

The Christian movement reflected the general situation. It was a time of reconstruction. Restored to health and with returning energy the leaders of church and schools made plans of renovation and building. In the schools, men of affairs on the boards of trustees were now back, giving wise guidance to the temporal side of the i nstitutions. Some of them had managed to salvage their business and were able to renew their financial help. Others unheard of before, emerged as captains of shipping, manufacturing and banking. Alumni of the schools joined hands to help in the work of reconstruction, and large fund-raising campaigns were common. The Southern Presbyterians established the Shikoku Christian College, at Zentsuji.

At this time a number of schools moved to new locations, obtained before the revival of life had made the purchase of land too difficult. Various schemes of a semi-commercial sort under government license brought in funds with which to rebuild and even to expand some of the institutions. The schools, however, were not affluent, They were in desperate need of reconditioning; and this took large sums of money. When all their local resources were cast up there was always a deficit. This was the point at which friends from the churches of the West with their financial assistance saved the day.

The rebuilding of churches was going on. Of the 1,600 major church buildings in the country about 500 had been lost. Many parsonages, too, were burned. After the Quonset huts, some prefabricated buildings of aluminum were imported. By 1950 it was possible to obtain materials including heating systems in Japan. Competent architects, reliable builders and efficient workmen could be had. Aid from abroad now took the form of financial grants.

In the Kyodan a Reconstruction Commission passed on every case. The general rule was that no local church would receive more than $3,000 from overseas, and that they must themselves meet a minimum of one-tenth of the cost. This may seem a small amount, but in the local churches pastor and people alike had very little income. Pastors were slightly better off than in 1946 when their average monthly income was less than the bill at the rice-shop, but they were still terribly under-paid. Supplementary work was frowned upon. Their libraries were gone, and had to be replenished, the children had to meet their school expenses. They were in a bad plight. The members, too, were not in the position of the few wealthy alumni mentioned with relation to the schools, most of whom were not Christians. The ordinary church members had little financial margin. Out of their poverty they gave sacrificially, and helped to re-house Protestant Christianity.

Christian social work revived. The distribution of relief by LARA had never stopped, and eight million dollars worth of supplies came during the five years. In addition, the postal authorities reported about a million dollars worth of CARE parcels sent to individuals every year. Under the new regime many enlightened laws had gone into effect. Social Security for old age, a Child Welfare law, and the organization of City Community Chests were all aimed at social amelioration.

In 1949 Communism reached its peak in numbers and conspicuous strength, when three million voters placed thirty-five members in the Diet. They were still obstructive, but some of their activities tended toward social justice. At times they joined with the more moderate Socialists in promoting social legislation. Labor unions were strong, and on a rising tide of prosperity they were able to obtain far better working conditions and wages than ever before. In all her history as a modern nation Japan had never been so near to being a welfare state under a free electorate.

There was, however, much room for improvement, and the social agencies of the churches, badly hurt by the war, were again called into service. In all the denominations there was renewed work for the blind and for disabled persons, and care of tuberculosis patients. Homes for the aged and orphanages sprang up, most of which were the lengthened shadow of some one dedicated person. With very little equipment they were nevertheless a Christian witness of compassion and made a wide appeal. Some new social settlements were established, such as that at Taura near the naval station of Yokosuka. A large officers' club reconditioned for many forms of social service became a busy center for an active program of community welfare. It was said that there was not a household in the entire city which was not in some way a beneficiary of the Center.

The YMCA and YWCA's with their large city plants suffered greatly, and were late in recovering their occupied or destroyed properties, but by 1950 they reported much progress. In most of the cities the local members had handled the campaigns and supervised the reconstruction. The national headquarters in Tokyo was rebuilt, the spacious city building was restored and the usual program was resumed. The YWCA in Tokyo was similarly restored and at work. In Nagoya a new social service project had been initiated.

Several visitors from abroad brought strength to the Christian movement. Dr. E. Stanley Jones in 1949 made his first evangelistic tour, and was welcomed everywhere. Thereafter he has made it a practice to go every second year, remaining for several months. His procedure has been to speak two and three times a day in sixty or seventy cities. In these campaigns sponsored by the Japan N.C.C. Dr. Jones has gathered decisions by signed cards in the scores of thousands. His energy is inexhaustible, and with deep dedication he gives himself utterly in this service. The postwar years would be hardly recognizable without Dr. Jones' periodic campaigns.

Another unusual service was rendered in 1950 by Lawrence Lacour who with his wife and four young ladies made up a musical troupe. In their caravan of cars and trailer they toured the cities and towns of Japan, giving concerts on assorted instruments, singing Gospel hymns and offering quiet meditations through an interpreter. It was altogether novel, and it met with a general welcome. Half a million people listened to the presentations, and thousands made decisions.

Dr. Emil Brunner, the eminent theologian of Switzerland visited Japan, and lectured in the seminaries, greatly stimulating the pastors and students. In the summer of 1950 Professor John C. Bennett of Union Theological Seminary, New York, spent some time in Japan holding seminars and giving lectures. His visit marked a turning point in the thinking of many theologians and pastors. He combined a solid theological grasp with a sensitive social awareness which was a new phenomenon in their experience. Hitherto the social witness in the Christian movement in Japan had tended to be accompanied by a somewhat casual attitude toward doctrine.

The history of Christian social thinking in Japan is a story of either retreat to the security of the study or else of a radical advance along social lines that have finally led outside the Christian circle. Among the church leaders and theologians there was very little application of Christian thought to social problems. As a result of the friendly discussions and interviews with Dr. Bennett some of the most influential thinkers in the church, such as President Hidenobu Kuwada of the Japan Union Theological Seminary testified to a new view of the social responsibility of the Christian.

In the same year, 1950, Miss Irma Highbaugh, experienced as a China Missionary and the Secretary of the Home and Family Life Commission of the International Missionary Council, spent several months in residence, conducting conferences and seminars. It was something of an innovation for the women to be told that they and their husbands would

302

be expected to attend meetings together. In all their lives many of them had never made such a venture, but now some did make the experiment. They found themselves in a new world of open discussion of family problems between men and women. It was a time when the laws provided women with complete political and economic rights, but when many of them did not know how to avail themselves of freedom from the conventional restraints of tradition. The Christian church had been a trail-blazer in youth guidance. It had also furnished examples of ideal home life among its ministers and members. Miss Highbaugh's visit added a new range of possible service to the family in the new Japan.

Another emphasis related to the home was brought by Harold H. MacConnell, of the Evangelism Department of the National Council of Churches of Christ, U.S.A. He came to commend the method of Visitation Evangelism in use by many American churches. In Tokyo and several other cities he demonstrated the techniques of systematic neighborhood visitation by Christian laymen and women.

In the early Occupation years no Japanese was permitted to travel abroad. Even by 1947, when the first postwar meeting of the International Missionary Council was held at Whitby in Canada, there had been no Japanese representative in attendance. The one single exception was the passport issued to Rev. Mrs. Tamaki Uemura, daughter of Masahisa Uemura and herself the pastor of a strong Church in Tokyo. In May, 1946 she came as a friendly ambassador on the invitation of the women of the Presbyterian Church, USA, and made a lasting impression by her modesty, and great ability. When she returned she took back for presentation to the Empress a beautifully bound copy of the Bible. For several years she made weekly visits to the Imperial Palace, by Imperial command, to give the Empress

303

Christian instruction, and to teach her Christian hymns.

By 1950 the ports were open and the waterways were carrying two-way traffic. Japanese church leaders were beginning to make visits abroad and to attend world conferences as before the war.

THE YEARS 1951 AND 1952 were a time of dramatic change. For the Christian movement they may be seen as years of Recovery. In Korea the tides of war rolled back and forth inconclusively. The desire of the United Nations was to effect a truce and settlement. President Truman communicated this policy to General MacArthur and instructed him in pushing back the North Korean forces to stop at the 38th Parallel. It was feared that any movement of troops beyond that point would mean involvement with China. General MacArthur held strongly dissenting views, and gave public utterance to them. On April 10, 1951 by a curt cable message he was suddenly relieved of his command, dismissed as Supreme Commander and ordered home. In silent obedience the mighty Shogun took plane and was gone.

At first the news was received with incredulity. But the nation came to see it as a striking demonstration of democracy in action. General Matthew B. Ridgway, the new Supreme Commander never aspired to the role of his predecessor. He viewed his task as that of liquidating an Occupation already spent in force and changed in direction. He gave the Japanese government a free hand, with permission to review every directive issued since the beginning. At once there followed the restoration of the purged persons, the reassembling of the commercial forces, and a modification of some of the other more extreme policies. Essentially, the state of the nation was not shaken, for already it had been exercising a large degree of freedom, and the constructive work of the Occupation was preserved.

The Allies proceeded with the preparation of the Peace

Treaty which was signed on September 3, 1951 at the San
Francisco Conference. It was ratified in October and November, and in April, 1952 it became effective. At long last
the Occupation had come to an end. It was time. Since the
Great Reversal of almost three years before, the moral
authority for the reform of militarism and the appeal of
the Allied Occupation reconstruction for freedom had largely gone. General MacArthur had repeatedly said that Japan
was ready to take the helm. The government and people felt
that this was true. It was with immense relief that they
assumed full responsibility for their recovered autonomy.
"Japan was out of its ashes."

In the Christian community, the recovery went on. In
downtown Tokyo on the busy Ginza, the Christian Headquarters building was renovated and became the home of
a wide range of Christian activities. Similarly in Osaka, the
Christian laymen under the leadership of Motoo Sakata had
projected a Christian center, and in western Japan at
Fukuoka another one was under construction. The schools
reported that most of the basic rebuilding was complete and
that they could turn to their pressing advance programs of
expansion. Many of the former middle schools and Girls'
higher schools were qualifying as junior colleges. The
former colleges were receiving charters as universities, and
some were starting graduate courses leading to higher
degrees. Student morale was restored, and the faculties were
working with zest in the more democratic atmosphere of
the new school system. The administration in most schools
was having trouble with the powerful left-wing Japan
Teachers' Union, but the agitation was sometimes in the
direction of progressive change.

The most conspicuous postwar Christian educational development was the founding of the Japan International
Christian University. A pastor in Richmond, Virginia,

called on the churches of America to make a gift to Japan as a token of penitence and reconciliation. The result was a plan for a Christian University, international in faculty and students, and supra-denominational in its support. For fifty years this had been the unrealized dream of Japanese Christians. It had always had to wait until the various Christian colleges in Japan had been provided for, and its turn had never come. Though encountering many difficulties the plan went forward under the leadership of Ralph E. Diffendorfer, then serving as Secretary of the Methodist Board of Missions. After his retirement, he became the full-time organizer of the movement and labored for it unsparingly until his death. In Japan an influential Committee undertook a large share of responsibility, and soon by their efforts a magnificent site and building near Tokyo had been purchased. Dr. Hachiro Yuasa resigned his presidency of Doshisha University and became the administrative head. The first class was admitted in 1951.

The Japan Union Theological Seminary, training institution for the men and women ministers of the Kyodan, found a fine site near the International Christian University, where after erecting six new buildings it moved in 1951. Embodying the united forces of fifteen former schools, it established a strong faculty; and its six classes of students came to a total of over two hundred. One fifth of the number were women. It received a university charter. In residential Tokyo, the Japan Biblical Seminary enlarged its work by evening classes, with a special emphasis on the training of women church workers. Among the newer mission groups several Bible Training schools were started.

The handling of overseas fellowships for Japanese theological students was systematized, through the NCC, and an annual group of about thirty was being sent.

The Kyodan celebrated its tenth anniversary in 1951.

Among the churches, too, the major work of rebuilding was complete, though everywhere there were calls for help in establishing new ones. The emphasis on evangelism became strong. In a national conference between church leaders and representative missionaries, ways were explored for a more full and vital integration of their work with the life of the Kyodan. This proved to be a great help to the morale of the missionaries, and it gave an impetus to new programs of aggressive evangelism within the church.

At the General Assembly of the Kyodan in 1951 the movement within the church for a degree of denominationalism came to an issue, and about forty churches withdrew. Most of the pastors were loyal disciples of Dr. Uemura. His daughter joined the movement. They re-organized under the name of their former Presbyterian Church. Since that time there have been no further withdrawals.

The Episcopal, Baptist, and Lutheran bodies reported a similar degree of recovery in their church life and related institutions. Among the Lutherans there was a stream of new missionary personnel representing churches in America and the Scandinavian countries which had not had work in Japan. Numbers of missionaries from various denominations had come from China when the revolution of 1949 forced them to leave.

Student Christian centers resumed work at full strength, with more young people coming than ever before. The YMCA moved into a Five Year Plan of balanced expansion of city work, student work and the establishment of centers in selected villages,—a new departure in "Y" strategy in Japan.

The production of Christian Literature received great encouragement when Professor Floyd Shacklock of Drew University was sent to Tokyo in 1950 to help plan a forward movement among the Christian publishing agencies. After the war, recovery had been slow. With the wholesale destruction of books, basic Christian works were an urgent necessity. Dr. Shacklock for two years held consultations and obtained united planning with publishers and booksellers in a program of cooperative publishing. A Christian Publishers Association was organized and a Christian Writers Association. With financial aid from the Western agencies a comprehensive range of publications new and old was projected. Christian classics, concordances and other reference books, and special series' for children and youth were among the first to be undertaken.

At the same time Mrs. Emily Hodder Shacklock, an expert in the field of Christian and missionary education, gathered together the scattered forces in the field of Church School work and achieved the beginnings of united work on a curriculum of study. The former National Sunday School Association of Japan in 1950 had been reorganized as the Japan Council of Christian Education and was again at work.

During the almost seven years of the postwar period Japan had moved swiftly but gradually back toward a normal life. There was still a long way to go, and it was to be in a world itself undergoing cataclysmic changes. But the main factors of change and decision within the nation had already appeared. The developments would be in the implementing of these, rather than in any sudden or unforeseen new directions. In the Christian community, too, the general courses and goals had been set, and the elements that were to be operative in the coming years were already in evidence.

Both in the Catholic and in the Protestant communities the groundwork for a continuance of normal life and growth had been laid. The periods of Relief for those in extreme need, of the Rehabilitation of the people, of the Reconstruction of destroyed properties, and of a general Renewal of church life, had been successfully passed with systematic co-operation from fellow-Christians outside Japan. All these tasks had cleared the way for the remaining years of advance that were to bring the Protestant churches to the celebration of their first century in modern Japan.

CHAPTER SIX

RENEWAL AND ADVANCE

1952—1959

Japanese Christianity
Faces the Future

EVENTS OF THE POST-OCCUPATION
YEARS IN THE NATION

1952–1959

With the return to autonomous national life Japan faced a double set of issues and problems. There was the bloodless revolution into the pattern of an Anglo-Saxon welfare State, which was the legacy of the Occupation. These new patterns required careful and detailed modification if they were to be absorbed into Japanese society. A second set of problems, however, came from the fact that the Treaty of Peace brought by Secretary of State Dulles in the name of the San Francisco signatory powers was matched by a Security Pact to be signed the same day. This attached Japan to the Western powers in the massive cold war developing with the Soviet Republic and its allies. The terms provided for a continuance of military bases in Japan, over seven hundred in number at the time. Within a few months an Administrative Agreement established something like extra-territoriality for the Western military and naval forces. Later by the requirement of the Mutual Security Aid plan Japan was forced to adopt a disguised but real re-armament program. The nation instead of being freed from a coercive post-war occupation now found itself bound under signed agreements to participate in what threatened to be a preparation for another war. As the outpost of the West in the East, Japan was obviously a potential battle-field.

Although deeply appreciative of the lenient terms of the Treaty, the public mind was plunged into renewed shock and apprehension by the new developments. Military alliances and wars no longer had any attraction for a people who had gone to ruin by that tragic path. Yet there seemed no escape from the new involvements. The history of the succeeding years has been one of the inter-twining of life with the West, especially with the United States, at the same time that there has been recoil at the terms under which that dependence has had to be bought.

Politically, there was a swing of responsible government toward the conservative position. Shigeru Yoshida, the "One Man Cabinet" held office until 1954, when the unpopularity of the Mutual Security compacts made him yield his office to his rival, Ichiro Hatoyama. Nobusuke Kishi became Premier in 1956. All this time the two or three conservative parties were splitting and finally coalescing into one group, the Liberal Democratic. In the meantime the groups to the left of center were doing the same until, in 1955, right- and left-wing sections of the Socialist Party were reunited.

The parties reflect the subterfuges of present political life in Japan. The popular outcry against rearmament, against a treaty as yet not signed by the Communist countries, and against the presence of large foreign forces and installation is a political rallying chorus. Any party assuming the responsibilities of office, however, must find ways of seeming to represent the public demand while at the same time acceding to the inescapable realities of Japan's precarious and dependent national position.

The Communist Party has followed an undulating course responsive to Moscow directions. Until 1951 it remained within legal bounds, but at that time a change of policy to aggressive tactics led to the "red purge" by the police, when the strength of the party seemed to have been broken. After the assumption of autonomy in the nation, on May Day, 1952, anti-foreign riots and street fighting with police took place in Tokyo. This was so strongly condemned by the public that thereafter there was little sign of violence. Instead of aiming at political power the movement has operated largely underground. Candidates for the Diet have been set up in great numbers, as the party has never been legally banned. The process of electioneering has offered an ample opportunity for spreading the doctrines of Communism. In 1958 there was but one member in the Diet. The actual size of the party was then thought to be about two hundred thousand, but the number of fellow-travellers was probably around one million. The official strategy seemed to be that of quiet waiting for some crisis to offer an occasion for vigorous action.

The political complexion of most Christians of the period under review cannot be sharply defined, though it was probably one of moderate conservatism. Of the eighteen Christian members of the Diet in 1958, however, a majority belonged to the right-wing Socialist group. They were solidly in support of the progressive features of the Occupation changes, and their affinities of spirit were with America; yet they were working for a position of neutrality, or better, for one of reconciliation in the cold war. They urged renewal of life with China.

312

In international relations Japan had made a creditable come-back. Eager to repair the damage to community in Asia and to restore friendly relations, the approach was usually one of economic agreements. These involved adjustment of reparations by payment in goods and services. There has been some prospecting by Japanese industrialists for openings in Indonesia, the Philippines, Thailand, and other countries of Asia.

In 1955 Hatoyama negotiated a treaty of friendship with Russia, though not an actual peace treaty. The fisheries arrangements were again operating, greatly to Japan's relief. Trade commissions had been exchanged with China. Japan belonged in the Colombo Plan sponsored by the West, and her delegates also attended the Bandung Conference of Afro-Asian nations in 1955. By the end of 1956 diplomatic relations had been restored with seventy-one nations.

Economic renewal has been a central issue. It is bound up with the matter of increasing population. During the war the casualties of a million and a half were more than replaced by births. The increase in some particular postwar years had been as high as a million and a half. Widespread and sometimes desperate measures of birth control have been employed to keep the increase to a smaller level, but the total inexorably rises. In 1959, the population approximated ninety-two millions. The food supply must be supplemented from abroad, payment to be made in manufactured goods or currency. Thus Japan's livelihood depends on manufactures and trade, upon natural resources from abroad and markets overseas. Every oscillation of economic life registers in jobs, wages, working conditions and in family life. Christians are deeply influenced by all this.

Farming has received a great impetus from the new laws. There was some hardship in the virtual expropriation of the land held by landowners. The sudden transfer of the

313

responsibility of ownership to men who had never borne it, also meant a risk. Without capital to carry costs around the crop-year till marketing, there is the danger of the land's slipping back into the money-loaning banks of the nearby towns, usually owned by the landlords. Encouragingly, the gain in the annual harvests for the past few years are an evidence of the capacity of former tenants to cooperate with government in increasing acreage, in the use of some new machinery, and in social organization, for mutual welfare. For the first time in the modern century in 1959, the Japanese farmers were getting a fair share of the "New Deal."

In the laboring world there has been parallel renewal and advance. The strong labor unions have been a force for humanizing industry. National laws have made great advances toward this goal. Between the lingering tradition of employer responsibility of the feudal days and the enlightened public demands of the present period, hand and machine workers, notwithstanding their many problems, are facing a better day.

The reforms in education have brought general improvement. A new atmosphere of free research and of teacher-student relationships is generally felt. Teachers of primary schools have always maintained a parental control of the pupils, but above those grades there has traditionally been very little personal contact. The new emphasis is on counselling through high school and into the college level. The accrediting of the many new universities has been taken seriously. In providing for the nine years of free public education the ten thousand new local boards of education are finding difficulties in current financing, in construction of new buildings, and in obtaining trained instructors. Following an immemorial impulse they are appealing to the central government for assistance.

The Ministry of Education is steadily renewing its strength—though possibly to the general good of public education. A national scholarship fund is drawn on by one half all students in higher schools. The search for a suitable dynamic for inculcating loyalty to the nation as well as for sound moral personal behavior goes on, but with no change in the curriculum as of 1959. There is a demand for a more adequate teaching of science in the atomic age.

From about 1950 the general religious situation began to show signs of recovery. The first postwar years of shock and confusion had been hard on the old faiths. Occupation policies regarding the separation of church and state drastically cut into their strength. There was a tendency for the public to make friendly inquiry into the claims of Christianity, the faith of the conquerors.

As energy returned, as the families became reunited and rehabilitated, and as life moved back into some of its old channels the hereditary religious systems resumed their hold. Shrine Shinto learned that it could command voluntary support which was more fruitful for a free program of activities than the former tax-maintenance system. Many shrines were rebuilt. Pilgrimages enlisted more people than before, At Isé, the central national shrine, there never were so many worshippers. The Yasukuni Shrine in Tokyo appealed for support to the relatives of the one and a half million of the war dead whose spirits were enshrined there. It received an unprecedented response in warm and generous loyalty. A powerful central Shrine Headquarters Association, assisted the one hundred thousand shrines of folk Shinto throughout the country to resume their central place in neighborhood life.

The Buddhist bodies, too, generally recovered their lost ground. Temples were rebuilt by the offerings of believers. Deprived of the income-earning lands attached to temples, many priests had to take up practical pursuits for a livelihood. They taught the tea ceremony, flower arrangement and the other cultural disciplines associated with Buddhism, which lie at the heart of refined living in Japan. These services have opened the way to household contacts other than those of the former customary funeral visits. This changed position of the priests has helped restore the pastoral ministry of Japanese Buddhism. When in the thirteenth century Japanese leaders broke away from the monastic type of the faith common in India and China they established a form of popular Buddhism. The priests were permitted to marry, and they lived their lives among the common people in an everyday ministry. Observers of the contemporaneous scene feel that with this renewed emphasis on neighborhood concern there is a new interest in the religious training of children, in lay activities, and in the teaching element in Buddhist life.

The mission of Buddhism to promote world peace is widely felt. When Muriel Lester, international secretary of the Fellowship of Reconciliation has come to Japan she has received a tumultuous welcome from a group of pacificists of the Nichiren sect. This sect has traditionally been Buddhism's fighting nationalist wing in Japan. A series of world conferences of Buddhists has drawn together the leaders from all the Asian nations, and Japanese Buddhists with the rest. In 1952 Japan was host to the second of these world conferences, which was held in Hirosaki of Northern Japan. The conference cited for meritorious services a Christian missionary formerly resident in the city. Buddhists are projecting foreign missions. Teachers of the Zen and True Land sects have been sent to North America and the Latin American countries. National evangelistic services are common. Such an outreach requires a popular presentation of Buddhism. It aims at a personal decision of conversion or of a return to the faith for the individual,—a concern which conventional Buddhism in the past has seldom felt.

Much has been written concerning the new religious sects in Japan, and their origin. Before 1940 there used to be some fifty or more officially recognized Buddhist sects, thirteen sects of voluntary Shinto, and perhaps seventy registered missions and Christian denominations. The control law of 1940 forced these all into a total of forty-one bodies, allowing Christians only two. In 1945, the Occupation removed all controls, whereupon the original sects separated, and in many cases they broke up still further under religious leaders with their separate followings. Some of these leaders were frauds, attempting to make money or to escape a purge under the cover of religion. Soon there were over seven hundred bodies listed. In 1951 as one of the last acts of the Occupation, a Religious Juridical Persons Law was recommended and was passed by the Diet. This was a modified statute, midway between the extremes of the controls of 1940 and the license of 1945. It called for registration and for suitable compliance with laws for property-holding and finance, as qualification for tax exemption and for other forms of recognition as religious bodies. Even this mild law strained out one half of the religions and left a total of about 375, or roughly two hundred started since the war.

Most of the new sects spring from Buddhist sources—many of them from Nichiren Buddhism—or from a Shinto tradition. Some of them have an infusion of Christian procedures and influence, but in most cases they do not acknowledge any debt from the West. They stress faith healing, communication with the spirits of the departed, mental tranquilization, family concord, world peace, and, in a subdued key, the prosperity of the nation. This latter

317

theme really means renewed loyalty to the Emperor. It is easy to see how these new bodies, with their group-fellowships, their emotional aspects, and their application of faith to the immediate areas of personal experience and need, do offer to their ten or fifteen million adherents an alternative to Christian conversion on one side, as real as Communism is on another side. As of 1959, however, the new religions do not seem to be adding greatly to their numbers.

EVENTS AND ACTIVITIES IN THE PROTESTANT MOVEMENT

1952-1959

During these years the National Christian Council was the clearing-house for the denominations that comprise two-thirds of all the Protestant community. It, therefore, makes a natural point of observation from which to view the events that were of national scale in significance. It has been the spokesman in voicing concern over problems arising out of the security affiliations with America, and related questions. A very able group of laymen, most of them prominent in public life, constitute the Commission on International Affairs. They have been alert to dangers arising from the. widening of the military installations, and have protested. In 1954 the NCC appealed to Christians in America to put an end to the testing of atomic weapons such as that on the Bikini Atoll in the Southern Pacific, when the fall-out poisoned the air and water and caused the death of a fisherman a hundred miles away. They repeated their protests when the secret weapon, "Honest John," was distributed to Japanese military forces. Again they spoke out when the military bases in Okinawa were to be enlarged. The Japanese delegation at the meeting of the General Assembly of the World Council of Churches in Evanston, Illinois in 1954 presented a request for repudiation of the cold war by the world's Christian forces, and called general attention to the agonizing desire for a peaceful world on the part of Japanese Christians.

At home, the Commission on General Affairs has addressed itself to current problems of society. They protested the suggested return of religio-ethical teaching in the public schools. When a repressive labor law and one to enlarge the authority of the police were presented in the Diet they publicly opposed them. They called attention to the looseness in controlling prostitution, and raised their voice against the craze of gambling at bicycle races, dog racing, and in the innumerable pinball dens that mushroomed all over Japan during the Occupation. The Protestant forces feel a responsibility for the moral welfare of the nation.

In 1952 a furor was raised by sensational reports of large numbers of children of mixed parentage who had been abandoned by their servicemen fathers. The Japanese people are no less fearful of an interfusion of alien blood than some of their Anglo-Saxon neighbors, and they were in a state of near-panic at the prospect of hundreds of thousands of such children. A special committee was set up, and a careful survey was made. The published results showed that there were five thousand in all, of whom nine-tenths were being cared for by their mothers, and that only five hundred were scattered in one hundred orphanages throughout the country. Most of them had reached school age at about 1955, and the adjustment to school life and to the neighborhood at that time seemed to be progressing successfully. A joint committee of Americans of all faiths undertook to assist in the adoption of the children in Japan, and to oversee the well-being of those left in institutions. Mrs. Renzo Sawada, whose husband was long in diplomatic service established in her villa at Odawara the Elizabeth Saunders Home for such youngsters until they might be taken for adoption.

The moral conditions surrounding the Occupation military installations cried out for action. Discipline stopped at the gate, where every conceivable temptation lurked for the lonely soldier, or for the one unused to discipline or decent living at home. Thousands of "pom-pom" girls in cafes or on the streets called themselves "heroines" because it was they who, in large part, drew from the pockets of the foreign servicemen the many million dollars each year that were spent on recreation. Without trying to allot the mutual blame between the American boys and the Japanese girls, Mrs. Ochimi Kubushiro, herself the heroine in many a battle for moral reform as the national director of the work of the WCTU, went to Kure Naval Station near Hiroshima, and got the pastor of a local church to open its doors in a welcome for the men from the installation. From this small beginning the project grew until six or seven centers were opened. The Presbyterian Church, U.S.A., sent out Norman Koehler and his wife for a three-months survey. They were so impressed by the needs and possibilities of the work that they remained for three years. Under the joint auspices of the Chaplains organization, the foreign missionary agencies in America, and the Japan National Christian Council, this ministry of Christian friendliness has continued going on.

From the side of the servicemen, too, there have been touching examples of friendliness. The Chaplains voluntarily established a scholarship fund at the Tokyo Union Theological Seminary, in honor of Chief of Chaplains Ivan L. Bennett, and by 1954, they had made offerings in various chapel-centers amounting to over thirty thousand dollars.

In preparation for the Evanston Conference of the World Council, the Japanese churches in 1953 held a conference on the Mission of the Church, and the following year they published its findings. These focussed attention on evangelism, as well as on service to society. Intensive evangelism by visitation had taken hold of the imagination of the churches when Dr. McConnell introduced it in 1951. Ryukichi Yoshida, associate to Dr. Kozaki in the pastorate of the Reinanzaka Church in Tokyo, had adapted it to Japanese patterns, and had put it to practice in what was called "volunter evangelism." He first selected five laymen—later increased to over sixty—and gave them training in Christian counselling, Bible study and the technique of evangelistic interviewing. They then went to the homes of neighbors as evangelists, to draw them into the church circle and to conversion. By 1954 Yoshida had proved the work of the plan by adding to the church each year over a hundred members. A national conference was held, with representatives of most of the 200 churches using the method, and practical training in workshops was done. Since then there has been a similar conference every year. The system calls for discipline, as the volunteer is to give from two to five evenings a week, to engage for long hours in prayer and Bible study, and to follow through with each new friend on a permanent basis of personal and family association. It is a very fruitful plan, though perhaps too exacting ever to become generally popular.

In the same year, 1954, another emphasis on evangelism developed to the point of national attention when the Joint Committee on Occupational Evangelism was set up. Since 1950 the Kyodan had turned its attention to the laboring people. In Kyushu several churches had been projected among miners. For years in Tokyo there had been training courses for laymen engaging in factory evangelism. A pastor in Yokohama gave up his church to devote himself exclusively to this work.

In 1954 Henry D. Jones, an experienced American home missionary worker in this field, and with experience overseas as well, was sent out by the Presbyterian Church, U.S.A. to coordinate the effort. By surveys, lectures, preparation of literature and by liaison work with laboring groups he was able to promote seven or eight centers of new work. Better still, he held before the attention of the Protestant community the necessity for entering the world of labor. In 1955 a "Labor Ashram" was held, and the following year, under the Social Problems Committee of the NCC, the Council of Labor Leaders and Christians was formed. At least a bridge had been thrown across the chasm separating labor and the church, and there was hope for the future.

Another form of intensive evangelism was tried in 1954. Lawrence Lacour, carrying the burden of the evangelization of Japan on his heart since his days as a Chaplain there, returned in 1954. He did not bring his musical troupe as in 1950, but had assembled for the project a score of American pastors, some of them accompanied by their wives. At their own costs they came and devoted the summer months to the project. Several small communities in Fukushima Prefecture were selected, and the visitors scattered among them, each one accompanied by a theological student assigned as an interpreter, and sometimes by a nearby pastor.

The difficulties of the Lacour plan seemed insurmountable, but once again, as in the case of the young "J-3s", it was proved that wherever direct and immediate personal contact is established between Western Christian workers of goodwill and Japanese people at large, a deep sense of community develops and friendships spring into life. Those villagers will never forget the strange, but lovable Americans who came in their friendly invasion. And all over America there

322

are ministers and their wives who never cease telling the story of village life in Fukushima Prefecture.

Every year from 1954 to 1959 such a Lacour mission has come. By 1957 twenty-seven churches had been founded as a result of these summer weeks of cultivation, and of them eleven were entirely self supporting. The plan could not have been successful without the cooperation and administration of a Japanese layman, Tomio Muto, editor of the *Christ News* and director of the Kyobunkwan, the commercial department of the Christian Literature Society.

Work among young people is stressed. All the major denominations have their own youth organizations, represented every year in the All-Japan Youth Conference sponsored by the NCC. In May an annual Japan Christian Youth Week is held, with discussion groups and workshops, as well as devotional disciplines. Young people crowd the frequent Peace Conferences that are held by various organizations in Japan, and also they go to the regional ones, throughout Asia. They express themselves vigorously on world issues, particularly on the atom and hydrogen bomb problems. In the summers, caravans are undertaken for evangelistic work in remote communities. International youth workshops are held, and delegates are sent to countries overseas for conferences. Japanese young people have a sense of their place in the Christian world.

The revision of the Japanese Old Testament had been going on throughout the war years; but by the time it was completed there had come a general demand for a more colloquial style of re-translation. The dignity of the old version had served its day; the new generation wanted a book that anyone might more easily read and comprehend. A committee of Japanese scholars was set up under the chairmanship of Senji Tsuru, Old Testament expert and later President of Meiji Gakuin. Working from 1951 to 1954 they completed the heavy task. It is a measure of the maturity of the church that with its comparative small numbers it could produce the scholarship to do this of its own strength, and financially that it could bear its equal share of the expense with the sponsoring American Bible Society and the British and Foreign Bible Society. With its accustomed energy the Japan Bible Society began to place the book in whole or in portions in the millions of homes of Japan. Since the war over twenty million copies of Scripture have been distributed, mostly through the seventy colporteurs who go in teams throughout the forty-six prefectures of the country.

Another eagerly awaited revision was that of the Union Hymnal. The vicissitudes of the book during the war were even more serious than those of Bible production, for the government, while permitting small editions of a few hymns, exercised the right of censorship. This kept the committee busy with attempts at compliance with wartime requirements rather than solely with supplying the worship needs of the congregations. After the war, publication slowly got under way again, but the musical advance of the church life was calling for a revised book. From 1950 to 1954 work was carried on by weekly meetings, under the careful direction of the Chairman Koh Yuki who had helped make the original book.

Again the church gave evidence of versatility with one half the committee Japanese professional musicians and the others men of national reputation in the field of literature. Fifty thousand copies of the book were sold as soon as published. The Committee has started a School for Church Music with a regular course and diploma recognition for work done. It conducts seminars and training institutes regionally in Japan, and offers prizes for hymns. The visit of Dean Williamson of the Westminster Musical School in

1957 was a great encouragement to the many choir directors who took his work, and transmitted the inspiration of this genius through church music to all their local choirs.

A personal tragedy in 1954 drew the Japanese Christian community near to the missionary body in sympathy when, in a storm off Hakodate, the ferry steamer foundered and Alfred R. Stone and Dean Leeper lost their lives. As a leader in rural evangelism and a selfless servant in every good cause, Stone, of the United Church of Canada had endeared himself to all Protestant Christianity. Dean Leeper a young YMCA secretary was proving himself in exceptional leadership of youth work. They were on their way to a conference on rural evangelism, and their mission, as well as the manner of their death, gave a tone of something almost like martyrdom to their lives of devoted service. When last seen both were helping others to safety.

The Japanese church took over the work of social welfare in a new way with the formation of Japan Church World Service in 1954. The original Church World service from America as a part of the work of LARA had come to an end of its work and was discontinued. The Japanese organization took up much of its task. In affiliation with the Division of Inter-Church Aid and Service to Refugees of the World Council of Churches, and working in collaboration with the Welfare Ministry of the Japanese government it carried on a wide ministry to those in need. About one half of its resources have gone through semi-official channels to institutions in all of the prefectures where, under branch organizations, it has been distributed. The rest has been held to meet emergency situations of flood, famine or fire.

The "returnees" from service overseas were rehabilitated on land which was too poor to support them, and they have been helped. Service is rendered persons about to emigrate.

Stateless European refugees from Siberia and Hongkong have been assisted through passport service and travel guidance to reach other countries. The American program of "Share Our Surplus", whereby grain and other foodstuffs are given free provided transportation in Japan is furnished, has been channelled through the Japan Church World Service as one of its main activities.

The Christian Children's Fund of Richmond, Virginia under the direction of J. C. C. Clarke has made possible continuous aid to nearly three thousand orphans, in over fifty institutions. Many of these gifts come from personal sponsors overseas. In 1957 the Bott Memorial Center was opened in Tokyo for service to mothers and children. This Center was named in honor of G. Ernest Bott, of the United Church of Canada, greatly loved leader in social work for a generation, and the organizer of relief and welfare work under LARA in the first years after the war. He literally gave his life in a service which received the recognition of the entire nation. In the Center there is a home for children, and also a training course for orphanage house-mothers. This in-service training is the first of its kind in Japan.

A ministry to inmates of prisons has marked the postwar years. Not since the earliest days had it been possible for Christian pastors to have ready access to prisoners, for the Buddhists had the traditional assignment as chaplains. With the freedom of the postwar period many pastors availed themselves of the opportunity to visit and, when permitted, to hold services. A Prison Evangelistic Association was formed, and when in 1956 there was a meeting of a National Conference of Prison Chaplains the Christians were included. Over two hundred and fifty do some systematic prison visitation. Herbert Nicholson, Quaker, and a frequent visitor in prisons says that few men under sentence of death are without the ministrations of a Christian clergyman, and that most of them have accepted not only Christian consolation but the faith itself.

In 1955 St. Luke's Medical Center in Tokyo was returned to its own directors after ten years use by the American military forces, and resumed its manifold services of help. The School of Nursing also was reopened. The Episcopal church and mission lead all other Protestant ones in medical work, with a total of 650 beds in a half dozen institutions. The Seventh Day Adventist mission is also conspicuous for its excellent hospitals and nurses training institution. The Salvation Army operates a number of sanitaria. The army authorities at Kinugusa, down the sea-coast from Tokyo, gave the Kyodan a hospital, which is now operated chiefly as a tuberculosis sanitarium. In 1956 the mission of the Presbyterian Church, U.S., erected the first unit in a new hospital in Osaka. The Southern Baptists purchased a large site in Kyoto and opened their first renovated building to receive patients. This new interest in medical work comes more from a desire to express Christian concern through a ministry of healing than from the thought of providing Japan with basic medical service. It is a significant trend in current Protestant mission policy.

The new laws abolishing the licensed quarters and registered prostitution were to be effective in 1957, and the Christian forces for moral reform prepared for the confusion that would ensue. The WCTU opened several rehabilitation centers in addition to those already in operation in Tokyo. Japanese visitors to Germany had been impressed by the institution of the "Mutterhaus" with its resident deaconesses serving neighborhood needs, and especially by their work for wayward girls. On invitation of the NCC three deaconesses came from Germany and two from the United States and opened two centers. Units in other cities were projected and further extension of deaconess work was contemplated. The Midnight Mission and some others, as well as the Salvation Army were ready to engage in this service to the freed victims of the licensed system, though still in 1959 the enforcement of the law was being postponed. An association of German Missions had been formed, and had taken associated membership in the NCC. It was expected that other features of German "Inner Missions" would be introduced to Japanese Christianity in the future.

The use of audio-visual aids in teaching and evangelism made slow progress before the war. From about 1950 one or two missionaries and Japanese ministers in several of the denominations had slowly gathered momentum in an organized movement to get equipment, a staff and a program. They were fortunate in finding a competent full-time secretary, Matthew Ogawa, and in enlisting the help of RAVEMCO the responsible division in the National Council of Churches of Christ, U.S.A. By splendid cooperation and generous assistance a site o nthe campus of Aoyama Gakuin University was obtained, and in 1955 the Audio-Visual Aids Commission of the NCC (AVACO) opened its new building. With studios, offices, assembly room, libraries of films and filmstrips, and laboratories for producing materials, this center served the entire Christian constituency. Workshops were held, seminars conducted regionally, and branches maintained in several cities.

Several programs a week were prepared by AVACO and broadcast on private radio stations. Time was taken on the government network each week. Recorded church programs of music, worship services, story-telling for children, and Bible instruction were sent out to churches for local broadcasting. AVACO in 1955 operated a six months Radio Drama School. It makes moving pictures, as well as filmstrips, and the *Kami-shibai*, or picture stories that have come to be a special technique given by Japan to world

328

Christianity. The products of this service are sent all over Asia. In the Far East AVACO is a recognized pioneer in the field of audio-vision among Protestants, and leaders from neighboring countries have come to Tokyo for observation and training. In 1958 it was host to the Asian Audio-Visual and Mass Communications Conference.

On the call of AVACO eleven Christian agencies met and formed the Japan Christian Broadcasters Association. This includes "The Lutheran Hour" (Missouri Synod), "Voice of Prophecy" (Seventh Day Adventist), "Time for Christ" (Southern Presbyterian) and several others. Another group of missions in Japan uses the facilities of the Far East Broadcasting Company, which with its powerful sending station in the Philippines can reach every part of the country.

The Rural Training Center at Hino in the outskirts of Tokyo served the churches well from the time of its establishment. The land, however, was claimed for municipal use, and it became necessary to move. The institution was re-established in 1956 at Tsurukawa a few miles away, with much better facilities. The main building is the Stone Memorial, in recognition of Alfred Stone's service. It has a truck and dairy farm for practical work, and it carries on a school for the training of rural pastors and laymen. With studies in the morning, work in the afternoons, and the week-ends spent in the churches the students are given an all-round preparation. This center, though operated by the Kyodan, serves persons of any Protestant denomination.

When in 1951 John H. Reisner, "father of world rural missions" visited Japan, a Rural Program for the next quarter-century was adopted. This is being kept in view. Up to 1958, twenty-eight Rural Centers had been established by the reconstruction or utilization of country churches in a wider service to their community. Rural

329

Gospel Schools continue to be a sound means of Christian evangelism and training for promising young farm leaders.

An important event in 1957 was the first graduation of students from the Japan International Christian University. The high goals and hopes of its founders had not been lowered. Ninety percent of its students had come from the top tenth in high school senior classes all over Japan on the recommendation of their principals. One third were young women. Students from other Asian countries and from America mingled in the classes. The highly qualified faculty gathered from various countries and all active Christians maintained close personal relations with the students. The residence and teaching of Dr. Emil Brunner from 1953–1955, greatly enriched the university life. Dr. Yuasa, the President was giving superb academic and spiritual leadership. Voluntary Christian services were crowded with students, and the University Church was the center of ICU's deepest life. The charter for advanced professional work was received in time for the most promising graduates to continue in residence and to go on toward a doctorate in Education. The university seems destined to become the dynamic training center for first class teaching in Christian schools as well as for a higher type of lay leadership in public service and in industry.

The National Christian Educational Association was reorganized in 1957, and became the Education Association of Christian Schools with Dr. Yoshimune Abe as its director. Its new role was to be less one of concern for the general problems of school administration, and more particularly one of assistance in promoting Christian programs and instruction. At every school level it was at work with recommendations for the religious programs of the schools as well as in the preparation of materials for Bible study and Christian counselling.

In the summer of 1958 the Japan Council of Christian Education was host to the Fourteenth World Convention on Christian Education, (the former World's Sunday School Association) held in Tokyo. Twelve hundred visitors from more than sixty countries were welcomed by nearly three thousand Japanese fellow-delegates. In connection with the convention a series of institutes was held throughout Japan. In these, Japanese church school workers were given the benefit of the lectures by three hundred world leaders in the field. An opening ceremony was held in the Sports Stadium, Tokyo at which twelve thousand persons viewed the spectacle of a procession of the delegates in foreign costumes. Premier Kishi gave a fine tribute to Christians in Japan when he said:

"Japan is not a Christian nation,...But Japanese Christians—humble followers as well as outstanding leaders—have made signal contributions to the social progress and spiritual uplift of the nation through their exemplary conduct, their piety, and their spirit of service and helpfulness."

It exactly stated the truth.

To this inspiring scene, however, the current report for 1957 of the general secretary Masatake Fujita for the work of the church schools in Japan was an anti-climax. Attendance had fallen off twelve percent in two years. The causes given were that the public schools had returned to a six day week after the five-day reprieve of the Occupation policies, and that Sundays were again as before the war, filled with all sorts of community activities, usually held at the schools. Reduced numbers in the church schools could not fail to cause concern. Even so, a quarter of a million students were in attendance at nearly four thousand schools.

The Literature Commission of the NCC also sponsored at

the same time an Asian Conference on Christian Literature. Since the war there has been no dearth of thinkers in the churches and especially in their seminaries. The Faculty of the Tokyo Union Theological Seminary is typical of a half dozen graduate schools for ministerial training. In every one of the disciplines there are men of first rank. On the occasion of the World Convention on Christian Education this Seminary bestowed the degree of Doctor of Theology upon six world leaders of the churches of Europe, Asia, Africa and America. A new day has come to the world church when this could happen in a country of a so-called "younger church." There are other able faculties at Kansei Gakuin and Doshisha in Western Japan, and elsewhere. These institutions publish learned journals and reviews. There is a wide stream of books covering many areas of Christian thought and action and aimed at various sorts of reader. Yet the impression persists that the full current of earlier periods has scarcely been matched, either in periodicals or in books, in the devastating war years and those that have followed.

The prevailing thought trend throughout the churches has continued to be that of the dialectic theology of crisis. The influence of Karl Barth in the pre-war years was strong. In recent years the trend has become more pronounced. Within the former Methodist group, especially among the younger men, this same Barthian emphasis has become clear. The mood of crisis was the atmosphere of the Evangelistic Manifesto issued by the Conference on the Mission of the Church in 1953 when it spoke of "the mission which our Lord entrusted to the church as it faces a hostile society... Now we who live in a hopeless world, filled with insecurity and excitement... must witness... at the risk of our lives." There are those who feel that if the devoted laymen and women of the church could make their own formulation of their faith it would have a more central place for the tender love of the Father-God, and for the capacity of His children to respond in obedience. Such a faith, less authoritarian and more dynamic would seem better suited to the spiritual leadership of the common life in the new world of today.

In its wider outreaches the Protestant movement is conscious of belonging to the ecumenical fellowship. Through the NCC it is a part of the International Missionary Council, and was represented at the meetings in Willingen, Germany in 1952 and at Ghana, West Africa in 1957. Its major denominations are affiliated with the World Council of Churches, and take a share in its work. In addition, the churches have been active in the movement begun in the East Asian Consultation on Ecumenical Mission at Hong Kong, 1954, which culminated in the formation of the East Asia Christian Conference, 1957. Here Japanese delegates meet intimately with their fellow-Christians of neighboring countries in a regional organization.

A list of the overseas conferences to which Japanese church leaders and staff members of councils and commissions have gone would be too long to enumerate. In fact, the multiplying of overhead networks of cooperation in the ecumenical movement threatens to become a major problem of time and expense for the constituent churches of limited size and resources such as those in Japan. Yet each person charged with any responsibility craves the experience of conference at the regional and world level. Each one brings back new experiences and skills and weaves another thread for the Japanese Christians in the fabric of worldwide Protestantism.

There is also a continuing stream of visitors from abroad who bring their varied gifts and stimulate the Japanese Church to new efforts. Never have members of the Japanese churches had the direct inspiration of the most representative world leaders in the Christian community to the degree that they have since 1952. To mention one or two in particular: in 1956, Billy Graham spent four days in the country, and in that time held mass rallies in Tokyo and Osaka at which tens of thousands of persons crowded into the great auditoriums and more stood in throngs outside.

Another quite different evangelist was Donald Soper, Christian socialist and labor-evangelist from London, who followed his Hyde-Park methods, and did his preaching on the streets and in the parks of the cities. In these open-air, free-for-all sessions criticism and questions from the public were invited. Andre Trocme, pacifist minister of the French Reformed church travelled through the country under the auspices of the Fellowship of Reconciliation, mingling in peace conferences with other pacifists of the "fellow-traveller" and Communist persuasions, challenging them in friendly head-on encounter, and encouraging Christians to give their witness even though it might invite misunderstandings from both sides of the embattled ideological field.

A genuine movement toward a foreign missionary outreach had begun. A YMCA secretary was loaned to herve on the staff at Colombo, Ceylon. Two young men were sent to Brazil, in Christian work. Frequent missionary visits are made to Okinawa—which has been on the heart of all the churches. Notably, Jiro Fukui, Kyodan pastor in Fukuoka, and moderator of the Kyushu District volunteered for service in the lonely island of Amami Oshima.

A CLOSER LOOK AT THE CHRISTIAN CHURCHES IN 1958

Among the Christian forces the Catholic Church has registered pronounced growth and advancement. During the long decades of the modern period the church with great patience waited for the traditional deep-seated fears and hatreds of the people to subside. All head-on collisions were avoided, no aggressive policies were followed. Churches were placed inconspicuously on side streets. Foreign priests were not often seen in public. But works of mercy were undertaken. Excellent schools were founded. Foreign clergy —many of them in the Society of Jesus—came to promote scholarship, especially through the Sophia University.

In the meantime a group of Japanese clergy was being given intensive training over long years. Japanese women workers were being taught to handle the manifold works of education, and mercy. In the excellent schools for girls and young women the future mothers of the Catholic community of tomorrow were carefully being molded into the pattern of the faith. Orphanages were nurturing large numbers of children. Many sick, baptized *in extremis* recovered to continue in the community. Unremitting application to long goals was winning the day.

Since the war, building operations have been numerous on desirable corners of cities, and in strategic secondary towns. There is a foreign missionary force of some 2,000 men and women. The bishop of every diocese and the archbishop are all Japanese. The Bible has been translated into the colloquial tongue. There is a wide range of church literature and periodicals. Radio broadcasting is being pushed. Laymen's activities are well organized. The growth of the community has been steady. From about 120,000 in 1941 and a drop probably to fewer than 100,000 during the war, it had by 1958 risen to 240,000 members in over five hundred parish churches. With baptisms approaching twenty-five thousand a year, and with a net increase of around ten thousand communicant members, the Catholic church moves with assurance on its path toward its clearly envisaged goal.

The life of the Eastern Orthodox Church in Japan is as difficult of appraisal as that of the Roman Church is sharply defined. Perhaps that is characteristic of the respective natures of the two churches. The Orthodox church has announced no programs or policies. During the war it was decimated, as were the other churches. After the war the Soviet diplomatic corps in Tokyo virtually took over the management of the headquarters. Metropolitan Sergius, the spiritual head of the church had died during the war, and there was no center for renewing the life of the scattered congregations. The wartime rivalries over leadership within the church continued, and were not settled until Bishop Ireney of the Orthodox Church in the United States came and established order, attaching the church to the jurisdiction of Metropolitan Benjamin of New York. The commanding Cathedral in Tokyo was damaged but not destroyed in the war, and has since been restored. The church consists of about one hundred parishes served by 65 priests. As to its membership, the familiar figure of thirty or thirty-five thousand recurs over so many years that it fails to give an impression of reality. It would seem that there may be an inner working core of around ten thousand members, and that with no special efforts toward growth or evangelism, but with loyal family life the church is about holding its own with a wider constituency of about thirty thousand— the figure of a quarter century ago. With no affiliated institutions, no assistance from outside its membership and almost no ecumenical contacts it is a miracle for it to have survived at all.

The Protestant Churches stand midway between the clearly outlined pattern of the Roman Church and the nebulous character of the Orthodox Church. At first glance there seems to be in the Protestant bodies a variety of structure, emphasis and affiliation so great as to defy

JAPANESE CHRISTIAN CHURCHES

1941   1958

The Protestant Bodies

	1941		1958
Presbyterian-Reformed Church	55,400	The Church of Christ (Kyodan)	172,000
Japan Methodist Church	50,500	Withdrawn from Kyodan:	
Congregational Churches	35,500	Presbyterian Church	10,000
United Brethren	3,400	Reformed Church	3,000
Churches of Christ, Disciples	3,400		
Methodist Protestant Church	3,300		
Evangelical Church	2,800		
	152,000		185,000
Episcopal-Anglican	26,000	Episcopal-Anglican	40,000
Holiness Churches (3 Denoms.)	23,000	Holiness Churches (7 Denoms.)	36,000
Evangelical Lutheran	7,000	Evangelical Lutheran	8,500
Baptist, East (No. Bapt. Conv.)	4,000	Baptist, East "New Life Assoc."	1,500
Baptist, West (So. Bapt. Conv.)	3,000	Baptist, West "Japan Bapt. Conv."	10,500
15 Other Church Bodies, (With many small independent Groups)	18,000	25 Same, with numerous split-offs	44,000
		About 40 Postwar Church Bodies	22,000
Total Protestants	233,000	Total Protestants	348,000

The Older Churches

	1941		1958
"The Japan Catholic Church" (Roman)	120,000	"The Japan Catholic Church" (Roman)	241,000
Eastern Orthodox Church	30,000	Eastern Orthodox Church	34,000

Others

	1941		1958
"Churchless Christians"	50,000(?)	"Churchless Christians"	70,000(?)
"Friends of Jesus" (Kagawa)	(?)	"Friends of Jesus" Many thousands.	(?)
Total Christian Membership	433,000	Total Christian Membership	693,300

337

analysis. But on closer study it is seen that there is a large element of continuity in them, and that they are not too difficult to classify with relation to the earlier periods of Japanese Christianity. A rough tabulation of the churches in 1941 when the curtain dropped, and again in 11958, may serve to make this more clear. Since published statistics contain many inaccuracies these figures are presented tentatively and in round numbers.

It will be seen that, essentially, the churches of 1958 are those of 1941, and much earlier. The only really new factor of a fresh start since the war is represented by the forty denominations averaging but five hundred members each, and totalling less than seven percent of the Protestant membership. For all the rest, the changing structure, shift in position or growth in numbers has gone on within a continuing church.

There has been a good deal of change. Foremost among the innovations of structure as well as of spirit is the Church of Christ (Kyodan). It is really a united church. Within the bonds of one living organism there are the diverse traditions of the episcopal, presbyterian and congregational systems. The historic backgrounds of Calvin, Wesley and the Pilgrim Fathers live in the church, with its various emphases on scholarship, evangelism, and the pastoral ministry. Its affiliations are with the United States and Canada. It is a diversified, but not a divided church.

The Confession of Faith of the Kyodan, finally adopted in 1956 is more detailed than the former Methodist and Congregationalist constituencies felt necessary, but somewhat less so than the Presbyterian-Reformed tradition would have called for. Nevertheless, it was cordially adopted by an almost unanimous vote of the General Assembly in a hearty spirit of loyalty to the fellowship. Almost every aspect of the life and work of the churches noted in connection with

338

the National Christian Council in recent years has had its counterpart in the organized work of this United Church which still numbers among its members one half of all Protestants in Japan.

Of the 200 Christian schools with their 125,000 students, three-fourths are related to the Kyodan. Its social institutions are similarly widespread. The relation with the missionary agencies in a fine balance of autonomy in its own life with an acceptance of assistance in projects of expansion or experiment may well prove to be a landmark in the developing science of relationships within the world church.

The Episcopal Church in Japan has undergone changes in that all its ten dioceses are administered by Japanese bishops. Yet it still knows itself as the Japan Province of the Anglican Communion in the world, and the course for its life is charted by that fact. Its care for beautiful and orderly worship and its many works of benevolence are an adornment to Japanese Protestantism.

The Holiness Churches have the strength and the weaknesses of their special emphasis. They are marked by sanctification of the personal Christian life, evangelism in society, and eager waiting for the return of the Lord. There is some stress on faith healing, and a good deal of emotionalism. They have ardor of service, but a vulnerability to division. Their history throughout the years has been one of separation into groups, loyal to different leaders.

The most conspicuous example of growth in these latter years is that of the Church of Jesus' Spirit, (Pentecostal), which, under Bishop Jun Murai has grown from a few hundred in 1941 to the third largest denomination in Japan, with 28,000 members. Possibly one fourth of the total baptisms currently reported in all the Protestant churches are in that one. A large part of its membership is among the people of Okinawa.

The Evangelical Lutheran Church moves within the traditions of historic Lutheranism, its creeds, church order, and sense of belonging to a world church. The energetic activities of the Missouri Synod are still in the early stages of foundation laying, and the Japanese church related to their work is as yet less than two thousand in number. The other ten postwar Lutheran missions have not gone far in establishing Japanese churches, and efforts are being made, before it is too late, to draw together the work of all of them into one single Lutheran church in Japan. A committee has offered a plan of union, and recommendations have been made to the various bodies for procedure but no action has been taken.

The Baptist Churches have also undergone changes. For the first three quarters of the modern century it was the northern church in America which carried the major responsibility for the Japan mission, with as wide a geographical spread of churches as any of the other large denominations, and with a comprehensive program of schools, social work, and pioneer evangelism. Since the war the initiative seems to have been taken by the Southern Baptists whose mission thrust all over the world is one of the current phenomena of American church life. Building up its numbers and with unceasing stress on evangelism, the mission has assisted its related churches to grow to three times their pre-war size. They are organized under the generic name "The Japan Baptist Convention." In the meantime the churches associated with the Northern Baptist mission appear to have shrunk to a third their former size. Even though this may have been to some extent a transfer of churches from one Baptist body to another, still the total registers a good gain in numbers, and it is a reflection of a new dynamic element that is evident in the Baptist forces in Japan.

The other twenty-five pre-war church bodies include some of those with work, which, though not large, was of fine quality. The Swedish Alliance, the Nazarenes, several Pentecostal and faith missions with their churches, the Seventh Day Adventists, the Church of Latter Day Saints, and a number of others had a worthy place in the harmonious orchestration of the years in Japanese Protestantism. They are still doing their work, and some of them have made gains relatively higher than those of the larger denominations. Since the baseline, however, was small, the totals still are not substantial enough for separate listing.

In the case of one or two of these denominations it is surprising that the churches are not more sizeable than they are, in view of the large expansion of the mission force. The Evangelical Alliance Mission for instance, building on the foundation already laid by the Swedish Alliance Mission and reporting a hundred and eighty missionaries has fewer than three thousand members of churches. The Mormons with ninety-three missionaries do not quite reach one thousand in membership. Others, however, have more than doubled their church membership, so that the total of such pre-war churches has now risen to almost forty thousand.

The last item in the Protestant tabulations is the most surprising of all. Of the large contingent of new missionaries numbering over fifteen hundred who arrived in Japan between 1949 and 1953, some belonged to the major denominations, others have been accounted for by the enlargement of smaller missions previously established in Japan. But many hundreds of missionaries came who had no connections in Japan, and they started new work. The surprising fact shown by the published statistics is that after ten years there still can be listed only twenty-two thousand Japanese Christians as the result in church membership of this large missionary accession. This total is less than the membership of the one denomination that Jun Murai has built up without the benefit of the work of a single foreign missionary.

It is a sign of promise that, notwithstanding the slow start, most of the new missions have stayed on, and are settling down for a long siege. The first concentration on immediate conversions through mass evangelism and literature distribution has deepened into an awareness that a Christian constituency has to be gradually gathered and trained. Missionaries are engaged in systematic language study. Bible schools are being started in several of the newer missions. The same problems that faced Hepburn and Greene a generation ago are being confronted. Publishing agencies are putting out tracts and books with an appeal to common people. There is in Japanese Christianity a great need for the "desperation evangelism" that Kagawa has been laying on the hearts of the churches for many years. It may well be that in 1959 the foundations for a strong church with this central emphasis were by the efforts of the newer evangelistic bodies, in the making.

RETROSPECT AND PROSPECT

Any analysis of Protestant Christianity in Japan during the modern century raises questions regarding the problem of growth in numbers. The smallness of the total is often an object of comment by observers. It is frequently said that the Christian movement has become stationary. These terms are at best relative. It is true that during the decade before the war the growth was extremely slow—if indeed there was any—and during the war there was a deep recession. But as the tabulations show, since the war there has been steady growth. By about 1948 the Catholic church had regained its pre-war level, and the Protestant churches, though slower, had done likewise by about 1951. The intervening years have shown enlargement among the Protestant bodies. In varying degrees, all have grown. It is interesting to note that no one pattern of church organization, or of missionary relationships or assistance stands out as the conspicuous cause of unusual growth. Wherever there has been that unaccountable moving of the Spirit to energize a mission, a church, or an individual, the results have been seen in added conversions. The wind bloweth where it listeth.

The fact remains, however, that there has been no such phenomenal growth as was commonly expected after the war. This expectation grew out of the "vacuum" theory. It was assumed that the people of Japan in their defeat had lost all belief in their old faiths but that, being still religious, they were ready to accept a new one, presumably Christianity. This superficial view was not borne out by events. There was no mass change of religious allegiance. The course of missions in other non-Christian societies indicates that mass conversions should not have been expected. In only certain restricted situations do these tidal movements take place. Preliterate, animistic tribes have often moved rapidly into the light and liberty of the Christian Gospel. It is a part of missionary history that if among peoples of ancient culture and religion there are rejected groups or aliens, they too, often become Christians in masses. But the dominant people with their integrated religious systems seldom do. During the colonial period in the Philippines, India, Indonesia, Indo-China, and in the Latin American countries large Christian communities grew up under favoring government auspices.

In Japan none of such conditions existed. There were no rejected peoples. Even the three million "hamlet" dwellers, cultural semi-outcastes though they may be, are members of the Shin Sect of Buddhism, in good standing. During the war, religious forces were carefully utilized by the government for maintaining national morale. They were never in disrepute. The Occupation policy sedulously avoided any affront toward a religious body or any repressive measures. Even in defeat, the Shinto pantheon still was intact. Though most Japanese would have been unable precisely to say who or what the Gods were, the shrine system was their own, Japanese and precious, and participation in its ceremonies was an essential element of community living. The Buddhist temple also was bound up with their life.

For most normal Japanese adults there were slight inducements to withdraw from this communal religious web of life and to enter the Christian household of faith with its exacting moral demands, and its separateness of living. Few really contemplated a change of faith. Each individual would have to be sought out, his friendship cultivated, teaching added to teaching, and finally the persuasive steps taken to lead him to his own decision. This is the slow but sure way Japanese pastors follow. There may be short-cuts, but thus far they have not proved very effective.

It is noteworthy that the mass evangelistic programs of recent years with the exception of Dr. Kagawa's campaigns have been done largely on the intiative of persons from the West. Their services have been courteously accepted, and they have been given access to the churches, but on the part of the Japanese Christians there has been nothing like the all-out efforts which took place at the turn of the century. Then a hundred of the leading ministers and laymen of the churches would travel the country for weeks at a time, in a national campaign. One reason for that method in the early days was that it gave an opportunity for Christians to make their case before their own people.

The aims were partly an apologetic and only partly the conversion of individuals.

Since the war Christianity is well known and generally understood. Permanent results in church membership following mass meetings are seen to be meager. Even Dr. Kagawa now enrolls his inquirers as "Friends of Jesus," and not as church members. Thus the work of propagating Christianity ultimately goes back to the local church, the pastor and the members. It may well be that to ask for growth averaging more than five or ten percent a year is to try to hurry a process that should be more like the germination of a seed toward a future harvest than like some hastily constructed work of an artisan, rushed to meet a contractor's deadline.

The matter of naturalization in Japanese life is a real problem for Protestant Christianity. From one point of view the Christian movement including churches, schools and social work is deeply and purely Japanese. The Christians are self reliant, fully conscious of themselves as being Japanese, and mature enough either to accept and utilize Western colleagues and money if offered, or if not, to plow their furrow with their own heifer.

There are indications, however, that the roots of the movement must go deeper still before it can claim the allegiance of the nation at large as an indigenous growth. The Roman Catholics entered the modern century with thousands of traditional Christian villagers in Kyushu as their nucleus. Grateful for this start they nevertheless persistently moved along the social scale with their schools and literature to reach all classes of society. The Protestants, in contrast, won their place first among the uprooted *samurai* and the townspeople, merchants and professional men. There they have stayed. They never really have come to grips with the common people.

345

Protestantism in Japan is an urban, middle class intellectual's religion. Cosmopolitan, international, enlightened, ethical and rational, it commends itself to the movable classes in the cities. This is a generalization which needs much qualification, and has many exceptions, but which in the main holds true. With an earnestness that deserves larger results, for fifty years the eyes of the church have been cast self-accusingly and wistfully, first at the rural peoples, and later at the laboring groups in its own city neighborhoods. Yet its feet have found it hard to go to them, and its hands have lacked the requisite skills for service. Neither the people of the villages nor the workers in the cities have been deeply reached, much less won.

Is it not an ironical fact that the initiative in both rural evangelism and occupational evangelism programs should have come so largely from the Western colleagues? The reason is not that these foreign observers were the first to see the need but rather that they knew so little of the stern difficulties which were only too obvious to Japanese Christians, within their own society. A clump of bamboo trees when young will put all its energy into sprouts that still belong to the mother-stock, and not till this is large, tough, and interlaced in support will the rootlings run underground far afield and push up sprouts to form another grove. The time will come when Japanese Christians will be sure enough of themselves as a community to move into these areas now touched only at long range by special projects from headquarters.

When that time comes a genuine acculturation of Japanese Christianity may be expected. There was something synthetic about the adjustment to national life dictated by the stern pressures of a war crisis. Both in thought and in practice it came from without rather than from the inner ponderings of free spirits or from the unconscious experimentation in everyday living of a Christian in his own hereditary non-Christian society. It was patriotic and political rather than cultural. Foreigners sometimes bewail the lack of any serious cultural adjustment in Christian buildings and furnishing, in church music and drama, in literary forms or artistic expression. It is true: there is very little. Even these results, though, are enough to offer the promise that when Japanese Christians really become Christian Japanese something splendid is destined to break upon the Christian world community. With the cultural commitment of centuries, and the tradition that a religious spirit must infuse all good workmanship and true art, Christians may yet produce a new and more meaningful orientation of Christian expression in indigenous forms.

Perhaps it will be not till then that Christian thinking will widen its base, from that of the traditional historic formulations of the West to include insights offered by Japan's own greatest truth-seekers and spiritual geniuses of the past. Baptized into new meaning and life this heritage may bring enrichment to the thinking of the world Christian community. In the few decades of the past century the Protestant Christians have laid a sufficient foundation for this hope to come to fulfilment.

James Moffatt the church historian notes that it took early Christians two hundred years to obtain a footing in the Roman Empire, and that during that period they accomplished little else. The next three centuries were devoted to the Church's beginning to assume responsibility for the spiritual permeation and leadership of the Empire. If that time-table holds for Japanese Christians at the close of their first century, it may be said that they are on the right track and are well ahead of schedule.

A review of modern Japan's fourth quarter-century confirms the impression of an almost unendurable confusion of crises and catastrophes. These years brought the fevers of expanding empire, the frustrations of a disastrous Asian war and the cold coercions of a military totalitarian society. The sufferings of the bombings, and terrors of an invasion ended in the humiliation of surrender, and the searing disgrace of a foreign armed occupation. There were the moral perplexities of the Occupation, and then the restraints on real freedom as an economic and military satellite in another nation's orbit. The precariousness of subsistence and the loneliness of alienation from Asian neighbors has been overshadowed by the frowning fear of one more last war. Did any people in modern times ever have to go through experiences such as these in one quarter-century? Yet in each of the trying experiences Japanese Christians took their full share. They suffered and endured with their people. They often took the lead in prophetic utterance and in ministering to human needs. They were usually ready to give a witness to their faith by word and by daily living.

The strength of Protestant Christianity lies in the thousands of little Christian local churches that dot the land. The faithful pastor day in and day out gives nurture to this small flock. The few families carry their weight of responsibilities in the community and stand as models of gracious and loyal living. The young people bring into schools and onto playgrounds the influence of a simple faith in Christ. Honorable Christian laymen witness in all walks of life. These are the tiny roots of personal and social redemption that have silently sunk into Japanese soil, never to be uprooted. It is because of the vitality in these roots that Protestant Christianity has come through crisis upon crisis until the present day.

There may be few Christian leaders of national stature matching the achievements of the giants of the early years. There may be no mass movements into the church. But the quality of the ordinary individual Christian, makes of him, quite without his knowledge, a light as of a city set upon a hill. Protestant Christianity has not yet won Japan as a nation, but it has already become the leaven put into the three measures of meal. One day in the future its task will be the open, bold challenge to discipleship for the whole nation.

Thus the Modern Century in Japan has drawn to its end, and with it the Christian movement has come to its centenary. The people have passed period by period through the classic phases of the modern revolution from feudal to industrial life, to that of a modern nation-state, to empire, and through ruin to renewal. Will that complete the cycle, and leave the nation on a plateau of peaceful living? Or are there mounting crises and even tragedies ahead? The answers to such questions lie with Japan's neighbors as well as with herself. In their determination the nations and particularly the Christians of the West must bear a heavy share of moral responsibility. In a peaceful world Japan may still be the keystone for a new Asia. Midway between the positions of the Eastern and Western peoples in geography and in national life, she may become the interpreter and the mediator between two worlds now so widely separated in outlook and understanding. Somewhere along her swift cycle of change moves every one of the Asian and African nations in revolution. Japan has much to teach, and the rest of the world has much to learn from her experiences.

In such a world of peaceful cooperation the Christians of Japan may play a formative role of leadership and interfusion of life with those of Asia and the West. Embodying in themselves elements both of an older church and of a younger church, they are both senders and receivers in the interchange of life within a worldwide Christianity. The Christians of Japan have been mellowed by the experiences

349

of adversity, deepened in spirit by crisis and enriched by the reconciliations of the postwar years. Now, quickened to fresh zeal by the challenge of a world newly born yet newly lost, they would reach out to their yoke-fellows in the other churches of the world for a new comradeship in the Gospel, to help lead a wandering generation back to the feet of God.

INDEX

INDEX

BIBLE: used as English language textbook, 30; translation started, 34; translation progresses, 36; Chinese Bibles imported in early days, 40; Wakasa studies Dutch Bible he found floating in the sea, 40; translation of New Testament prog. esses, 43; translation completed, 83; Bible societies active, 131; revision of translation of New Testament started, 162; inexpensive editions of New Testament distributed by Bible societies, 199; shortage after the war, 281; Old Testament translated, 323; distributed by Japanese Bible Society, 324

BICKEL, LUKE, skipper-missionary of *Gospel Ship*, 91

BICKERSTETH, BISHOP, comes from Britain, 1885, 81; a tireless worker, 102

" BIG FIVE ", name given to a group of major protestant denominations, 81

BLACK DRAGON SOCIETY becomes active, 196

BLACK MAGIC, 24

BLIND: helped, 84; school opened in Yokohama, 106

BONIN ISLANDS visited by Anglican workers, 91

BOOKS: import unrestricted by Harris' agreement, 30

BOOTH, WILLIAM, visits Japan, 129

BOTT, G. ERNEST, helps establish service centers, 184; organizes overseas relief, 282; Memorial Center opened, 326

BOVENKERK, HENRY G., member of postwar commission, 282

BOWLES, GILBERT, campaigns for peace, 207

BRAZIL visited by Japanese Christian leaders, 144

BROTHEL VICTIMS helped by Salvation Army, 91

BROWN, FRANK, introduces new concept of sports, 161

BROWN, FRANK L., visits Japan, 130

BROWN, SAMUEL R., early missionary for Dutch Reformed Church, 32; greatest of early missionary schoolmen, 32; early missionary, 34; converts Japanese, 50; refuses diplomatic immunity, 60

BRUMBAUGH, THOBURN T., establishes Methodist Student Center, 181

BRUNER, GLEN, serves postwar Japan, 273

BRUNNER, EMIL, lectures in Japan, 302; teaches at the Japan International Christian University, 330

BUCHMANISM popular, 208

BUDDHISM: background, 17; temples used to house Christian missionaries, 34; priests spy on Christians, 34; moribund, 61; opposes Christianity, 61; priests become Christian ministers, 62; major characteristics of Buddhism, 64; religion of the common man, 68; increased opposition to Christianity, 79; loses ground, 80; forcibly fights Christians, 92; borrow elements of Christianity, 174; has a revival, 174; engages in welfare work, 175; postwar recovery, 315; missionaries sent abroad, 316

BURIALS: Christians barred from Buddhist cemetaries, 61, 142

BUTTERFIELD KENYON, sent to help with rural work, 202; studies Japan's agrarian problems, 203

BUXTON, BARCLAY, heads the Evangelistic Band, 90

elder of Yokohama Church, 53; leader of Hirosaki Band, 56; active in politics, 78; forced to resign principalship of a Christian school, 79; gives up politics, 99; active with Wartime Service Association, 101; Chairman of National War Service Commission, 118; makes goodwill trips abroad, 142; attends Edinburgh Conference, 149

HORI, M., leads two weeks of meetings celebrating Doshisha anniversary, 180

HORTON, DOUGLAS, visits postwar Japan, 270

HOSTELS for Christian students increase, 206

HOSTILITY: towards foreigners, 30, 33; towards Catholics, 34; towards Christians, 37, 60

HOUSE OF THE OPEN DOOR established by T. D. Walser, 181

HOUSE-TO-HOUSE EVANGELISM conducted, 163

HOWE, ANNIE L., founds first training school for kindergarten teachers, 125

HOZUMI, YASOKU, promotes emperor worship at Imperial University, 138

HYMNS: "All People Who on Earth do Dwell," played by band on Perry's ship, 29; first attempts at translation made, 58; first hymnal issued in Japanese, 1878, 59; hymnal published in Nagasaki, 83; union hymnal published in 1903, 131; hymns copied by Buddhists, 174; hymnal for Sunday schools published, 176; hymnals changed because of war, 248; shortage after war, 281; union hymnal revised, 324

IBUKA, KAJINOSUKE, makes good-

will trips abroad, 142; attends Edinburgh Conference, 149

IEYASU; see TOKUGAWA, IEYASU

IGLEHART, EDWIN T,, returns to Aoyama Gakuin, 288

IMAGE OF CHRIST defiled, 34

IMITATION by Japanese, 19

IMPERIAL PALACE, TOKYO: Emperor installed, 1868, 41

IMPERIAL RESCRIPT ON EDUCATION issued, 88; considered to be ethical in nature, 100; read at Christian ceremonies, 103; enforcement stressed, 205; causes trouble for Christians, 220

IMPERIAL RULE ASSOCIATION formed, 228

IMPERIAL UNIVERSITY, TOKYO, founded, 49; professors oppose Christianity, 60; small Christian group formed, 103

IMPORTS: opium and firearms barred by Harris' agreement, 30; books duty free, 30

INDIA: kinship, 19

INDUSTRY: development, 46, 65; expositions used for revival meetings, 75; industrialists grow powerful, 89; leaders support Christianity, 190; attempt to practice Christian principles, 201; Industrial Harmonization Movement under way, 215; great industrial growth, 226

ING, JOHN, goes to Hirosaki, 53

INLAND SEA GOSPEL SHIP launched, 91

INSTITUTE OF JAPANESE LANGUAGE AND CULTURE founded in Tokyo by the Conference of Federated Missions, 146; headed by Darley Downs, 146; aided by Baron Sakatani, 146

INSTITUTE OF PACIFIC RELATIONS

INDEX

anti-Christian, 118

KATSUTA donates building to Aoyama Gakuin, 190

KAWAI, MICHI heads YWCA work, 121; founds Keisen school, 121; warns against materialistic education, 225; in group sent to America to avoid war, 237

KAWASAKI: dockyard workers strike, 158

KAWASUMI, S., Secretary of National Sunday School Association, 176

KEIKI, last of shoguns, resigns, 37

KEIO UNIVERSITY: founded by Yukichi Fukuzawa, 61; adds Christian to its faculty, 79

KEISEN SCHOOL AND COLLEGE founded, 121

KEISHEISHA publishes hymnal, 132

KELLOG PACT signed, 192

KERR, WILLIAM C., counsels Japanese Christians, 273

KIERKEGAARD'S WORKS studied by Uchimura, 95

KILBURN, ELIZABETH, active in postwar Japan, 272

KILLING OF CHRISTIANS: 1600, Sekigahara, 30,000, 24; 1638, Shimabara Castle, 37,000, 24

KIMURA, SEIMATSU, conducts evangelistic campaign, 119; holds large anti-vice meetings, 180; stresses imminent return of Christ, 181; wins converts at Kwansei Gakuin, 205

KINDERGARTENS increase in number, 125

KINGDOM OF GOD movement headed Kagawa, 198; weekly starts publication, 199; movement undertakes social work, 201

KINOSHITA, NAOE, opposes wars of expansion, 117

KIRISUTO KOKWAI founded by Ballagh, 43

KISHI, PREMIER, lauds Christians, 331

KNAPP, A. M., introduces Unitarian Christianity, 79

KOBE: ten places of worship in Kansai in 1875, 54; churches attempt organic union, 57; Kagawa concerned with underprivileged, 157; Roy Smith teaches at University of Commerce, 181; Theological Seminary develops training of rural workers, 203

KOCHI: home of Itagaki who helped establish church here, 78

KOKUTAI (NATIONAL STRUCTURE) emphasized, 153

KONOYE, PRINCE, becomes Premier, 214

KOREA: relationship to Japan, 19; taken over, 89; oppression of criticized by Uchimura, 101; annexed, 135

KOREAN CHRISTIAN COUNCIL sends pastor to Osaka area, 202

KOREAN CHURCH OF CHRIST IN JAPAN organized, 202; joins National Christian Council in Japan, 202

KOREAN CHURCHES established, 144

KOREANS IN JAPAN, status lamentable, 202

KOTOKU, SHUSUI, executed, 140; conspiracy against Emperor questioned, 156

KOZAKI, HIROMICHI, converted to Christianity, 51; joins Kumamoto Band, 51; founds Cosmos Magazine, 59; establishes YMCA, 59; heads Bancho Church, Tokyo, 78; champions Christianity, 80; lectures on Karl Marx, 95; produces robust apologetic writing, 98; active in YMCA summer conference,

366

INDEX

formed, 169

LEIPER, HENRY, expresses good will of China toward Japan, 178

LEPERS helped, 84; Miss Riddell work with them, 106; lepers call for government assistance, 169

LESTER, MURIEL, welcomed by pacifists, 316

LIBERAL GERMAN MISSION establishes Unity Hall near Tokyo Imperial University, 104

LIBERAL THEOLOGY upsets ministers, 93

LIBERALISM spreads, 209

LIGGINS, JOHN, transferred from China to Japan, 31; serves as early missionary, 34

LINCOLN, ABRAHAM, admired, 68

LITERATURE; see CHRISTIAN LITERATURE

LOO CHOO (RYUKYUAN) NAVAL MISSION, 1845; failure of Naha missionary, 29

LOOMIS, HENRY, distributes Bibles in army camps, 101

LUTHERANS: United Lutheran Church sends missionaries, 91; concentrates work in West Japan, 91; establish kindergartens, 125; "Lutheran Hour" radio broadcast heard widely, 296; Missouri Synod establishes a strong mission, 296; extend activity, 307; Evangelical Lutheran Church appraised, 340

MACARTHUR, DOUGLAS, heads Occupation, 262; initiates revolutionary social change, 267

MACAULEY, H. CLAY, Disavowes unusual practices, 163

MACCONNELL, HAROLD H., encourages Visitation Evangelism, 303

MACDONALD, CAROLINE, heads YWCA work, 121

MACKENZIE, D. R., leader in evangelistic campaign, 151; advocates church administration by the Japanese church, 188

MCKIM, BISHOP, leaves Episcopal Church, 81

MACNAIR, THOMAS, urges the writing of hymns, 132

MAGIC, 24

MANCHURIA: Christian chaplains accompany troops, 101; taken by Japan, 115; Japanese expansion frustrated by Chinese immigration, 167; government taken over by Japanese Army, 193

MANN, JOHN, sent to reestablish Episcopal Church in Japan, 286

MARCO POLO BRIDGE incident occurs, 212

MARRIAGES, PLURAL, campaigned against by Madame Yajima, 99

MASS MEETINGS successful, 74

MARTIN'S *Evidences of Christianity* distributed by Townsend Harris, 40

MARTYRDOM accepted by common people, 23; Nagasaki martyrs, 39

MARX, KARL, lectured on by Kozaki, 95

MASSACHUSETTS AGRICULTURE COLLEGE President sent to Hokkaido, 52

MATSUMOTO, TAKUO, pleads for real missionary effort during war years, 225

MATSUNO, KIKUTARO, visits Manchuria and China, 144

MATSUYAMA, TSUNEJIRO, writes hymns, 132; in group sent to America to avoid war, 237; helps with work of pacification, 246

MATTHEWS, SHAILER, visits Japan, 147

MAYER, PAUL S., works with SCAP on return of missionaries, 282

371

INDEX

INDEX

established, 84; Seventh Day Adventists established, 91; Tetsuzo Okada influential Christian leader, 100; small Christian group formed at Tokyo University, 103; liberal German mission establishes Unity Hall near Imperial University, 104; Christians help with earthquake relief, 105; WCTU establishes home for unfortunate girls, 106; site of Missionary Conference, 1900, 112; Shingakusha founded, 124; World Student Christian Federation meets here, 130; Conference of Federated Missions founds Japanese language school, 146; Churchless Christianity taught here, 154; Sarah Bauernfiend engages in social work, 158; Misaki Kaikan (institutional church) sounded, 159; Women's Christian College founded, 161; decimated by earthquake and fire, 166; one half of City Couucil in jail for corruption, 170; host to World Sunday School convention, 175; Fujimi-cho Church has many members, 197; Methodist Student Center established, 181; Shinanomachi Church headed by Tokutaro Takakura, 182; Fujimi-cho Church members transfer to Shinanomachi Church, 182; earthquake sufferers aided by National Christian Council, 183; Kagawa called to serve as Counsellor, 184; East Tokyo Mission established, 184; Ai-Kei Gakuen Christian Center established, 184; S. Motoda, first Japanese bishop, 187; Kegawa's pawnshops famous, 201; St. Luke's Medical Center established, 202; St. Paul College professor forced to resign, 221; churches pledge

to unify, 233; Ginza Church holds 24-hour Prayer Vigil, 243; Ginza Church active in postwar Japan, 272; "The Messiah" performed in Hibiya Hall, 273; Christian Headquarters renovated, 305; Union Theological Seminary given scholarship fund, 320; has first-rate faculty, 332; Bott Memorial Center opens, 326; St. Luke's Medical Center returned to Japanese after the Occupation, 327; Billy Graham holds rallies, 334; Ugo Nakada in charge of music at Chapel Center, 274;

TOMEOKA, KOSUKE, founds home for delinquent boys, 84;

TOMITA, MITSURU urges patriotic endeavor, 242; received by Emperor, 249; Moderator for the Kyodan, 285

TOMOMATSU, ENTAI preaches Buddhism on radio, 174

TŌ-O GIJUKU connected witn Christian Band, 53

TOPPING, HELEN, studies social conditions, 159

TOPPING, MRS. opens house to all after war, 272

TOYO EIWA SCHOOL established in Tokyo, 84

TRADE, see FOREIGN TRADE

TRANSLATION OF BIBLE: started, 34; progresses, 36, 43; completed, 83; revision of New Testament started, 162; Old Testament translated, 323

TRAVEL by missionaries allowed, 54

TREATIES: Perry's, 28; Harris' 29; 1859, 33; block national development, 46; revision needed, 66; Shimonoseki, 1895, 89

TROCME, ANDRE, visits Japan 334

TRUE LINE written by Uemura,

380

INDEX

80

TSUNAJIMA, KAKICHI, observer at Washington Conference on Disarmament, 178

UCHIMURA, KANZO, member of Sapporo Band, 53; leads Sapporo Band, 56; establishes Churchless Christianity, 56; studies works of Kierkegaard, 95; becomes teacher of English, 99; fails to honor Rescript scroll, 99; resigns teaching post, 100; turns to journalism, 101; opposes wars of expansion, 117; has nothing to do with the Three Religions Conference movement, 140; concentrates on Bible studies, 154; studies Prophets and the Book of Revelation, 181, 209; works published in 15 volumes, 207; Tadao Yanaihara, a true disciple of his, 223

UEMURA, COLONEL (Salvation Army), arrested for espionage, 230

UEMURA, MASAHISA: Protestant leader, 50; joins Yokohama Band, 56; champions Christianity, 80; translates hymns, 83; produces robust apologetic writing, 98; participates in theological controversy, 111; leader in independence movement, 123; able Christian leader, 127; has nothing to do with the Three Religions Conference movement, 140; heads evangelistic campaign, 151; abstains from public affairs, 155; heads Fujimicho Church in Tokyo, 179; has great influence on other clergymen, 182; leaves the scene, 182; works published in 8 volumes, 207; withdraws from outside world, 209

UEMURA, TAMAKI, visits the U.S., 303; gives Empress Christian instruction, 304

UNDERGROUND : Japanese Christians maintain their faith, 39

UNION CHURCHES supervised by the Conference of Federated Missions, 146

UNION HYMNAL published, 131; revised, 324

UNION OF CHURCHES attempted, 57, 82, 229, 233

UNITARIANS arrive in Japan, 1885, 71; A. M. Knapp active, 79; concerned with social change, 105

UNITED BRETHREN send missionaries, 91

UNITED CHURCH issues pamphlets, 251

UNITED CHURCH OF CANADA conducts social work, 184

UNITED CHURCH OF CHRIST IN JAPAN formed, 1877, 55

UNITED LUTHERAN CHURCH, see LUTHERANS

UNITY HALL established by liberal German missionaries near Tokyo Imperial University, 140; members, unitarian, concerned with social change, 105

UNIVERSAL SUFFRAGE advocated, 157; movement gains ground, 169 bad effects, 170

UNIVERSALISTS send missionaries, 91

UNIVERSITY, CHRISTIAN, needed, 128; planned, 160; considered desirable, 204

UNIVERSITY PROFESSORS oppose Christianity, 60

UOKI, PROF. T., follower of Ashida, 209; publishes *The True Nature of Japanese Christianity*, 252

URBAN NATURE of Christian effort, 64

UZAKI, KYUGORO, member of church-and-state state study com-

381

mission, 186; observer at Washington Conference on Disarmament, 178

VAN KIRK, WALTER, visits postwar Japan, 270

VERBECK, GUIDO F., early missionary of Dutch Reformed Church, 32; brilliant, 32; counsels national leaders, 32, government advisor, 32; early missionary, 34; goes to Nagasaki, 40, visited by Wakasa, 40; baptizes Wakasa, 40; summarizes progress, 44; head of one of two schools which formed the Imperial University, Tokyo, 49; recommends Captain L. L. Janes to head new Kumamoto school, 50; writes first church history, 70

VICE rampant, 171

VIRGIN MARY: explained by Catholic priest, 39

VISIONS, 17

VISITATION EVANGELISM encouraged, 303

VOLUNTEER EVANGELISM effective, 321

VORIES, MERRILL, serves needs of rural people, 159

WAINRIGHT, SAMUEL H., establishes Oito Band, 73; active with Christian Literature Society, 147

WAKASA, LORD, finds Dutch floating in sea (1855) and studies it, 40; studies Chinese Bible, 40; questions Verbeck, 40; is baptized by Verbeck, 40

WALNE, E. L., active distributor of Christian literature, 147

WALSER, T. D., conducts voluntary classes, 181

WALTON, H. MURRAY, directs Japanese Christian News Agency, 208

WAR CRY puzzles Japanese, 91

WAR IN CHINA affects Christians in Japan, 100

WAR WORK engaged in by churches, 101, 119, 223, 245

WASEDA: "Garden of Service" work expanded, 181

WATASE, TORAJIRO, establishes churches in Korea, 144

WATER LEVEL SOCIETY: rallying point for depressed classes, 169

WEEK OF PRAYER held in Yokohama, 42, 72

WEEKLY MISCELLANY first published, 59

WELFARE WORK; see SOCIAL SERVICE WORK

WESTERNIZATION: western ways studied; 47; change rapid, 67; slows down, 85; discontent with Westerners shown, 94; creates juvenile delinquency, 170

WILLIAMS, CHANNING M., transferred from China to Japan, 31; first Episcopal Bishop in Japan, 31; prophesizes that new middle class will be open-minded toward Christianity, 31; early missionary, 34; establishes nucleus of Japanese Episcopal Church, 53; retires, 81

WILLIAMS, S. WELLS, arrives in Japan, 1838, 30; translator for Perry expedition, 30; back in Nagasaki, 31;

WILLIAMSON, DEAN, stimulates interest in church music, 324

WILMINA GIRLS' SCHOOL established in Kyoto, 84

WISHARD, LUTHER D., institutes first summer YMCA conference, 1889, 103

WIVES OF MISSIONARIES active, 77

WOMEN: social position improved, 68; women evangelists increase